ASHES OF VIETNAM

Stuart Rintoul is a Melbourne journalist. He graduated from Monash University with an Honours degree in English and History, and has worked for the Melbourne *Age,* the *Sun News-Pictorial,* the ABC and the *Australian. Ashes of Vietnam* is the product of three years work.

GW00725528

ASHES OF VIETNAM

Australian Voices

Stuart Rintoul

William Heinemann Australia

First published 1987 by
William Heinemann Australia
85 Abinger Street, Richmond, Victoria 3121
in association with the
Australian Broadcasting Corporation
First published in paperback 1988

Designed by Green Poles Design
Typeset in 12/13 Bembo
by Mackenzie Typesetting (Vic) Pty Ltd
Printed in Australia
by Australian Print Group

National Library of Australia
Cataloguing-in-Publication data:

Rintoul, Stuart.
    Ashes of Vietnam.
    ISBN 0 85561 167 7
    1. Vietnamese Conflict, 1961—1975 — Personal
    narratives, Australian. I. Title
959.704'38

CONTENTS

For my mother and father

PREFACE

The veteran begins: 'I can tell you things that happened in Vietnam, but they're just incidental memories, scenes from that place. It was the whole picture — the lies, the corruption, the stupidity, seeing people die for no reason. It was just so sick. I could never justify in my own mind why we were there. That's my basic conscience problem.'

Almost fifty thousand Australians went to the Vietnam war between 1962 and 1972. Five hundred and one died there, two thousand four hundred were wounded physically. Most of them were scarred. Few who went to Vietnam came away uninjured.

They were young, most of them in their early twenties but some as young as nineteen, predominantly working-class and patriotic. They were raised on the Anzac mythology and John Wayne films. They knew nothing about Vietnam. They only knew that their government told them that to fight in Vietnam was the right thing.

They didn't know that the French had taken Vietnam in 1887 after twenty years of trying and in the next fifty years turned the country into a prosperous but repressed colony. They didn't know that America supported Ho Chi Minh against the Japanese during the Second World War, or that after the war occupying British forces handed the country back to the French with the consent of the Americans, or that Ho Chi Minh then began fighting to again drive out the French. He succeeded at Dien Bien Phu in 1954. They didn't know that more than ninety thousand French troops had died in Vietnam.

They didn't know that America had committed itself at Geneva in 1954 to the idea of free elections in a united Vietnam, but later reversed that decision because it was known that Ho Chi Minh would win. They didn't know that America had installed an oppressive and corrupt leader, Diem, and was later implicated in his overthrow and murder.

And they didn't know that the Menzies Government had contrived to become involved in Vietnam and that the South Vietnamese government of Dr Pham Huy Quat, which was supposed to have requested Australian military assistance, lasted less than four months in office before it was replaced by a military regime headed by Nguyen Cao Ky, who later became famous for his admiration of Adolf Hitler.

What they were told and what they believed was that they were going to Vietnam to contain communism in South-East Asia, to preserve freedom in South Vietnam and to support the American alliance. Most of them didn't even know where Vietnam was.

Australia followed America into Vietnam, stupid with anti-communism and xenophobia, and indifferent to the interests of the Vietnamese people to a point beyond immorality. Ultimately, the war in Vietnam was America's war and America's tragedy, but successive conservative governments in Australia were content, even eager, to play the role of the willing accomplice.

The Menzies perspective now seems simply inept: 'The take-over of South Vietnam would be a direct military threat to Australia and all the countries of South and South-East Asia. It must be seen as part of a thrust by communist China between the Indian and Pacific oceans.'

This was in contrast to the prescience of Arthur Calwell: 'The people of Vietnam may, therefore, be divided into three kinds: those who support the present government and are actively anti-communist; those who are communist and of whom the Viet Cong are actively and openly engaged in subversion; and those who are indifferent. I have not the slightest doubt that the overwhelming majority of the ordinary people of Vietnam fall into the last category. They watch uncomprehendingly the ebb and flow of this frightful war around them, and as each day threatens some new horror, they become even more uncomprehending.'

A veteran remembers the day he left for Vietnam: 'We were marching down the Strand, one of my proudest moments I thought, and I've since spoken to blokes and they said they cried that day. Our chests were that far out our shoulder blades must have been showing. Townsville had finished up adopting us and the people were marvellous to us and they were lining up five, six deep through the main street and we were done up in our starched pressed greens and polished brass and our weapons were absolutely brilliant and you could comb your hair on the spit-polish of our boots. We marched the full battalion and it really was emotional. People cheering us and our own pipe band.

'We got down to the quay and our wives and girlfriends were saying goodbye to us. I've got a photograph of my mate,

Johnny, who was killed later on and it's him saying goodbye to his wife. They'd only been married a month but two and a half months later he was buried in the same church. Whenever I think of that time we were going away, of how final it was, I picture my wife and I walking along and right behind me is Johnny smoking his Viscount cigarette with his arm around his wife...the last thing, you know.'

It is twenty years since Vietnam for most of those who were there and many veterans have retreated into a world of almost hysterical bitterness, disillusionment, anger, grief, guilt and sickness.

The lives of many Vietnam veterans are characterised by violence, alcoholism, divorce, self-destruction. There is an intertwining of medical and psychological problems: rashes, damage to the peripheral nervous system, constant fatigue, depression, inability to concentrate, nervousness and irritability, insomnia, vertigo, loss of sex drive, recurring headaches, nausea, gastro-intestinal disorders.

There are numerous and varied birth defects in the children of some Vietnam veterans.

Collectively, these have been called the Agent Orange problem.

There was bitterness first for the way they came home. Many Vietnam veterans remember that coming home meant arriving back at Mascot airport in Sydney after dark to avoid the demonstrators and then afterwards being met with scorn and derision, or indifference.

In their minds, they had expected to be heroes, just as their fathers and grandfathers had been. Instead, they found themselves the untouchables, almost the unmentionables of Australian society, which had changed so rapidly that they barely understood it.

In 1965, according to the Morgan Gallup poll, a majority of Australians supported involvement in the Vietnam war, as they supported conscription, although not necessarily conscription for service in Vietnam.

By late 1969, public opinion had swung against involvement in the war, propelled by the issue of conscription and by nightly television reports. The images of the Vietnam war were abhorrent and seemed interminable.

In 1970, reflecting America's changed mood, over one hundred thousand people throughout Australia demonstrated for peace in the first of the big moratorium marches; and when finally the last soldiers were withdrawn from Vietnam the Australian public drew a collective sigh of relief.

A veteran remembers his homecoming: 'I copped some flak in my home town. A woman that taught me at school spat at me. She was in the Save Our Sons. She spat at me and I adored that woman, you know. The best teacher I ever had, I thought. You remember one or two teachers in your life and she was a magnificent woman. I didn't think any less of her. She had her axe to grind. It was just surprising more than anything else.'

Another recalls settling back in: 'I went to a party a few weeks after I got back and nobody was interested in anything I said. You could feel it all around you. A few months later a little kid stepped out of a phone box and he called me a murderer. It turned out to be the son of somebody that I'd known since I was a kid.'

Confronted by this, Vietnam veterans began a long retreat. They never told anybody about Vietnam. Some even denied that they had been there. At first, there was no-one to listen and afterwards they came to believe that no-one could understand.

There was disillusionment, with the realisation that Vietnam was not a 'just' war and that they were sent there to support a political end which was untenable.

'I look back and even today I think that the only hero out of the whole Vietnam fiasco was Simon Townsend. He was the hero, because he stood by his principles and he went to jail because of it. I thought if only the rest of us as twenty-year-olds had had the foresight to get up and do the same thing. He knew it was wrong, morally and every other way, and I look back and I think if only I could meet that man personally I would give him every medal that I supposedly earned and I would pin them all over him because to me he is my hero.

'I burnt all my Army gear. The slouch hat, the battalion lanyards and all that. I just had a sacrificial fire one afternoon. It was something that got in my head. I didn't want anything else to remind me of it. I felt like part of a crazy system that got me involved in something that shouldn't have been in the first place was being burnt along with it.'

Sometimes from bitterness and disillusionment came anger towards the society that sent them to Vietnam, but gave them no way to come home.

'I got shot out of a lot of towns for fighting, breaking into joints, shit like that. I didn't give a fuck about nothing. I had no morals. All my morals were knocked out of me when I was nineteen. I was in Darwin jail and I tried to hang myself.'

This veteran dreams such nightmares that he sleeps in his living room with the television on so that when he wakes up screaming he can relate to something other than Vietnam.

Vietnam was not like other wars. Tim O'Brien said it best, in *Going after Cacciato*: 'They did not know even the simple things: a sense of victory, or satisfaction, or necessary sacrifice. They did not know the feeling of taking a place and keeping it, securing a village and then raising the flag and calling it victory. No sense of order or momentum. No front, no rear, no trenches laid out in neat parallels. No Patton rushing for the Rhine, no beachheads to storm and win and hold for the duration. They did not have targets. They did not have a cause. They did not know if it was a war of ideology or economics or hegemony or spite. On a given day they did not know where they were in Quang Ngai, or how being there might influence larger outcomes.

'They did not know the names of most villages. They did not know which villages were critical. They did not know strategies. They did not know the terms of the war, its architecture, the rules of fair play. When they took prisoners, which was rare, they did not know the questions to ask, whether to release a suspect or beat on him. They did not know how to feel.'

Mark Baker, in *Nam*, wrote: 'The war billed on the marquee as a John Wayne shoot-'em-up test of manhood turns out to be a warped version of Peter Pan. Vietnam was a brutal never-never land, outside time and space, where little boys didn't have to grow up. They just grew old before their time.'

There were no marching songs for Vietnam, no George M. Cohan to sing them over there, or Gracie Fields to wish them luck.

Instead there was Country Joe McDonald:

    'And it's one, two, three
    What are we fighting for?
    Don't ask me, I don't give a damn
    Next stop is Vietnam
    And it's five, six, seven
    Open up the pearly gates
    Ain't no time to wonder why
    Whoopee we're all gonna die.'

There was so much guilt that came out of the Vietnam war. Guilt for going there, guilt for surviving when friends did not, guilt for seeing friends die and thinking, 'Thank Christ it wasn't me,' guilt for coming home before the war was ended, guilt for losing, and guilt for the things that were done there most of all.

Australians in Vietnam were guilty of acts of barbarity. There were Australians whose morality was so eroded that they murdered villagers, raped women, tortured and killed wounded enemy soldiers and mutilated corpses. But they were not like that before they went to Vietnam. No nineteen- or twenty- or twenty-one-year-old went to Vietnam thinking, 'Now I will be evil.' That was what Vietnam made them and in that they were no different from the Americans or the French before them.

In Sydney, a veteran recalls an interrogation in a village.

'We dragged two young boys out of a pit in a house, an air-raid shelter. They wouldn't have been fourteen, fifteen I suppose. We had a Vietnamese interpreter with us and we were trying to get information out of these two young kids.

'One of the blokes said, "There's only one way to make them talk, that's do what the Yanks do, shoot one of them." One of the guys walked up and he just shot one of these kids, just standing there. He just walked up and he just went bang and shot him through the head. His brains went all over the ground and this Vietnamese interpreter pushed the other kid down onto the brains and pushed his face into it.

'If anything out of Vietnam worried me it was that — that we as human beings could do that. That's probably my biggest regret. That was pretty close to us coming home.'

In the dreams of Vietnam veterans the most common is the dream about being alone with Vietnamese all around and a weapon that won't work, or whose bullets fall short of their intended target. Other dreams, both abstract and specific, derive as much from losing in Vietnam as from the ordinary, or extraordinary, experience of war. A veteran dreams this:

'I just looked at the doorway and he was there, a young Vietnamese bloke, like you'd see hanging around Vungers or any of the villages. Baria, or anywhere like that. It just scared the hell out of me when I saw him there. There are other times when I've dreamed I've had a gun in the bed with me and he's been standing there and as I've grabbed the gun to shoot him he just disappears and then I start screaming and my wife will wake me up and I'm saying, "He was at the doorway," and she's saying, "No-one's there."

'When I see him I think I'm fully awake, but I know it's in my dreams. I can see everything as plain as day and he's just standing there. He's not smiling or nothing. He's just there and sometimes he's saying, "I've come to get you."'

Another veteran dreams that he is back in Vietnam.

'I have dreams about when my mate Doug was killed, but they're never quite the way it was. Something is always missing from the dream, and I know that there is something wrong.

'I dream that I'm walking through mud, walking up mountains of mud; just getting to the top and seeing another one and then just getting to the top of that one and finding another one and turning around and yelling out, "I ain't going any further."

'Dreams of being in a hotel room with my wife, and a little kid will walk in and it's a little Vietnamese kid and he's laughing, then all of a sudden his face changes from a Vietnamese kid to Doug's face, but he's a little kid and he's laughing at me and all of a sudden my wife's arms and legs will start falling off. Things like that. Crazy dreams. Some of them are so real and frighten me so much that I come and sit in the living room and just wait until the sun comes up.'

Night is a bad time. It was bad in Vietnam, when they were waiting and it was so dark they couldn't see the tips of their rifle barrels and someone or something triggered an ambush and the area was lit up by the spectral light of illumination flares.

Memories about friends who were killed, doubt about the reasons why, which makes them all the harder to carry, questions they ask themselves like, 'What would he be doing now? Would he have a family like mine?'

A veteran relates the death of two of his friends. They died when somebody stepped on a mine. It was a common way to die in Vietnam.

'We'd only just sat down off the side of a track and the platoon commander came across and he said something like, "Trust you lot to be in the way." The next thing I recall was seeing a lot of smoke, different coloured smoke and then I realised that I was numb and hot all at the same time. Although it probably only took seconds I can remember lying back and a spout of blood running across my left eye and I couldn't work out what it was, how come this red stuff was running down from my head.

'I saw Jacko, but I can't remember what I saw. I remember looking at him and my mind was so shocked with what I saw that it blacked it out.

'I turned to John Kennedy and he was screaming and frothy red blood was bubbling up through his back.

'I remember reaching for my rifle and it was blown in half, so that when I dragged it towards me it came in two disjointed parts. I tore off my field dressing, but I didn't have enough strength to get over to John and all I could do was sort of throw it to where he was, but by that time the medics had come in and got to him.

'I know that when I did that John was still alive, but that the screams were in bursts and they got shorter and shorter and shorter and they just ended up fading away and I knew that he couldn't live. I knew that he was going to die. There was just no way that someone could have had those injuries and lived.

'Neither of them said anything. I remember one of the medics ran up to me and looked at me and...'

At this point the veteran put his head in his hands and wept convulsively, saying, 'It hurts. It still hurts so much.'

Most veterans haven't cried yet. Some of them feel that if they ever started they might not be able to stop.

Another veteran says that he has lost the capacity to show emotion. In Vietnam, there was never time or opportunity or encouragement to show emotion.

He comes to the part of his story he seems to have been heading towards all along.

'The first sight I saw when I got to that position was my best mate. He was as white as a sheet, and bloated. I don't know what happens but he was just bloated in the face and just totally white.

'They'd pulled him back from where he got hit and I saw him die and that was the most horrifying experience, that was the most terrible experience I ever had.

'He'd been hit with an RPG (rocket-propelled grenade). His face wasn't affected, he must have been hit in the side that was away from me. He was still alive for a while and then he went. He was totally unconscious. He just twitched and quivered and that was it.

'But the thing is that I had no feeling of anger, I had no feeling of revenge. It was just a total disassociation from every-thing. No feeling of anything. Nothing.'

Perhaps as many as one-third of the fifty thousand Australians who went to Vietnam are suffering from a range of neurological, dermatological, gastro-intestinal and psychological disorders caused by the spraying of toxic chemicals in Vietnam as part of a massive defoliation program to destroy jungle cover and crops.

The chemical most used during the war was known as Agent Orange, a mixture of the n-butyl esters of 2,4-D and 2,4,5-T, a contaminant of which is TCDD or dioxin — the most potent cancer-causing agent known and a powerful teratogen causing birth defects and reproductive toxicity such as stillbirths and miscarriages.

The use of Agent Orange in Vietnam was halted in 1970 because of concern over its possible role in producing birth defects. In July, 1985, a royal commissioner, Mr Justice Evatt, QC, concluded, however, that on the evidence presented to him, Agent Orange was not guilty and that problems complained of by veterans were attributable to post-traumatic stress from the nature of the Vietnam war and the poor homecoming the veterans received. He found no evidence to suggest that there were higher than normal rates of cancer, birth abnormalities or suicide among veterans and suggested that periods of psychological counselling for the veterans and a public awareness campaign would put matters right. That finding is now under review by the federal government, but has already been widely criticised by experts in the field.

All military personnel can be presumed to have been exposed to toxic chemicals in Vietnam, to varying degrees. Along with the defoliation of jungle canopy, forests and croplands, herbicides were sprayed around basecamp perimeters, landing zones, fire-support bases and along roadways and riverbanks. It was sprayed directly over waterways and large amounts of herbicide were washed into streams.

The sight of chemicals being sprayed was as much a part of the Vietnam war as was the artillery used there and the soldiers paid it no attention because they were told it was doing them no harm.

It has been estimated that between 17.4 and 19.1 million gallons of herbicide were aerially sprayed over South Vietnam — 107 million pounds of herbicide applied over about six million square miles.

From 1965, Operation Ranch Hand sprayed between 10.6

and 11.7 million gallons of Herbicide Orange, between 5.2 and 5.6 million gallons of Herbicide White and between 1.1 and 2.1 million gallons of Herbicide Blue. The area most heavily sprayed was Military Region Three, where the Australians operated.

In addition, unknown amounts of herbicide were regularly sprayed by engineering units and riverine forces; additional unknown amounts were sprayed by the South Vietnamese military. Some areas were sprayed with more than one herbicide; other areas were sprayed with both herbicides and large amounts of pesticide; some herbicides were used undiluted or in cocktails of more than one chemical agent.

'I've lost a daughter. She had only half a heart. That was my first child and then David, my eldest boy, he's got perforated ears. He used to lip-read when he was young. He was really a bright kid. He used to lip-read everybody but we couldn't pick it up, that he was partially deaf. It was hard for him, really hard, because all his mates used to call him the dummy.

'My other son has got incurable skin diseases. They tell me it's hereditary — that's the answer I get from them — but it's nowhere in the family. He comes out in blotches and big scabs. He's also got turned hips, pigeon toes, locked knees.

'Kim, my wife, has had three curettes, where the babies died inside her so they removed them, and she's miscarried four or five times. She's had a lot of vaginal infections.

'I don't know whether all these things are associated with the chemicals that were sprayed in Vietnam, but I was definitely sprayed. In fact, I sprayed them myself out of knapsacks.

'I remember seeing a chopper going over me with a couple of bars hanging out the back and a fog coming off and then in 8 Field Ambulance we did fogging every night for mosquitoes and other times we would spray to keep down the weeds.

'We would mix up the chemicals from one drum to another and away we'd go. I didn't have a clue what was in the drums, would not know.'

In Sydney: 'I've got rashes under the arms, groin. I get headaches all the time. They get bad. Flashes of temper. It's like a boiler without a pressure-release valve. It builds up and builds up until it explodes. Sometimes with me it takes two weeks, other times it might take six weeks, but eventually I explode.

'I can't mix with people. I've got no sex drive. At one stage I went to the doctor to give me hormone injections, which didn't work. I was married twice. My first wife had quite a few miscarriages. That was back in the early '70s.

'I used to unduly pick on the kids, isolate myself from their lives, behave irrationally until it got to a stage where they just couldn't take any more.

'Unfortunately, I realised the problem just a little too late. That's the trouble. When you are having these problems you don't realise it until it's too late.'

In Melbourne: 'The symptoms that I've got are nausea, dry retching, anxiety, a total inability to concentrate, blurred vision, an inability to take any form of stress or responsibility, loss of appetite, I suppose I could say depression.

'I don't feel any self-pity, although occasionally in outbursts when someone questions me and they say, "Why are you like this?" I just scream out and say, "Well you don't bloody well know what I'm going through." But then, I don't know what I'm going through myself.'

ACKNOWLEDGEMENTS

The first debt is to those Vietnam veterans who were willing, often at great personal cost, to tell their stories. I hope I have justified the faith they showed in me to give an honest account.

I want to thank Phil Thompson for his assistance and encouragement. It hurt like hell when he died. Also Paula Voltz, who was there when it started, Tim Bowden, Max and Iris Cameron, Charles Chen, Dennis and Sue Cole, Ted and Margaret Cowell, Micheal and Maree Crawford, Michael Currie, Greg Earl, Jill Favero, my sister — Anne Feehan, Brian Griffin, Chil Hutchings, John Kerr, Peter Molloy, Cecily Morton, John and Marion Skinner, Garry Starr, Graham Walker, Ted Warner, Laurie Woods, Gough Whitlam, and my editor, Michael Langley.

I also gratefully acknowledge the assistance of the Vietnam Veterans Association of Australia, the Vietnam Veterans Counselling Service, the Herald and Weekly Times, the *Age*, the *Australian*, the Australian Broadcasting Corporation, staff of the Latrobe Library, Melbourne, and the Australian War Memorial; and Lansdowne Press for material from *The Eagle and the Lotus* by Dr Jim Cairns (1969) and Longman Cheshire for permission to quote from 'The Gift of the Gods' in *Sometimes Gladness — Collected Poems, 1954–1978* by Bruce Dawe.

To my mother, Eleanor, for her patience and support, thank you.

To the other members of my family and friends, *slàinte*.

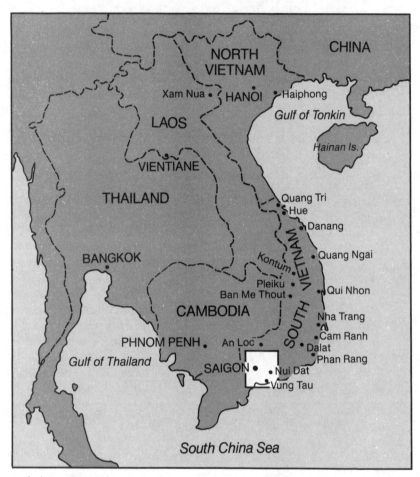

Indochina, 1970

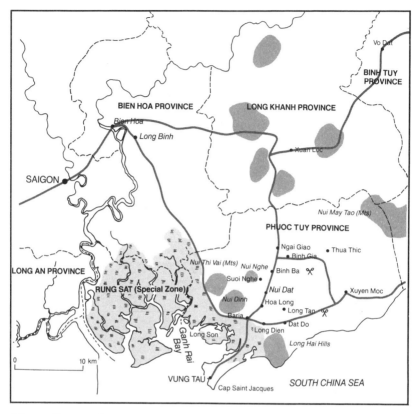

Major villages in Phuoc Tuy Province

then the trucks to carry off the living
then the bulldozers to cover over the rest
then the night
and the sound of ashes
sifting subsiding
then the silence along which in single file
squads of politicians advance
with the wreaths of their breath.

from 'The Gift of the Gods'
by Bruce Dawe

1

Illusions

'It took us not five minutes to decide that when this thing came to the point of action we would be in it, if invited by the government of South Vietnam. We had no hesitation, no doubts and I've never had any regrets.'

Former prime minister Sir Robert Menzies in an interview in 1969

BOB GIBSON

He was a shearer when he was called up at twenty.

'I grew up with the glorious stories of the Second World War, how the Japs were coming down here and we stopped them. In a little town on Anzac Day as a school you'd line up and you'd see the men with their medals marching down the street and they were heroes, they were the most respected people in town. They were like the Phantom, they would never die.

'My grandfather was shot through the lung in the First World War. He died when he was about twenty. His picture was on the wall at home. I idolised him. He looks identical to my father and I've got the same set of eyes and everything as him.'

I left school at fourteen and I haven't got one certificate to say I was at school. I started shearing at fifteen. I come from a shearing family.

I went to Dubbo for my first medical and I was knocked back on the grounds of low blood pressure. I thought that was strange, because being a shearer is pretty hard work and I wasn't a bad shearer either. I felt a sense of not being good enough.

I was from a little town and a lot of people had died from that one town in Australia's wars, and I thought, 'Well, everyone's going to think he didn't make the grade.'

They prescribed iron tablets for me and after twelve months I got another appointment to go to Dubbo and I passed with flying colours.

The only thing I knew about Vietnam was what the military had told us and from the films that we'd seen: that there were a lot of communists running around cutting people's heads off, disembowelling people, killing school teachers, raping the land and that they were heading this way and if we didn't get over there and kick their arse real soon they'll be down here and they'll be raping your sister and they'll be raping your mother. We were going to stop that.

The time came when we had to decide what corps we wanted to go into and the whole lot of us sat down and decided as many of us as possible wanted to stick together. We'd become close. It's hard to believe that in six or seven weeks a group of civilians, country and city boys, could knit together as a group and become soldiers and so close in that short a time.

I wanted infantry and another couple of guys from the

country wanted infantry so we had a vote and most of the guys wanted infantry then.

From there we went to Singleton where we did our infantry training. We had a choice after Singleton of what battalion we wanted to go into. I went to the reinforcement wing at Ingleburn, on standby to replace blokes who were medevaced home from Vietnam, or were due to come home: the one for one system — one went over there, one would come home. It was the fastest way to Vietnam. At that time I thought everyone in the Army wanted to get there.

JOHN ROBBINS

He went to Vietnam as an infantry soldier in 1966. He is a quiet, thoughtful man. He discusses Vietnam rarely. 'I think I've put it out of my mind. I don't wear an RSL badge or anything like that. I talk about it with fellows that I know, but most people wouldn't even know I've been there. How can you pick someone who's been there?' He is forty years old and lives in Brisbane.

I was in a private company in Brisbane in 1964. I was a jackaroo in north-west Queensland. I'd been a jackaroo since I'd left school and I left home in Townsville on my seventeenth birthday. My father was in the bank and I wasn't brilliant at school. I applied for a job in the bank. I didn't really think it'd suit me, the lifestyle, not that I thought that being a jackaroo would either. I spent two and a half years jackarooing, getting £12 a week. After that, I worked with a contractor, putting up tank stands and pumps and windmills in central and northern Queensland. Then I was offered a job with a livestock company. I started with them and it was difficult enough, because I was doing a lot of clerical work which I hadn't been used to, but there was a fair bit of outdoor work involved in the sale yards and things so I didn't mind. But then the call-up came.

In a way, I was quite pleased when my birthdate came out. I was looking forward to it really, with no idea about going to Vietnam at that particular time.

JOHN QUINCEY

He was getting towards the end of a butcher's apprenticeship when he was called up in the first draft of national service in 1965.

I didn't think enough about conscription, as conscription was. I had no ill-feelings about being called up for national service. I was quite looking forward to it actually. I even looked forward to going to the city and having the medicals and all that sort of thing. It was interesting.

I thought about being stuck in four walls in a butcher's shop for four years too: I was ready for a change. I had always been a person that loved the outdoors. I was always playing sport and out shooting and fishing and what have you, and then taking on a job where you were shoved in four walls five and a half days a week, I was quite looking forward to getting out. But at that time it was far from my mind that we would be going to Vietnam to get shot at. I think at that stage of the game, in 1965, the government was denying that they were introducing national service to send troops to Vietnam.

WAYNE

It is the psychiatric ward of a repatriation hospital. Old men from Australia's various wars wander the corridors in dressing-gowns. It smells of urine and strong antiseptic. In the background, somebody plays on a piano, 'Pack up your troubles in your old kitbag and smile, smile, smile…' He is thirty-six years old.

In 1969 I went up to Hurstville, that's where I lived, and I had to register by 31 January.

You just went to the post office, got a yellow form, filled in your name and address, date of birth, and just posted it back to the national service.

I don't know where the card went from there, but then they used to bring the marble out. Certain numbers would be drawn from a lottery barrel and if your birthdate corresponded to the number on the marble then you were called up for national service.

The chances of going in were supposed to be one in seven by the marble, but my birthday came out every year from '65 to '71. In my class at Kingsgrove High there were twenty-eight blokes and twenty-eight were called up.

I got a letter to say I'd been posted to Puckapunyal. I didn't even know where bloody Puckapunyal was.

My father was very pro-Labor. He didn't want me to go to Vietnam because he was against it. My mother died when I was two and when I went over he gave me the New Testament he got from her in 1942 when he went overseas. I used to always keep it in the left pocket of my shirt.

I believed at the time I went into the Army that we were doing the right thing, because I thought we didn't need communism in Australia, even though we had a free society.

I can remember that year, 1969. It was when Whitlam nearly got into government and we couldn't even fucking vote.

MICK RAINEY

He is a strongly built man of forty-two with conservative and uncomplicated views of men and war.

'My belief is that if your country says you're going to war then you should go, whether you want to or not. I don't believe in this conscientious objector crap.' He served twenty years in the Army and was a tank commander in Vietnam in 1968. He lives in Seymour, Victoria, not far from the Army base at Puckapunyal.

I joined up in 1960. I was seventeen at the time and I evidently had a bit of a chip on my shoulder as a young kid working on a farm. I was brought up in an orphanage and I went back there after leaving a job they had found for me. A bloke from the orphanage said to me one day, 'You've got a bloody chip on your shoulder, young fellow, that needs to be knocked off. If you joined the Army they'd bloody sort you right out.' I just let it pass and then the following week I went down and joined up. Whether that was in the back of my mind I don't know.

ALAN ASHMORE

He went to Vietnam in 1970 as a company clerk. He lives in a comfortable house in the hills near Melbourne.

I would have been about twenty when I was conscripted. I couldn't see anything wrong with it. I didn't believe it was practical for everyone to get called up. I believe you don't knock the current system unless you can come up with a better alternative and I couldn't really think of one. I guess if I hadn't gone into the Army I probably would have left my job and gone around Australia or done something like that. Not that I saw it as an adventure, but it was a change.

When I was doing my training a lot of my friends were saying to me, 'I bet you're getting brainwashed.' Now, the only talk of politics I can recall in my two years was from a really good sergeant at recruit training who said to us, 'If anyone ever says communism is a good thing just ask them one question and it will kill all arguments, all discussions — Why do they build the walls: to stop us getting in or them getting out?' That was the only political comment I heard the whole time.

BOB MILLARD

He was an electrician at Nui Dat in 1967–8. Today, he lives on a farm at Holgate, New South Wales, with his wife and two children. At forty, he receives a service pension for permanent incapacitation.

I was brought up well by a couple of good parents and you always did the right thing. Everyone had to register for national service, so you did the right thing and you registered. I wasn't a rebel in any way. I registered and I just sort of hoped. I had never won a lottery before, but I hoped my number wouldn't come up. When it did, well, I just accepted it.

JEFF SCULLEY

At thirty-six, he works as a gardener at the Lakeside psychiatric hospital in Ballarat, Victoria. In Vietnam in 1969–70 he was a platoon medic.

I started in a book and stationery shop. I worked there for $14.20 a week. I missed out on the call up, but I then volunteered for it and naturally enough got accepted.

I always had in the back of my mind that I wanted to go in the Army. I don't know, for some reason I'd followed Vietnam right through in the newspapers from when the Americans were supposed to have been attacked in the Gulf of Tonkin.

I did my medical about October '68 and I went in at the end of January '69 with the fifteenth intake. I treated the whole thing from the word go as something different in my life and as an adventure, because I'd never done anything outlandish or anything. I had a lot of parent problems at home. They were both alcoholic and the job I was in was a rut of a job and so I thought, 'Well, this will be something different, I'll really change my life around.'

MARK ROSE

He was an infantry corporal in Vietnam in 1968. At forty, he is bearded and pot-bellied and receives a pension for being 'totally, temporarily incapacitated'. He has been on a drinking binge for the past two weeks. He begins, 'I was mentioned in despatches in a war I wish I'd never heard of.'

I didn't have a hard childhood, but I won't say I had a luxurious childhood either. I was looked after, I was provided for. I went to the local state school until sixth grade and then went to Oakleigh Tech up to fourth form.

My boyhood was a very romantic sort of thing. I've only got half the books I had at one stage, but I used to have all sorts of things, from Rudyard Kipling through to *Horatio Hornblower* and wild west by the dozen, and Henry Lawson and Banjo Paterson.

I decided I wanted to be a policeman, so I became a cadet for two years in the Victorian Police Force, which was virtually like doing high school anyway.

I left that. I got my Leaving Certificate there and left at eighteen and walked about in the bush for a few years, came back to Melbourne, and got myself a job in the local pub. I missed out on national service, found my mates were getting called up, and I was looking for something to do with myself so I joined the Army. There was a war on and I was young and idealistic and fairly ignorant. I definitely joined the Army to go to Vietnam. As I saw Vietnam at that stage it was a matter of stopping the yellow peril.

PADDY

A conscript, he was from a farming background at Lyndhurst, Victoria. 'The day before we left for Vietnam I was called into an office and a lieutenant said, 'Look, this is not going to be recorded anywhere, but if you don't want to go you don't have to.' I said, 'Well, you've got to fight these things I suppose. My grandfathers fought in the World Wars. I suppose we've got to do the right thing too.' He served in Vietnam as an infantry soldier in 1966.

When I got called up the only thing I knew about Vietnam, or communism, was that someone said in the paper something like you're better off killing a snake outside before it gets in the house. That was my idea of communism — that it was a snake in South-East Asia and unless we stopped it there it was going to come into Australia.

CHRIS LUCAS

He was working for the railways when he was called up in 1970. He went to Vietnam as an infantry soldier the following year. He lives in the small Victorian town of Briagalong where he works as a farrier.

There wasn't much you could do about it. I was twenty. I had my twenty-first birthday at Puckapunyal four or five weeks after I went in the Army. I just went along with it. There wasn't much you could do. If you didn't go in they could send you to jail for two years; if you burnt your draft card you had to go bush or hide in the city and then your whole family didn't think much of you I suppose. That's what would have happened.

My old man was a deserter in the Second World War and I thought, 'No, I couldn't do that.' He wasn't around, but I'd never thought much of him and I wouldn't have thought much of myself if I hadn't sort of stayed in. I knew I wasn't really suited in the end.

LES MYERS

He was an infantry soldier in Vietnam in 1970.

I went over there for the same reason thousands did, just to see what it was like. But then, my father was an alcoholic caused through war experiences. He was a prisoner of the Japanese on the Burma–Thailand railway. He was an alco, he didn't drink at all before he went in the Army, he was a teetotaller.

I guess I wanted to find out what he went through. I knew the experiences probably had nothing in common, but it was the closest I was going to go to it. That was mainly why, although it's always in your mind, that you want to know how you would perform in a life–death situation.

GEOFF COLLINS

He was a field engineer in Vietnam in 1969. We meet at Torquay, a Victorian beach resort.

I was really bitter about having to go to Vietnam. I enjoyed surfing and I didn't want anything to interfere with that. There was a big group of us used to surf down at Torquay back in those days; everyone knew everyone. And out of it all there were only two of us who ended up going in the Army, out of about thirty or forty. I think two or three just bolted and the rest of them didn't pass their medicals and that.

We tried everything going in for our medical. We were told if you had three or four quick whiskeys you didn't pass the urine test.

I tried to get out through my ears, tried to pretend I had a hearing problem. And I got it right twice, but the third test I completely messed up.

I felt like jumping out of the bus going up to Puckapunyal. I knew a lot of guys went AWOL and stayed up in the snow or stayed round the back beaches. They got away with it in the end when the government changed. I just didn't think I was capable of doing that. They lived off the smell of an oily rag and I would have liked to go and see my folks and that, and in the end I preferred to put up with what I had to put up with.

RIC

The room is a confusion of moods. On one wall hangs a print of Frederick McCubbin's Down On His Luck, *on another a portrait of a pretty girl, the type that sells cheaply at markets. Elsewhere: a Groucho Marx novelty lamp; a few books; a stereo, which is playing a Brahms concerto; and plastic models he has built for an incomplete diorama set in Vietnam. He was an artillery forward observer in 1969. As we talk he snorts speed.*

I volunteered for Vietnam. I wanted to go. Quest of youth, I guess, adventure, the whole bit, you know. There was no moral issue involved. I wanted to go to a war. I had the foreign legion syndrome. I saw myself as Beau Geste, I really did.

RAY PAYNE

He is a florist in Sydney, a placid man. We talk at the back of his shop, which smells sweetly of hyacinth and tuberose. He went to Vietnam in 1965 as a regular soldier. 'They called us the last of the professionals, the last professional soldiers before Menzies introduced conscription, and we were professional, we were bloody good.'

The dominant figure in my childhood was my grandfather. He was a gentleman, an absolute and complete gentleman. He was a very fine, very clean-cut sort of man who always had the right answer. No matter what you asked him, he was always worldly and wise. Very Army, regimented, a major who had the most fantastic handwriting. It was magnificent. He wrote with an Indian ink pen. The image of the Army that I had was very much his image.

When I went into the Army I went with a lot of preconceived ideas, ideas that he'd put forward, about what a soldier should do and how a soldier should go about being a soldier. That's why I never questioned anything or what anybody told me in the Army, because it wasn't my right to question. I was a professional soldier and I did what I was told. If someone said to me jump, my only question would be how high.

MICK CRAWFORD

He was an infantry soldier in Vietnam in 1970.

I was a nasho, from a small town I guess. Yarrawonga's not very big. How did I feel about it? I really didn't have any feelings at all. For a start, it seemed like the right thing to do, a great adventure — an Aussie soldier, you know, a big bronzed Anzac. They made you feel like that in the Army, until you got there and then it hit you: what in the hell am I doing here?

I enjoyed the training. Maybe I was young at the time, maybe I was brainwashed, I don't know, but I enjoyed it. I guess before I went over there you could call me a layabout. The Army certainly drilled something into me. It gave you mateship, responsibilities. It just made you feel part of something, whereas before, when you were more or less kicking around on your own, all you wanted was a girl and a fast car. It was just different, to me anyway, being brought up in a small town and all of a sudden you're with all these guys, you're all doing the same, you're all wearing the same.

For a start, it seemed like a good thing. They'd tell you about all these benefits you were going to get when you got home. You were entitled to a house through Defence Service Homes, you could get business loans, the RSL was the greatest thing going and returned servicemen were among the best liked people in Australia. You would be one of them, you would be on a par with the guys from the Second World War.

RAY ORCHARD

The last sounds of a Saturday night drift up from the street. He is the son of an Aboriginal slaughterman from Bundaberg, Queensland. One of nine children, he enlisted in 1962 and went to Vietnam as an infantry soldier four years later. At forty, he lives in a flat on the south side of Brisbane, a tough part of the city. Like many veterans he has never talked about Vietnam before and his wife interrupts constantly, 'Why are you telling this white boy?'

I left school after Intermediate, worked in the cane fields till I joined the Army, among other things. Went out cotton picking, ringbarking, worked on stations, everything like that, been right around through the system.

In the place where I came from, we used to live in an area with all my relations, I suppose you could say in a tribal system. There was about three different families, but they were all, in the old tribal way, related down through. Everybody was uncle, no relation like the white society. The bloody white society couldn't live like that. I always remember the greatest time was when we used to live in that way. No electricity to worry about. You used to have to do your own thing. That's when I first learned to go out and hunt.

People used to live in tin bloody bag huts all in the same area. We were the only ones that had a house because of my father's job. They had a house set aside for the person that looked after the slaughter yard.

I started to want to join the Army when I was seventeen and I had the biggest fight in the world. My mother died in 1961 and my father wanted me home because I was the eldest lad there at the time. He wanted me home to give him a hand, because I had four young sisters plus a younger brother. I'd go down and cut cane with him and run the truck home loaded with cane.

I had twelve months to fight him and one day in 1962 I took his smoko down to him and said, 'Here dad, sign this paper.' He took it in his old cane black hand, I'll never forget that, and he said, 'If you want to go, well go.' He signed it and he can only sign his name. He can't read or write.

Well, I had the biggest pride when I left. That was the first time I'd been to Brisbane, when I came down, the first time I'd left them all and I could feel it in my own head that this was going to be something big for me, something else. I knew I wouldn't be coming back for a fair spell.

FRANK HUNT

He was a sharefarmer in the north-west of Victoria when the war began in Vietnam. He went there as an infantry soldier in 1969. He lives in Bega, New South Wales. We meet in the local RSL.

I was born in a place called Birchip, in the Mallee in Victoria. My father was a soldier settler. He had probably about 1100 or 1200 acres to farm. He fought in the Second World War, served in Borneo and New Guinea. There were eight children and I was the eldest, the twin brother and I. At the age of about fourteen I left school to farm with my father because he had a drinking problem and the farm wasn't being worked to its full capacity.

I worked there for three years with all the family and we had two droughts. I always felt that I was going backwards on the farm, I wasn't getting paid. I was sharefarming at the same time and that was my only reward, but when the dry season came there was no reward whatsoever, just a lot of expenditure with nothing coming in. So, at the age of seventeen I decided to join the Army. Even then, when I went into my feelings, I wanted to be like my father, like my grandfather before him. I knew my father would be proud of me, that I was a third-generation Hunt in a direct line to put on the Australian uniform.

I joined the Army, against my mother's wishes. She didn't want to sign the papers, but my father said yes, because with him it was the old male ego thing too; he had something to skite about in the pub I suppose.

I was really a very naive bloody kid from the bush, a real bushy.

After a few weeks they were talking about Vietnam and I didn't even know bloody Vietnam existed and this is about 1967. I'd never even heard of the country. I didn't know what type of people they were, I didn't know where Laos or Cambodia or any of those countries were or what they were involved with. I didn't know the French had been in Vietnam.

We did our training in Townsville and we were really well trained. By Jesus we were well trained. We were bloody fit and keen, like a football team that had been training for eighteen months and the game's on tomorrow and this is what we're waiting for.

The day we sailed was one of my proudest moments, and

I've since spoken to blokes and they said they cried that day. Our chests were that far out our shoulder-blades must have been showing. Townsville had finished up adopting us and the people were marvellous to us; they were lining up five, six deep through the main street, all through the Strand, and we're done up in our starched pressed greens and polished brass and our weapons were absolutely brilliant and you could comb your hair on the bloody spit-polish of your boots.

We marched the full battalion and it really was emotional. People cheering us, and the bagpipes, our own pipe band, and we get down to the quay and our wives and girlfriends saying goodbye to us.

Connie was very teary, I was too. I've got a photo at home of my mate Johnny Needs who was killed in a mine accident later on. It's of him saying goodbye to his wife Donna. They'd only been married a month, and two and a half months later he was being buried in the same church.

Whenever I think of this time when we were going away I picture Connie and I walking along and right behind me is Johnny Needs smoking his Viscount cigarette with his arms around his wife and how final it was; the last thing, you know.

COLIN NICOLE

He was an infantry soldier in Vietnam in 1969.

I don't like the word 'indoctrination'. Indoctrination isn't what they did and also it implies that the people who have been indoctrinated are stupid. I wasn't a fool. I mean, I had my HSC and I was young, but I wasn't a fool. In fact, I can only re-member once ever being shown anything that you could call indoctrination; that was a black and white film of blokes in Vietnam, scouts, and what it was like and so on. It was like watching a John Wayne movie. It didn't mean anything to me at all, just these blokes talking about nothing. It was hot. I could hear the fans going around, thinking how bloody hot it is and when does this film finish because it didn't mean anything to me. The scout meant nothing to me. He was a soldier, but big deal. I don't remember lectures ever on propaganda or things like that, ever.

The only thing that struck home to me was when a CSM, by the name of Smiley Myles, said once, 'Everything's going well, but you've got to get a bit more aggro into you.' I thought, that's a funny thing to say; why is he saying that? It was just before we went to Vietnam.

BOB HOBBS

He was an infantry soldier in Vietnam in 1969.

I was having a pretty good time, enjoying life to the fullest when I received my call-up notice. I was pretty upset about it. I didn't particularly want to go into the Army. Some people from the Save Our Sons movement came around home to see me and my folks, but by that stage I had decided that conscription was in. It was the law and if it was good enough for all the other fellows to abide by, it was good enough for me.

As my induction into the Army drew nearer I suppose my attitude mellowed a bit. I was very keen while I was in school cadets. I really enjoyed cadets and I thought maybe that's what the Army would be like. Besides, it wasn't for an indefinite period, it was for two years. Maybe I would learn something and it would be a challenge, so I went in. I didn't try to fight it.

I hardly knew anything about Vietnam. Vietnam was something that was happening a million miles away and it wasn't affecting me or my lifestyle. The only time I started to take any real interest or to worry about Vietnam was when it looked like I might be going to participate in the whole thing.

I don't think the Army could have done much more to prepare us, short of putting us through the real thing. To be fair I would imagine that we were probably better prepared than a lot of our fathers and grandfathers were when they were given a couple of months training and shipped off to their wars.

I didn't volunteer for infantry. I wanted to be a musician at the Army school of music in Victoria. During recruit training the instructors would tell us that if we worked hard and really tried they would recommend that we get our choice of corps. Well, I worked my freckle off because the last thing in the Army I wanted to be was an infantry soldier. At the end of recruit training I was allocated to infantry.

During my infantry training, which took about three months more, I would go down to the orderly room every Friday and request a corps transfer to band corps, but it never eventuated until about three weeks before we left for Vietnam.

This sergeant asked me if I still wanted a band posting because there was a vacancy in the Artillery Band at North Head and if I wanted it he could probably arrange it. I thought about it and I looked at the other guys and thought, 'They've got no way of getting out of going.' Besides, it was a chance to travel, see a bit of the world and it was sort of like a big adventure.

MIKE BOLAND

He went to Vietnam in 1968. Today, he is a public servant in Canberra.

We had a CSM at recruit training who believed that if he didn't break you then there was no way you would break under fire; he reckoned you would be meaner and tougher and nastier than the Viet Cong were ever going to be. At times the discipline was harsh and at times unfair. There is a device in the Army called a Redress of Wrongs and the platoon had its leave stopped on some stupid pretext at one stage so a mate and myself told the CSM that we were going to bring a Redress of Wrongs action against him. The result was that everyone else went on leave and we spent the whole of the weekend scraping all the polish off the floor in the company headquarters with bayonets and repolishing it by hand and from then on we couldn't do a thing right.

His nickname was 'The Coon'. He was a very hard man and, in his own way, a very fair man.

BOB PRIDE

He was a land clearing engineer in Vietnam in 1967.

We had a couple of conscientious objectors with us at recruit training. The corporals fell on them pretty hard at the start, because the corporals at basic training were real dogs. I'm sure they were dragged up somewhere and just sort of poured into their uniforms and told, 'Get them boys.'

They would try to trick these guys. They would say, 'Go and pick that rifle up, sonny.'

'No, corporal, I don't want to pick it up.'

'Oh what's the matter with you son, go over and pick it up.'

'No, I don't want to.'

After a couple of weeks even these corporals worked out that they were fair dinkum.

MALCOLM McLEAN

'I was footloose and fancy-free at the time I was conscripted. I thought about nothing other than my mates, girls and good times. I found it hard to accept the military machine, all these people running around screaming at you twenty-four hours a day, giving us duties if we couldn't remember our regimental number when it was asked for. We used to sit up all night in the hut and recite our regimental numbers to each other. It was all part of losing your individuality. That's what it was all about.' He was an infantry soldier in Vietnam in 1968.

Where it really all started was in Canungra — the brain-washing and the propaganda part of it — and that's where I started to really dig my toes in against the system.

It was well into the second week when you used to get a lot of lectures and stuff like that, part of the process.

We walked into this particular assembly hall one afternoon, there were two or three hundred of us. There was a lectern at the front with two lights on it and that was the only lighting in the hall. A second lieutenant and a couple of NCOs got up near this bloody lectern and they had this big map of Vietnam on the wall. The place was just about in darkness.

We walked down and everybody's whispering and carrying on, saying 'What in the bloody hell's this all about?' They sat us all down and this officer pointed at the map with a stick. There was complete silence. The next minute he just brought this stick down — wham! — on the table to get everyone's attention and then all this crap is flying out of his mouth: 'You've been inducted into the Army, you're in this camp now, because you're going to Vietnam to kill, kill, kill. This is your enemy ...' And they had a silhouette of a North Vietnamese regular. 'You're going over there to kill, kill, kill.'

This was totally foreign to my upbringing, totally foreign to what I'd been taught at school about a fair deal for everybody, so-called democracy, all that crap. I couldn't believe that I was part of this system and this was happening to me.

BOB MILLARD

The main thing I remember is at Canungra. The first night we were up there we had a big lecture. I remember it was a crowded hall. It seemed like about five hundred to a thousand blokes in there to me. They asked how many of us wanted to go to Vietnam and I think about ten arms went up and they were all regs who had volunteered for it. But no other arms went up, so the man said, 'Oh well, we'll see how you feel at the end of your training.'

It was three weeks blitz training, the hardest training I'd ever done and I used to play Rugby Union. The first week we were absolutely buggered. Every muscle in your body ached all the way through and they kept telling you to run until you just couldn't run any more.

Halfway through the second week we started to feel a little bit fitter — we weren't getting any sorer — and the third week we just sort of laughed at anything they could do to us. Whatever they told us to do we did and there wasn't a worry in the world.

We'd had quite a few of those nightly lectures, but about the second last night before we left they asked the same question. They said, 'Who *now* wants to go to Vietnam?' and I don't think there was an arm in the room that was down. Everyone wanted to go.

BOB WALKER

A regular soldier, he was a loader-operator in a Centurian tank in Vietnam in 1969. He lives in Canberra.

I can remember our OC asked the entire squadron about two weeks prior to embarkation did anybody not want to go and there was only one person and he was a regular soldier. It was on religious grounds as far as I can remember and to our everlasting shame I suppose that ninety-five per cent of us called him a coward, gave him a hell of a time. I'll never forget that fellow.

He was a nervous wreck after that. They did some rotten things to him — the boot polish on the privates, scrubbed him in the showers, incredible name calling, that sort of stuff, really gave him a hard time. It was bad news. He cracked. He ended up with the Army psychs and a discharge so he did get what he wanted, but at what cost to him. Now probably we'd all pat him on the back for his guts.

BERNARD SZAPIEL

He was born in Germany during the Second World War in a labour camp. 'I remember particularly in Germany when I was five, going through wheatfields after the harvesters had gone through, picking up individual grains so that my parents could have sufficient grain to grind into flour for bread. I remember that the Germans prevented my mother from getting any milk to feed me.'

He arrived in Australia with his parents in 1950 and was conscripted in 1967. Today he is a potter in Melbourne.

I think I settled into the Army reasonably well from the first few weeks. I was a very malleable type of person; I was sort of easy to push where most people wanted to push me. I had no set ideas of my own, I had no political affiliations, I had no moral convictions on the Vietnam war. In fact, prior to actually going into the Army I don't think I could even say that I'd heard of the Vietnam war. This is 1967, because I was conscripted in February 1967.

After a few weeks we went to a session where we were broken up into various religious groups — Roman Catholic, Church of England and so forth. I attended the Roman Catholic seminar and the priest there actually advocated the war. I started thinking about 'Thou must not kill' and even though I was politically naive at that stage I felt we were not endangered by the Vietnam war and yet this person was telling me very clearly that if I went over there I was allowed to kill. I think I remember asking a question of the priest and I think he gave me some sort of an answer which didn't satisfy me intellectually, but as far as the moral issue was concerned it satisfied me. I felt that if the priest said it was okay to kill it must be okay, although I was very uneasy about it.

When we got our boots, our steel-lined boots, that was the reality, you knew that you were going; that was the calling card. I think I had a week's leave after that and I went home to Ballarat. My mother was devastated; she obviously knew more than I did about the whole thing. My father was very proud. My sisters I don't think knew much about it.

I came back after a week's leave, having had a great time in Ballarat with my folks, and we had a great piss-up in the canteen and I woke up that morning — it was the day before I was supposed to leave — and that was the first time that it really struck me. I thought, 'My God, I'm going there.' For the first time it struck me that I was going there to kill people and that I could die. Up to that stage it was a fairy-tale type of thing, there wasn't any reality to it.

The morning we left I got up very early, and we were transported to Mascot Airport and boarded a flight there. My parents were in Ballarat and they didn't come up. I remember making a phone call to Ballarat just a few hours before I left. That was the last contact that I had.

I remember seeing these guys who were going over, on the tarmac with their girlfriends and their mothers and their brothers and their sisters and their relatives, and I was the only guy on the plane looking out at all these people and I thought 'Gee, this is bloody sad, this is sad.' Well, I sort of laughed it off again. I'm that sort of person who can look at a situation and think, 'Oh well, poor bum' and then laugh at it.

All the guys eventually boarded the plane and this guy sat next to me who I'd made great friends with; we'd gone through corps training together and reo at Ingleburn and I knew his fiancée very well. On the plane we had kangaroo-tail soup. It was great, it was fantastic. It was a real party although there wasn't any booze served. Soon after we took off — I don't know whether it was a premonition or what — I remember saying clearly to myself, clearly in words in my own mind, 'One of us isn't going to come back, one of us isn't going to come back.'

GARRY

He was an infantry soldier in Vietnam in 1968.

I was a regular soldier, signed up in '67 at the age of nineteen. Before I went in I was getting into a bit of trouble. I was a bit of a blue artist when I was a kid and I wasn't having a lot of luck with jobs, so I decided the Army was the best shot. That was one reason. The other reason was that, the way I was going, it didn't look like I'd ever get a house and I thought a war service loan would make it a bit easier. I reckoned that I'd probably end up in Vietnam, but I didn't think a lot about it one way or the other. We were training to do a job and we only had twelve months to learn it and we poured everything into it.

When we went over in 1968 there was a song on the charts, one of Roy Orbison's: 'There won't be many coming home'. We were eleven days on the *Sydney* going over there and it had its own radio station and DJ who used to play requests. This song, 'There won't be many coming home', was requested about every twenty minutes. You'd hear that, then you'd hear four or five other songs, then you'd get this one up again. Our CO ended up banning it, wouldn't allow it to be played again. Bad for morale.

BARRY KELLY

He served as an engineer in Vietnam in 1966.

We only realised we were going to Vietnam about a week before we went. We thought we were going to go to Borneo.

After Christmas leave, '65, we came back and all of a sudden started doing all this jungle warfare training. We were doing a lot of work with landmines and anti-personnel mines.

Finally they told us we were going to Vietnam and we said, 'Where the bloody hell is Vietnam?' I'd never heard of it. We had to go and get a map of the world, one of those big round balls, in the RSM's office to find out where Vietnam was.

...oops embark for Vietnam at Garden Island, April 1965. They left believing that in ...eir year the war would be won. (Photographs courtesy of John Fairfax and Sons.)

Newly arrived troops are trucked from Vung Tau to Nui Dat. While the Australians saw themselves as part of a liberating army, the attitude of the local population was often

The ancient and agrarian culture of Vietnam was a constant source of bewilderment to the predominantly urban, working-class Australian troops. The Vietnamese were equally bewildered by the Australians. (Photograph courtesy of 5/7 Battalion, Holsworthy.)

For most Australian troops, the Vietnam war was endless plodding across flooded rice fields and tangled jungle trails in search of an elusive enemy. Most often, the soldiers were harassed more by heat and leeches than by the communists. (Photograph courtesy of Australian War Memorial.)

Soldiers move through a village, 1967. Australians patrolled roads and villages by day; at night these returned to the control of the Viet Cong. (Photograph courtesy of Australian War Memorial.)

Soldiers fill their water bottles from a creek before continuing their patrol. Entire ecological systems, including waterways, were contaminated by aerially-sprayed defoliants. (Photograph courtesy of Australian War Memorial.)

Australian soldiers sometimes carried more than half their body-weight into action. (Photograph courtesy of Australian War Memorial.)

An Australian soldier is carried out of the bush for medical evacuation by helicopter. Wounded soldiers could be picked out of the jungle and in hospital in half an hour. (Photograph courtesy of Australian War Memorial.)

Australian soldiers watch a bombing attack on the Long Hai hills, where many Australians were killed. More bombs were dropped on Vietnam in a single year than in the whole of the Second World War. (Photograph courtesy of Australian War Memorial.)

TREVOR MORRIS

He was raised in the tough western suburbs of Melbourne, where he still lives. He was called up in the sixth intake of national service in September, 1966, and served with a mortar platoon in Vietnam in 1968.

We boarded the *HMAS Sydney* at Garden Island. My mother was there and my fiancée and my sister and it was pretty hard. Everyone's doing their farewells. A band was playing 'Waltzing Matilda' and all that patriotic stuff. I didn't think the Aussies were like that, but they rose to the occasion. They must have taken a leaf out of the Yankees' book. All the kids had little Australian flags.

BRIAN GRIFFIN

He was a cavalry commander in Vietnam in 1969–70.
  'I knew where Vietnam was. My father had been a prisoner of war of the Japanese on Hainan, off the Gulf of Tonkin. He was pretty well able to tell me what was going on, and I had read a little bit of the history of the French in Vietnam, but after that it was just a big void.
  'The thing was to get your name up on the list of reinforcements to go over and that was a terrible thing really because in that situation there were either people coming home or people being hurt for you to get there.'
  He lives on a five-acre farm at Clunes, New South Wales.

We flew out of Mascot in the middle of the night, eleven o'clock I think the plane left. The trip out of Mascot was pretty funny. They sent us out alphabetically and the blokes who were next in line came out to see us off. I can remember them standing there singing, 'You'll come home in a plastic bag, doo da, doo da...' which didn't go down too well with the immediate family when they chorused it for you.

PETER VANDENBERG

He served two tours of Vietnam, in 1965 and 1967, as a platoon medic.

'For me Vietnam came onto the scene in May, 1965, when we saw on the television news that Australia was going to commit combat troops, only at that stage they hadn't announced what outfit was going. The funny thing was that as soon as they said that Australia was going there I got a real sweaty feeling at the back of my neck, a cold, clammy feeling, and I thought, "Hey mate, this is for real".'

We had a parade before we went, in the afternoon, where the Minister for the Army, Dr Forbes, made his 'die for Australia and uphold the Anzac tradition' speech. It was a lot of crap as far as I was concerned.

We then got in the back of trucks with our old Second World War weaponry, went to Central Station in Sydney where we unloaded our bulk equipment and from there we went to the dockyard. When we drove in, it was like driving into a bloody great prison camp because they shut the gates behind us. There was to be no families, no nothing.

I still remember — I think they called him a commo — a bloke with a limp who was handing out pamphlets at the dockyard gates when we drove in. I think that's why they called him a commo, because he was handing out anti-war pamphlets saying Australia shouldn't be involved.

We pulled away, I think it was just after midnight. Most of us were still at the card game anyhow. Nothing said, like we're going to leave at such and such time. I think a lot of it was because of the protesters, even then. That was in 1965.

I must have dozed off for a while and I got up, I remember it was after midnight with a hell of a racket going on. It was different from what it was when we embarked, the sound was different, and when I looked out the quay was two hundred yards away. I sort of got the feeling we snuck out under cover of bloody darkness just like a bloody mongrel dog. Disappeared like a mongrel dog.

BRUCE POULTON

He has his eyes fixed on some point outside the window. 'I had heard about Vietnam, I knew there was something going on there, but it didn't mean a great deal to me. I had left home when I was fourteen, went to live in Sydney in a boarding house. I was eighteen when I joined the Army. I was nineteen when I went to Vietnam.' That was in 1969.

We were taken by bus in the night from the reinforcement wing through all the back streets to Mascot. I think the plane landed about eleven p.m., after the airport had closed.

They kept the bar open for us. I never had anyone to see me off, or anything like that, even though my family lived in the state. This mate of mine from Tasmania and I just sat at the bar and got pissed.

We got on the plane and flew from there to Darwin, had a break there and then flew with Qantas from Darwin to Singapore for breakfast.

You had about a hundred and thirty blokes riding on that plane, different corps, all reinforcements, and we were ordered to carry a civilian shirt to put on at Singapore because it wasn't supposed to be a stopoff area for a war zone. So you'd see blokes with polyester greens on, with GP boots on, with short hair and a civilian shirt — about a hundred and thirty of them running around the joint, all keeping in groups with authority figures calling them into line and all that. We had breakfast and tried to sneak a few cans into us and then got back onto the plane.

It was daytime when we flew over Vietnam and it looked really peaceful from up in the air. The only blokes who would have realised just what was going on — the cancer that was running around underneath all that greenery — were probably the blokes who had been there before. Where we were going was just ratshit, but it looked good from on top. The cover of it looked nice and green and all serene.

2

At Vietnam

'Our men will be fighting the largely indigenous Viet Cong in their own home territory. They will be fighting in the midst of a largely indifferent, if not resentful, and frightened population. They will be fighting at the request of, and in support, and presumably under the direction of an unstable, inefficient, partially corrupt military regime which lacks even the semblance of being, or becoming, democratically based.'

Arthur Calwell, 1965

BILL DOBELL

*He was a volunteer, who served six months as an infantry soldier in
Vietnam in 1969, aged nineteen.*

*'I left school when I was fourteen and I was a bootmaker until I went
into the Army. I was pretty well hemmed in — just front up in town,
mend a few shoes six days a week, and go home again. I don't know
whether I was actually looking for a war, but I think it would be safe
to say that when I joined the Army I did it to go for a look — just
for a look.'*

I was very, very scared when we arrived. I remember coming in
by air and that was when I first realised I was there. This was
where it was going to happen, there was a war after all. Up
until then it was in the paper, on the telly, but all of a sudden,
shit, it's here, it's real, it's happening.

I just felt helpless. I'm on the plane. Once it touches down
that's it, I'm stuck, I've got to go, I've got no choice, I can't stay
on it. Around me now there's heaps of fighter aircraft, bombers,
God knows what. I didn't recognise any of them, just that they
were war planes.

They moved us onto a bus. I remember it had wire mesh over
all the windows and as we moved off I'm seeing soldiers, South
Vietnamese. They were all armed and wandering around. This
is really war. They're all there, they're armed and ready to go.
I felt lost, helpless.

JEFF SCULLEY

We went through all bloody mad stages on the ship going up
there, grabbing blokes and shaving the hair off their balls, just
generally killing time. A couple of blokes were told by the
RSM to have a haircut so two of them shaved their hair completely off and another bloke done a big mohawk.

We had a big hurricane going over. It went on for three days
and we had to do a battalion parade on deck with the ship going
up and down and rolling from side to side and the RSM was

screaming out 'Keep still'. We could have been washed overboard.

The last night on board we went up the coast past An Thuy, in the Mekong Delta area south of Saigon, and there was a bit of firefighting going on. We could see the tracers and the choppers and the planes flying around and we could hear all types of machine-gun fire. I don't know what everybody else thought but I couldn't get a front seat quick enough to have a look at it all.

We anchored in Vung Tau harbour and they took us ashore on landing craft. When we got off we were still swaying in the gut from the ship and I felt crook. I can remember looking around and getting hit by the smell of the place. I thought, 'Well Christ, what a stinking bloody hole we've had to come to.'

Our platoon sergeant was running up and down giving everybody ammunition and I missed out and I thought, 'Christ, I've got no ammo.' I was too scared to speak up and I was thinking what'd happen if they hit us on the road?

They took us to Nui Dat by truck and for the first mile I was thinking, 'Well, here we are, we've come to save you from the communists.' I expected we'd get a few cheers going through the streets, no worries. But the first bitch I seen, she spat at us, at the Australians! I thought, 'What the fuck is going on here?'

When we got to Nui Dat our platoon commander met us, showed us which hoochies we were in and once we got all our gear chucked in he says, 'I'll show you around our area of responsibility,' because we immediately had to start manning the wire. He took us down and the first thing he said to me, which stuck in my mind, was, 'Everything you learnt back in Australia, forget it; it'll be a different ball game here.'

PETER VANDENBERG

I remember the thing running through my mind was one of old John Wayne's war movies. It sounds stupid I guess, but we were expecting that we might have to hit the beach under machine-gun fire. The next thing that happened was an almighty thud and the ramp dropped down and there's about five hundred Vietnamese kids standing there and I thought, 'What the bloody hell is going on here?' I said to one of the blokes behind me, 'What are we supposed to do, for Christ's sake; are we supposed to fan out on the beach or what?'

We became so disorientated within those first few minutes that everything they'd told us seemed like utter crap. It was an anticlimax.

MALCOLM McLEAN

At Tan Son Nhut, when they unloaded us off the plane, they had us all lined up on the tarmac and I think it must have been about lunchtime or something because they brought out these cut lunches — sandwiches and all this sort of crap. While we were standing there looking around there must have been a dozen Vietnamese, I'd say airport workers, just sitting there watching, sitting on their haunches watching us eat all this food. A lot of the blokes, after the long flight and because of the unbearable humidity, didn't eat anything and just threw the sandwiches and the fruit and everything into these forty-four gallon drum garbage cans. These people on the tarmac were just so patient; they just sat there and they were just watching us, not even looking at each other, just sat watching us. To me it was a first impression of what patient people they are.

After we lined up and got moving, the next thing you knew these people were like bloody flies, straight for the garbage cans, ripping into half eaten sandwiches and fruit and all this sort of thing. They were literally starving! That was a big awakening for me, because you never read about this in a school book. Nobody told you about anything like this, that people were starving on the other side of the world.

WAYNE

My first impression of Vietnam was that it was a stinking dirty hole. It stunk like hell, it was like going into a sewer. It was really shocking. Looking at the people, you could tell they hated you, as soon as you walked off the plane. They really hated you.

The first day was 21 January, 1971, I'll always remember it. I got off the plane and there was a Vietnamese kid with one arm and no legs. He just had these hessian bandages on his knees. He was a beggar. I went to give him ten Australian dollars, put it in his hat, and this big Negro — he must have been six foot eight — picked me up, took the ten dollars off me and he says, 'You don't give those motherfuckers any money.' That really turned me off. I just couldn't understand.

BOB WALKER

I think the only contact I'd ever had with South-East Asia was in movies, or television, and it was always portrayed as a very busy, vibrant place and that came up to expectations. Busy, hot of course, but really pulsing. It was exciting, really exciting.

TREVOR MORRIS

We arrived at Vung Tau and got off the ship in landing barges. Well, talk about a joke. It was just like you see in the bloody movies: 'Keep your heads down boys, keep your heads down.' Everybody got in the back of the barge, no-one was up the front; you're waiting for the bullets to come whizzing over and when they dropped the ramp no-one moved. They had to kick us out.

We finally hit the beach and there's all these Yanks and Aussies on R&C, sitting drinking cans of beer with sheilas. There was a stunned silence. They sat up and said, 'Have a look at these silly bastards, will you.' We're like storming the beaches and they've got deck chairs and umbrellas, if you don't mind. I felt really embarrassed. Fair dinkum, I felt small.

Seven Battalion was in the background waiting to get back on the barges to go onto the boat. One of the first blokes I bumped into was big Johnny who I'd gone through training with in Australia and he was going home. He said to me, 'Sucker.'

BARRY KELLY

The thing that was so ironical was that all through our training we were taught that the Cong wears black pyjamas and a panama hat and that's your enemy. Well, bugger me, we landed on the *HMAS Sydney* a couple of mile off Vung Tau and we went in by American landing barge with weapons, ammunition, the whole thing, and every mother's son standing there was dressed in black pyjamas and a panama hat, selling Coca-Cola and pineapples. We were just looking at each other. We felt so bloody stupid.

GIL SCOLYER

From Smithton in Tasmania, he enlisted when he was twenty-one and went to Vietnam as a platoon medic in 1970.

My first impression was, fuck, the place stinks. There were nogs hanging out of shanties and it just stunk of filth. 'What are we doing here?'

The further towards the Dat you got the worse the country looked. It wasn't worth fuckin' fighting for.

FRANK HUNT

Johnny Needs was in our landing craft. He'd been over there with Six Battalion previously and he'd come back. John was a very thin, wiry fellow, a tremendously fit man, very caring, a real Ginger Meggs in behaviour; if anyone was going to get into bloody trouble he would, but somehow he'd cover himself and he'd get out of it. He had told us, 'Look, be prepared, rifles at the ready, make sure your water bottle belt is tied up, nothing loose, be prepared.'

The adrenalin was fair running through us. We were tense, we're not saying boo to each other and he's up the end: 'Just keep cool, boys, just keep cool, you'll be right fellas, remember you've been well trained, you're the top bloody troops in the Australian Army. Now all I want, when that board goes down, you hit the beach and you get onto your guts and you get into the ready-to-fire position; this is it boys, the fucking game's over, this is the fair dinkum stuff.'

The landing craft hits the beach, down goes the plank, out we go, head down, arse up, hit the sand, at the ready, look up and see people riding bicycles! Fucking hell, what are we into here, what type of war is this? And there's Johnny, standing on the bloody landing craft laughing his head off.

JOHN ROBBINS

They put us on cattle trucks. We all stood up and, of course, we were all peering over the tops to try and see what was happening and I saw this bloke having a shit in the street. I thought, 'This is a little bit different from what we're used to.'

TERRY HOLDEN

He was a driver in Vietnam in 1970.

'When the government introduced the conscription ballot I hoped I wouldn't be called up, but when I was I accepted it. I thought it was right that Australia contribute to Vietnam because of the American alliance. I didn't know very much about the war, only what I had read in the press and seen on the news. They didn't tell us a great deal.'

He lives in Stawell, Victoria, where he is a farmer.

The first day we had to do the rubbish run. We went out with the bloke we were replacing, around the camp picking up all the dustbins full of swill and that sort of thing, all the rubbish, to take to the tip.

We came to an area of Vung Tau where there was a wooden landing, as high as a truck, and we stopped and I said, 'What are you stopping for, there's no rubbish bins here?' I must admit we were a bit toey our first few months over there because you didn't know what was going to happen next, if some guy was going to come out from behind a tree or a corner of a building and let you have it.

We got two rubbish bins off the back of the truck and put them on the landing. Well, you should have seen them come out, in their hundreds, the Vietnamese. They were carrying anything they possibly could to take the swill back to their huts to cook and eat it. They'd dive in with their pots and pans and whatever. I was nearly ill.

RAY ORCHARD

They shipped us down to the back beach at Vung Tau, down to the sand dunes. We spent two weeks there, firing weapons and going to lectures on what was going to happen. Then a mob came down and flew us up into Nui Dat. Yanks were every-where there.

When I was on the chopper we had that much gear I thought, 'Oh shit, I'm going to fall out of this bastard.' You could fit seven or eight troops with just basic equipment on, but we had all these things. I was hanging on so tight I was weak. I just fell straight out when we landed, and my arm was numb because it was about a twenty-minute trip. I looked up at all these bloody Yanks, running around and shouting orders. They had greens on, but all red from the soil. The big guns were up there where we jumped off, and they were firing. I thought, 'Shit, we're here, we're in it, we're right in amongst it now, bloody hell.'

JIM FRANGOS

He was born in Greece and emigrated to Australia with his family in 1952. 'I couldn't have been a conscientious objector, I respected my father too much. He had fought in the First World War and was a patriot and a royalist. The law of the land to him was absolutely everything, so it was everything to me.'

He was an Army cook in Vietnam in 1969–70. He now owns a cafe in Ballarat, Victoria, and we talk between orders.

We got off the plane and got on a bus with wire grilles on the windows. When we got to the base there were sirens going and you name it and next thing I know I've got a two hundred-pound Negro lying flat on top of me and I'm in the mud. He's sitting on top of me with a gun saying, 'Sit there guy, I'm going to save you.' It was just before Christmas 1969 and the VC had mortared us. I'm lying in the mud and he's using me as a rug so he wouldn't get wet. I was genuinely frightened.

BRIAN GRIFFIN

I was out on operations the first day. We were wiring on down the road, escorting some American 155 howitzers from Nui Dat to a place called The Horseshoe. We're going down the road and everybody stops and I can see smoke ahead of us and there's Yanks jumping up and down. I said, 'Has someone blown a radiator?' I still hadn't switched on. They said, 'No, we've just been rocketed.'

FAY LEWIS

She was an Army nurse in Vietnam in 1970.

I'd been at the apprentices' school at Balcombe, which was basically an RAP, where you looked after all the apprentices' colds and tinea and played mum, but I went to Vietnam in charge of intensive care and triage and I just wasn't prepared for the mass casualties. I'd never seen intensive care. My main experience had been in labour wards, delivering babies. We arrived at Tan Son Nhut and landed beside planes taking coffins back to America. I think that was the first thing we saw.

RIC

On my first day there an old digger came in and said, 'Hoa Long dance is tonight, put on your polyesters and your finery.' Hoa Long was a village just down the road from Nui Dat. I thought, 'That'll be good, I'll enjoy that.'

I got myself all dressed up and the RSM came in and inspected me and all of a sudden everyone was laughing at the new guy. They were rolling on the floor they were laughing so hard. I didn't know what the hell they were laughing about until someone explained to me that Hoa Long was controlled by the Viet Cong at night time.

MICK CRAWFORD

You're there for about a day and a half and you want to go home again. I think everybody had a calendar and every time I wrote home it was only so many days to go and you'd be home. You just don't realise until you hit there what happens to you, you just don't. You become entirely disorientated. You don't know where in hell you are, which way is home anymore.

DON DUFFUS

'Just before the end of recruit training we could nominate for different corps and that was about the only thing in my two years in the Army that I put in for and got. I put in for engineers. I certainly never volunteered for Vietnam. I was just sent and that was it.'

He was an engineer.

My first day in Vietnam we ended up in the boozer and we ended up pretty pissed. I found my way back to my tent and jumped in the sack. About two, half past two in the morning there's an almighty kaboom. I jumped out of the stretcher and landed on my kitbags, just crouching there thinking what was that? The other blokes in the tent are all snoring away and I thought I couldn't be dreaming. Next thing kaboom again. I'm looking around. I thought I have to wake these guys up, the nogs are belting hell out of the joint. I'm yelling at them, 'Wake up, wake up.' One of the blokes said, 'Go back to sleep, they're ours.' It was our artillery firing out harassment and interdiction to stop the nogs moving around.

I suppose it was only a fortnight and I learned to distinguish incoming from outgoing.

JEFF SCULLEY

It was a funny fear, the first night on picket. Everything is new to you. I was in a bunker with this guy, Herb. It was about ten feet square, all sandbags over the top, a gun mounted inside facing out, and a big wire net out in front to stop grenades being thrown in from the wire.

They had these fireflies in Vietnam and they looked like torches and we're staring into the dark, looking at these lights down on the wire. Our eyes were like saucers.

'Is that a torch?'

'I don't know.'

Next minute we hear a noise out to the left, a rustle. We were underneath rubber trees and there were all these dead leaves on the ground. We hear this rustle through them and Herb says, 'What's that?'

'I don't know.'

'It's out there, go and have a look.'

'You go and have a look.'

'You go out.'

'I'm not going out.'

I end up going out. I open the back door and as soon as I step out this mongoose cuts away through the leaves. I've gone cold. I'm sweating and I'm cold. God Jesus, you've got no idea of the fear.

DAVID COWDREY

'All my mates were going into national service, but I was too old for the marble, I was twenty-four, so I went down to Martin Place in Sydney one day and signed the papers. I went into the Army as a regular soldier a few weeks later.' He is still serving in the Army.

We were taken first to a little place at Nui Dat called the Australian Reinforcement Unit which was designed to train you in procedures before you were sent to a battalion. I can remember they showed us how to let off a claymore mine and they introduced us to the Armalite rifle. Before I went over to Vietnam I'd never seen an Armalite in my life. All of a sudden you get there and they say, 'Here is an Armalite, this is how it works.'

I was sent to One Battalion. The first day there we march in and the RSM got us in a little room and says, 'Okay, you're now with the Fighting One. You are now a member of the killing, fighting One Battalion.' I thought what a load of shit.

On my first patrol we came across a small bunker system. The bunkers were there, the food and everything, and we'd gone through the lot but no-one was there. We were just walking out when the Viet Cong who were staying there came around the corner and virtually bumped into our forward scout.

Everyone went down, there was a lot of fire and a lot of tracers around my head. When it was over, we'd shot two and the rest had gone. My mate came up and said, 'How are you feeling?' I said, 'Good.'

Our lieutenant came around and told me to go out and search the bodies. We'd been told how when they're dying they put a grenade underneath themselves with the pin pulled out and when you turn them over you get blown up — so I took a guy out with me and we did what we'd been trained: we put a rope around the wrist, got behind a tree and pulled. The only trouble was when we yanked it felt pretty soft. I said to my mate, 'This guy must be a half-back because I've just pulled that rope and I don't feel nothing.' When I looked out I'd pulled him in half.

He'd been shot in the stomach about eight times so when I gave a big yank the top half came away and the bottom half just stayed where it was. He'd been blown in half, this fella. I think I started purking then and I didn't eat for three days. You'd cook up, say, corn, beef and rice and that would be it, I'd just be looking at that bloke's stomach and I'd be throwing up.

We got in a couple more after that. I saw a guy get his head blown off and my best mate got killed. A bloke who I became mates with over there, who was only nineteen, got about four bullets in his stomach; and then I just found that I couldn't sleep of a night. Everyone was weaving things, trying to get the best job, even all these heroes who went over there. I know so many guys who were supposed to be heroes who tried to weave their way into little jobs so they didn't have to do it. They wanted a batman for the dentist at Vung Tau. I put in for that. I tried to get that real bad.

BOB HOBBS

I was terrified of mines and the first patrol I remember going on I was immediately behind our sergeant, and I know that everytime he lifted up his foot I would put my boot into his footprint in front of me.

I was a 'new boy' in the platoon, a reo. The majority of the platoon had already been in-country a couple of months and everything was different to what I was used to: the rain, vegetation, smells, everything. It was all very alien. I wanted to be accepted by the other guys. I wanted to do well and not stuff anything up. I felt I was being appraised by the other guys in the platoon and later in the year I found myself treating the new guys with the same caution and apprehension.

FRANK HUNT

In my first contact I was that keen I remember the platoon commander yelling out to me, 'For Christ's sake, get back here.' Here I was virtually standing up firing into this bloody creek at these three fellows and to this day I swear I got one, but because we were only sent out to do a certain job we couldn't be sidetracked. By Jesus I was keen. It was like going rabbiting for the first time.

LACHLAN IRVINE

'I joined the Army in February 1966 and thought our training was pretty good, but we were trained by guys who had been to Vietnam in 1965 and they were training us to fight local farmers who were Viet Cong by night. When we got over there we walked right into the 1968 Tet Offensive* and we were fighting against a well equipped North Vietnamese Army. We just had to forget about what we had been taught and start learning all over again.'

He lives in Sydney.

We started patrolling pretty much straight away and I can remember my first patrol very well because I was carrying live grenades for the first time. I'd thrown them in basic training, but I went out on this first patrol carrying a live grenade in each of my shirt pockets and that was all I thought about the whole patrol. I didn't give a thought to the Viet Cong. I was just aware that there were live grenades in my pockets.

MAX CAMERON

'Originally I joined the Army for a bet. My brother was in the Army and his wife reckoned I wouldn't be able to handle it. Also I used to do things like borrow other people's cars and beat up people just for the hell of it. The way I was heading I would have ended up a crim for sure.'

He served two tours of duty as an infantry soldier in Vietnam, in 1965–6 and in 1969. He lives in Brisbane.

The first training operation was the best. It sticks in my memory. We went out from Vung Tau, where we were camped on the back beach, to a swampy area. They dropped us off and we were heading back towards camp, or supposed to have been, when all of a sudden all hell broke loose up front — bullets everywhere — and the whole company started running

---

**The Tet Offensive was a surprise offensive launched by communist forces throughout Vietnam during the Chinese and Vietnamese lunar New Year (known as Tet).*

towards where the fire was coming from. I couldn't believe it. They all started running towards it. I think I went from being up near the front of the company to tail-end Charlie in the blink of an eye.

We got pinned down and there's yelling and screaming and carrying on. It was bloody hot. The next thing I know they were all running back past me. I was trying to find out what was going on; all of a sudden I end up tail-end Charlie and now I'm up the front again. I had to get up and follow them otherwise I would have been there on my own, so I got up and chased after them.

We ended up with six heat-exhaustion cases and one guy got a slight graze on the arm from a stray bullet. We found out later that we'd walked in behind a practice firing range. I'd never seen such a shemozzel in all my life.

BRUCE POULTON

'In that first contact was all the realisation of what was going on. I think the hardest thing to come to grips with was that I had been taught to shoot someone and at the same time they had been taught to shoot me; I was out there to kill someone, but they were out there to kill me. It was a two-way game.'

We got ambushed in a swamp, water up to our guts. We threw ourselves into the water and I could feel my pack weighing me down, but I was terrified of what would happen when I came up. When I did, there was a bit of reed on the lever of the machine-gun that released the barrel. I grabbed hold of it and pulled it off but I pulled the lever and the barrel fell off into the water. I'm standing there with a heap of rounds going into a stock and no barrel.

People were screaming, 'Get the gun going, get the gun going' and all this shit, and I'm looking for the barrel and people are groping around in the water looking for the barrel. By the time we found it things had settled down, but I realised then that we weren't playing games.

GEOFF COLLINS

I'd been there about two weeks and I was really raw, I had no idea what was going on. A field engineer is completely different to anyone else. When the infantry went out, or the artillery, or the tanks, two engineers always went with them in case they came across any booby traps, or mines, or bunker systems that needed to be exploded. We were always there and caught up in it.

The first time I went out the APCs took us up into the Nui Thi Vai mountains just out of Nui Dat, the Warbies we used to call them because they reminded us of the Warburton Mountains back home. We ended up right up in the top of the Warbies and we walked around there for about a week and a half, had one or two contacts. I think the first three or four nights all I did was just lay there with my pistol on my chest, more or less like a kid cuddles his teddy bear for security. I didn't know what the hell was going on.

After a while if you were lucky — and I consider myself lucky — you were able to put yourself in a state of semi-shock. If you could get yourself into that, where you could just see things happening and just accept them, that they're happening because you're there, you didn't seem to crack up that much.

MICK RAINEY

It was a strange situation because we didn't know jungle tactics. We'd never been taught them, never practised them at Puckapunyal with its open, rolling hills. It was an entirely new ball game. I'd never driven a tank in jungle of that nature before. You just had to learn as you went along and modify things, and in most cases as far as tactics were concerned it was always compromise, compromise.

LES MYERS

The first time I was ever in a helicopter was in Vietnam. I'd never even seen inside one. The correct way to get out of the things was explained to me in about two minutes flat on the way in, which was bloody ridiculous. Bunker systems were the same. I didn't even know what a bunker system was when we went over there. Didn't take long to find out though.

BERNARD SZAPIEL

I remember the first night we spent outside the camp. I think it was in a rubber plantation and there was a full moon, everything was totally lit up and I think the rubber trees had lost their leaves or something. I don't know whether it was defoliation or what, but you could see every guy on the ground, a whole platoon, and I was really shit-scared then. A leaf would rustle, someone would cough and I was ready to shit.

After a while you became accustomed to it. No-one attacked you, you never shot anyone, you didn't hear any gunfire. It was sort of boring, hot, humid. You got wet, you got eaten by the mosquitoes, the leeches. You were tramping around in water, fighting your way through bamboo and you became very, very blasé. I think for the first two months that I was out with the battalion we'd had not one single contact.

Eventually our platoon was the only one that hadn't made a kill, or made any contact, and I thought, 'This is stupid, this is unreal, there's no bloody enemy out here.'

The first time we came in contact we had camped on an embankment above a track and two of us were on sentry; we were just smoking, talking out loud and laughing. I'd finished my sentry duty and gone back to my hoochie, just piled myself on the side of the shell scrape, when bloody hell broke out, shooting all over the place, just from where I'd left my mate by himself.

Apparently he'd lit up another fag and put his feet up, right up in the air, with his rifle more than an arm's length away from him, peacefully puffing away waiting for the next guy to come to accompany him in sentry duty. He saw a face peering at him and he thought, 'This face doesn't look familiar.' It was quite a moonlit night and he was under a hoochie so the guy who was looking at him, barely three or four feet away, couldn't see in. With this face staring at him, he edged over for his rifle, brought it around slowly, hardly daring to breathe, fired and got him.

It was incredible. I don't know how it happened that this guy didn't see him when he was only a few feet away. He fired a few more rounds and there must have been three or four of them there because he got two. He killed one outright and another one was just lying there severely wounded because all you could hear was him groaning, groaning, which just died and died and that was it.

That was the first time I'd heard a person dying and I thought, Jesus. I couldn't believe it. There was this guy, the breath just coming out of him, just pant and gasp and cough to the end. That was one hell of an experience. I'll never forget that, never, never.

In the morning, I, with a few other guys, were told to go down and search the bodies and then bury them. They were stiff as boards, their arms were stretched out, their legs were splattered all over the place. I looked at them and they didn't seem human to me, although the sounds the night before were human, the bloke dying; but in the reality of the morning they weren't human.

We were in a hurry, so we dug very shallow graves but they wouldn't fit so we started jumping on the arms and bodies to get them to go in. But that didn't work so we thought, 'Oh well, we'll make an easy job of it,' so we just cut the arms off with machetes and threw them in and piled the dirt over the top. It was like cutting up a sheep. Our training was so good that you never saw them as people; they were just an animal, really, nothing else but an animal.

After leaving there we went through an area that the Yanks had gone through. It was just totally devastated, there wasn't a thing living, the ground was all blown up. It was obviously a North Vietnamese encampment, and being a forward scout I suddenly noticed this white mound which I thought was rice. I signalled back to the company that I'd found a rice cache. We stopped and on further inspection there were a few of these heaps. They turned out to be bodies covered in maggots, just totally covered in maggots — and I thought it was rice.

The Americans never buried their dead in my experience.

PHILLIP BARWICK

'I went through rookie training at Kapooka in October 1969 and I was fortunate enough there to win a trophy for the most outstanding soldier in the platoon. I joined armoured corps and went to Vietnam in 1970. I wanted to go to Vietnam. I guess I saw it as an adventure.'

He lives in Tamworth. He is blind.

I suppose I expected all of the South Vietnamese people to be a hundred per cent on our side. It was fairly obvious in pretty quick time that wasn't the case.

The feeling that I received from the Vietnamese was one ranging from total indifference to absolute hostility, and in a lot of cases you suspected that the farmer you saw working in the field in the daytime would be a Viet Cong soldier at night time. It was impossible to tell which were goodies and which were baddies.

There had been an incident not long before I got there. A Vietnamese guy used to have a stall on the side of the road not far from Nui Dat and the Australians would buy drinks from him. He was there for quite some time. One night there was a contact on the outer wire at Nui Dat and one of the Viet Cong killed was this very same bloke who would set up his stall on the side of the road.

TERRY BURSTALL

Author and pub bouncer. He left school when he was fourteen, worked around as a horse-breaker and drover, married at nineteen, divorced. He joined the Army specifically to go to Vietnam. 'I didn't know where Vietnam was, I had no idea what the situation was in Vietnam, I believed the bullshit that was put to us by our political leaders that Vietnam was a direct threat to Australia.'

He lives in Brisbane.

We went on an operation called Operation Enoggera, to search and destroy the village of Long Phuoc, and when I say destroy I mean fuckin' destroy. It's one of the things that's stuck in my craw all these years because Long Phuoc wasn't a little grass-hut village, Long Phuoc was a town.

The houses were on fairly large plots of land, probably half an acre to two acres. The houses were beautifully solid, set on concrete bases with tiled floors and big ceramic gables, and beautiful fruit trees and everything around. Wells were brick-sided, and a lot of the community sheds for rice storage were really large and beautifully mortared together, with timber. The roads were brick-paved roads.

We just absolutely destroyed the whole bloody lot. We pulled it to the ground and burnt it and blew it up. There was absolutely nothing left of Long Phuoc when we left, absolutely nothing.

I can remember pulling down this beautiful great big shed: we just piled it all together and set a match to it and burnt it. Anything that we couldn't pull down we got the engineers in and blew it up.

The people were resettled at Hoa Long, but they were resettled in shanties compared to what they had.

GLEN ANDERSON

The first three months I was there I tried to help the people. I tried to get along, learn a bit of their language, but after three months I'd decided they were bad news. The kids would always be trying to pinch what you had in your pockets, or else sell you their sister, sell you something or other. It was nothing for a kid to come up and say, 'You want my sister?'

You'd buy cigarette lighters till you got sick of buying them. You'd put them in your pocket and they'd be gone five seconds later. It really was bad news.

BOB GIBSON

I was there about a week and we were out on patrol not far from Baria. I was carrying the radio — buggered if I know why because I knew nothing much about signalling. It was just as well we weren't mortared or attacked or ambushed because I'd only been trained as a rifleman.

We ran across this old lady. Oh God, she was older than Ho Chi Minh. She'd have been eighty, ninety; she had black pyjamas on, long grey hair and she was carrying a banana cutter. She was just shaking all over, bowing and shaking. The sergeant asked her for her ID. She showed it and the bananas she'd been cutting and he said all right, *didi mau*, take off.

That was the first time I saw the look of terror that I saw many times in my tour there, of the old people. Not so much the young kids, but the old people.

She ran away from us but she must have doubled back around because she ran right back into the platoon and one of the guys fired three shots and hit her three times and killed her. We thought we'd run into Charlie, but instead here's this poor old lady, one through the neck, one through the jaw and one through the shoulder.

We called in for a jeep and they took her into the local village. From what I can gather, because I asked later what happened to her, they just took her to the family and said that they were going to pay so much to compensate her death.

The guy who shot her, he cracked up, he went troppo. He was gone within a week. I don't know what happened to him. I often wonder if he's even alive today. He just couldn't handle it, that he'd shot an old lady. He'd gone through all that training for his first shot in anger to be an old lady with a handful of bananas.

STRUAN ROBERTSON

He is thirty-seven, a homosexual who has been 'out of the closet' since 1974, when he was discharged from the Army because of his sexual preference. His living-room is decorated with large photographs of the dancer Mikhail Baryshnikov.
He served in Vietnam in 1970–1.

I didn't realise what it was all about till our company had its first kill. I switched on then.

I think we were up near the Courtenay rubber and a couple of nog medics who had been into one of the towns around the place for a leave ran through a trip wire into a machine-gun. The whole company had to go back and look at the two bodies. That was one of the smart moves by our OC, who was a very good soldier.

The first guy who was lying there in the pile, he got shot through the head. He got stitched across the eyebrows and the inside of his head was empty. It blew everything out, like an eggshell after you've eaten a hard-boiled egg and then I thought, 'Well fuck, now I know what I'm doing here, wake up, wake up and be a good soldier.'

They were the first kills in the battalion. We'd been running around the jungle for about four weeks and they were the first ones we got.

LACHLAN IRVINE

Either the first or second morning I was at Nui Dat, an aeroplane flew over spraying chemicals. I asked somebody what this was all about and he told me it was an insecticide flight. They did this regularly over Nui Dat, it was just something you got used to and it seemed to be almost a daily event. The smell of insecticide just became something you associated with shaving in the morning. I guess it was Malathion*, but nobody ever told us. All we knew was that it was there and it was being sprayed to kill the mossies and if any young soldier asked you what they were doing you just played the old soldier and said, 'Don't worry, son, they're just spraying to kill the mossies.' We didn't know anything about herbicides; we only thought that they were spraying to kill mossies.

BOB STEPHENS

Coraki is a sleepy, backblocks town in northern New South Wales. He came here several years ago looking for work, but the area is depressed and he's thinking of moving on, maybe back into the Airforce. He was a helicopter crewman in Vietnam in 1970–1.

This guy was lying on the floor of the aircraft. He was dead, but his eyes were open and he was just looking up to the roof and there was just no more life left in that guy and I just couldn't help but just sit and watch him like that. You see in the movies, in the westerns and war films, when a bloke dies they close his eyes. To this day I don't know why I didn't do it. I was just taken aback by the way he looked.

*An insecticide.

COLIN NICOLE

Our first contact was probably the biggest contact we had for the whole year. We were walking up a track as a company and I was in charge of the machine-gun group. You couldn't see anything, nothing at all. It was just thick jungle. I turned around to Corporal Noel Islop and I said, 'What's the matter with you?' I mean, to even talk showed my inexperience. He was white and looked really, like scared. I was puzzled at why he was looking the way he was looking. He'd been to Vietnam before and he knew what was going to happen: I didn't. I turned around and I'm thinking, 'What's the matter with him?' and then all of a sudden there was a bang, just one shot I think it was, and then all this tracer fire started coming down the track and it didn't mean anything to me, just all these pretty lights. It was the only time I ever saw tracer in twelve months.

We were just off the side of the track, just behind a big tree and it was amazing. You couldn't hear anything, you couldn't see anything except the machine-gunner and the number two. I didn't feel any fear, because we'd been fired at by 'the enemy' in Canungra and it was all good fun. We'd got 'shot' in Canungra many a time.

Then I said to someone, 'That's a funny way for our blokes to be firing.' That's what I said, exact words: 'That's a funny way for our blokes to be firing.' They said, 'That's not our blokes, that's the enemy.'

Right at that exact instant I felt fear, absolute fear. From then on I was fearful for the whole time, virtually day and night, unless I was absolutely exhausted and then I didn't give a stuff.

PETER MOLLOY

Before being conscripted in 1968 he was an apprentice motor mechanic in the small New South Wales town of Merriwa. 'I was a pretty immature, naive sort of country kid. Actually I was quite excited about going into the Army. I mean, I didn't have the foresight to think about the possibilities. I didn't know anything about Vietnam. I couldn't have even told you where it was.' At thirty-eight, he lives on a farm near Tamworth. He wears an artificial right leg.

We had a few short patrols outside the wire a few days after we were there, just to acclimatise to the heat and the humidity. We were only there about a week when we did a cordon and search of Hoa Long. I think every battalion that went there did its cordon and search of Hoa Long. That was a big stuff-up that was.

D Company cut through some wire or went over a fence or something into a minefield and we lost three blokes there. That was our first real taste of what it was like.

I remember lying in a bomb crater in a banana plantation there. I was just sort of lying there and you could see fire coming back at us and it was cutting the banana trees to pieces. We had tanks in there and they were blowing hell out of houses. You felt sorry for the actual villagers. They were all sort of crying about their houses being knocked down and things like that. There were a lot of guerrillas in there. We got quite a few of them.

From there on we got stuck into it and did a lot of bush work. You just sort of hung in there. Twelve months is a long time; there was nothing you could do about going home. It would have been great if they'd have said it's finished, we're going home. But that wasn't the case. It was only just starting for us.

After Hoa Long we were up in the Nui Thi Vai mountains for a couple of weeks and we had quite a few contacts up there, ambushes of a night. We didn't lose anybody at all.

We'd just sat down for a breather and about four guerrillas came wandering along the track. I opened up on them and we got one straight away. I went out with a toggle rope to drag in this bit of a kid. He was wearing the Ho Chi Minh sandals, a bit of plastic stuff wrapped around his genitals, backside and over his shoulders, and he had an AK-47 rifle and a water bottle and that was it, nothing else.

I dug a bit of a grave and the old sergeant came up and just pulled out his machete and whacked into his legs and busted them all up. I had never seen a body mutilated like that before and every time I closed my eyes of a night after that I could see this young kid. He was quite young. They're only a small frame of a man and that makes it hard to guess, but I would have said he was about fourteen or sixteen, around that age.

I don't think the sergeant should have done that. I think we should have just dug his grave and left him.

RAY PAYNE

I'd been sitting on this ridge about an hour, an hour and a half. There was a village down the road and they were doing a clear and search and we were waiting back for anyone who left the village. I was sitting there pretty casual, pretty slack, and I turned around and looking at me just over the ridgeline was a face with a floppy camouflage hat. I looked and quickly turned away. I didn't want to believe it. I thought, no, it's not there, then I turned around again and thought, oh shit, that's a noggy. Everything that I'd ever been taught just went out the window. Instead of just raising the machine-gun up on the bi-pod I picked it up and stood upright, totally upright, and I started firing it without even aiming at him and all I did was shoot trees down about fifteen feet above his head and I watched him run away. He crossed the side of this little ridgeline into the scrub on the other side and just disappeared.

I know today that everything that I was trained to do, that should have been an instant reaction, just disappeared, just went away.

That was the second operation because the first time we saw nothing. We walked back along a bloody railway line for miles and miles and miles and there was no point to it.

MICHAEL

When he was seventeen he tried to enlist in the Army by forging his parents' signatures. He left school early to help pay the way for his younger brothers and sisters. Eventually he volunteered for national service and went to Vietnam in 1971.

It was patently obvious when I joined my unit that the young second lieutenant who was in charge of us had one thing in mind. He called them coons. 'I want as many coons as you can get me,' he'd say. For a young fellow who hadn't been shaving very long and who hadn't been up the front very long that was a funny thing to say. Everybody else called them nogs. He called them coons and he wanted as many as he could get.

DENNIS COLE

He was an infantry soldier in Vietnam in 1969. 'In the jungle I think it was as much good luck as good judgement if you turned up at the right place. You'd get a map with three creeks on it and you'd have crossed five creeks before you got to the first one on the map. It was just so inaccurate. Plus you couldn't take a bearing on anything. You'd hit a clump of bamboo and you'd have to go right around it, plus you've got a guy whose job it is to count every step and you've got to translate steps into yards, which depends on the territory. Normally I think it was one hundred and twenty steps to one hundred yards in open going, but you get into jungle and you're stepping over rocks and roots and tree stumps and you just have to take an educated guess. It was bloody near impossible. We lost one or two platoon commanders early in the piece by walking back into harbours from the wrong direction and being brassed up.'

I think it was pretty heavily timbered country. It was very flat. We came across a rise in the ground, crawled up, and there was a creek at the bottom and then across the other side there were all these trees, about seven foot tall, very heavily leafed all the way down to the ground. It didn't look natural. It was a strange sort of setting.

The creek was only eight or nine foot wide, not deep, and the order came down for me to take a section across and clear the other side, which we did, but it was very hairy because you couldn't see anyone next to you the foliage was that thick. They were a very strange sort of tree. I don't really know how to describe them. We cleared it as much as we could, probably fifty yards, and came back and the whole company went over and then they found a fish trap where the creek swung around.

Bob Carr had hurt his ankle so I took over his section and the platoon commander grabbed my section and set off up one side of the track. By the time I'd got hold of Bob's section and moved off I was probably level with the last man on the other side. We got about three-quarters of the way up level with them, moving around a left-hand bend when the claymore went off.

I just happened to look across to the right as it went off and a piece of shrapnel went through my ear and round the back of my skull. It was like someone had hit me across the head with a cricket bat and the next thing I knew I was on the ground. My head was ringing like a church bell and I didn't have much idea what was going on. I didn't even hear the gunfire. I sort of scrambled off the track, but then I could hear Johnny Higgins calling out. He was ratshit. I thought he'd been hit by something, but he just couldn't move, he just lay there in the middle of the track. I was shit scared, but I went back and dragged him off the track into the bamboo. He was just lying there saying, 'I can't move, I can't move.'

I could hear the screams from the guys up in front. Two of my best mates were killed, another one lost both his legs and another fellow lost his mind.

I moved up with the medic and all I could see were my mates littered all over the place, bits and pieces of them. One guy I could see was stone dead, George Neagle. He was just lying there with his eyes open, virtually unmarked, but as white as a bloody ghost. Then I saw Johnny Hallam. He'd lost his legs.

Somehow or other we got a hoochie underneath him and sort of carted him back. I thought he was gone. One leg was completely gone and the other leg was just hanging by a shred of skin and he was sort of in shock. I thought he wouldn't even see out the helicopter ride, wherever he's going.

They carried Midge back. He looked okay. He was laying there having a smoke and they said he'd just been wounded in the stomach and he looked okay. He died within an hour or so. We'd been hoochie mates for nine months. Apparently he'd got one through the throat as well which you couldn't see and he was dead before they hit the hospital. He'd only had a baby three months before he came overseas and when his wife found out she put her head in the oven and killed herself. That was probably a bigger shock than anything, really, when we heard that. You know, it was bad enough believing that he was killed.

Jimmy came back. Half his head seemed to be missing. They were carrying him, but you could see half his head was shot away. I don't think I'll ever forget the sight, or the way I felt. I couldn't believe it could happen to us.

They took the first chopper out with the badly wounded guys then they put me and Johnny Higgins and George Neagle, the dead bloke, on the second or third chopper. He had a poncho over him and his boots were sticking out the bottom and you knew who it was and knew he was dead.

We'd been in-country less than a month.

TOMMY BROWN

He went absent without official leave twice after being drafted in 1967. He spent time in Holsworthy military prison, and in Vietnam had 'something like fourteen' charges against him for AWOL and insubordination. He served in Vietnam in 1968–9.

'I never thought about joining the Army or the Navy or Airforce. It didn't turn me on; I wasn't interested. But my number came up and I was in. Didn't worry me. I didn't know much about Vietnam at the time, only what I'd read in the papers.'

He lives in Melbourne.

My mother used to send me over the *Sporting Globe* because I was a mad punter. She used to send me over the sport and I used to always try and read up on the form and all that. And she'd send me the *Herald* and the *Sun*. I'll never forget it, I picked up the *Sun* and there was a little bit on the front page: 'Diggers hurt in Vietnam' and it had their names: 'Johnny Hallam — satisfactory'. Fuck, both his legs were off. It didn't have 'both legs amputated', it's just got 'satisfactory'. I think there were eleven wounded in B Company. They were all 'satisfactory'. I think there was one with an arm off, one has never got out of the mental hospital, Jimmy. You never heard about that, you know, that he was off his head.

GORDON PIPER

He was born in a car between the towns of Gulgong and Dunedoo in New South Wales. When he was three years old he was put in an orphanage. He spent nine years there. 'I came out of that orphanage at twelve years old and then sat my time around Balmain, Leichhardt area until I joined the Army. I was getting in a bit of strife with the police, even though I was going to the police Boys Club doing boxing and wrestling. It was actually a police sergeant who recommended I join the Army and get out of the neighbourhood.'

He served two tours as an infantry soldier in Vietnam, in 1965 and in 1969. He lives in Brisbane where he owns and drives a truck.

We were walking along a railway track to get choppered out and Billy Carroll, who wasn't an easy walker, tripped a couple of times. He was a bit of a tanglefoot the way he walked. 'Listen, you better get those grenades inside your pouch,' I said. He had them tucked on the sides of his pouches. 'Yeah, mate, she'll be right.' Well, that's what Billy was like. Rough and ready, but a good hand.

We lifted out to Bien Hoa and then went back to our company lines on cattle trucks. They reckon Billy climbed out over the front of the truck when we got there and a grenade fell out of his pouch and went off. I didn't actually see what happened.

There was an explosion, everybody scrambling to get out of the trucks because we thought it was incoming mortar fire. I looked around and saw Stoney Burke. He was peppered to buggery, still alive. Harry Van Valen, he was still there, and a few others who were trying to work out where they were. I looked over the side and I saw a leg, which was I think Billy Carroll's leg.

Stoney Burke died in my arms, falling back saying, 'Help me, help me, oh God help me.' Blood was pouring out of him. He was ashen. He was a fair complexioned guy anyway, Stoney, but he was ashen. I suppose you'd say the colour of death, if ever you've seen death. He was just peppered all the way through.

I know my feeling then, which held for a long time, was I just wanted revenge. It was senseless, being killed there. Billy Carroll gone, Stoney gone, Harry Van Valen dying a few days later. It was then a revenge thing. We're here, we've done nothing yet, but this has happened, we've lost three of our mates. From there in I became a little bit hard and callous. I had no scruples from there on in, no compunction whatsoever to do whatever I had to do, no second thoughts about it. They didn't have to worry about me doing my job because I had a good reason then to do it, apart from the fact I was a soldier and it was expected of me. I had a good personal reason then to do it and do it the best I could do it and as effectively.

I hated the Vietnamese from then on. I used to get into punch ups and deliberately give them a hard time when we were on leave. Whenever we got a bodycount I was happy. It made you feel a little bit better. It was the progress of the war.

3

Illumination

'I would like for every Aussie that stands there in the rice paddies on this warm summer day, to know that every American and LBJ is with Australia all the way.'

US President Johnson

'You are right to be where you are, and we are right to be there with you.'

Australian Prime Minister Harold Holt

RIC

'You know that movie The Deerhunter. *Well I always, always, felt I was going on a hunting trip. I prepared myself to go on a hunting trip. I treated it like a hunt, I geared up for it. I had my ammunition, I carried my radio and I had all my clobber which I needed for that four-week period and I knew I was going to get clean uniforms and stuff like that choppered in from time to time. I treated it like a deer hunt. Except when we had a contact. Then it changed dramatically, then the adrenalin took over and the whole scene changed. You became totally aware that all of a sudden you were not on your own any more. There were people shooting back at you. Deer that shoot back.'*

My first experience of seeing someone shot was one of our own blokes. One of our guys shot a nasho, shot him in the chest from the hip with one round from his M-16. It happened quite a lot over there. Like, you'd double up on your own section.

We were in a creek bed and one section went to the left and one section went up the middle, and this nasho popped up. He was an Italian and he looked like a nog. 'Tex' just saw this movement and went blat.

I got a disease called leptospirosis over there and I just flaked after that incident, I passed out in the bush. When I came to I was in a chopper lying next to this young Italian guy and he's gushing blood all over the place. I didn't know what to do. I was screaming at him, 'Don't die, don't die.'

DAVID COWDREY

You'd get to a landing zone and you hit a bunker system and you virtually know it's thirteen-year-old kids shooting at you and then you go in there afterwards and you see what you've shot and you think, 'Jesus Christ, this is not the Second World War that we heard about from Dad. This is altogether different.'

GARRY

'Ninety per cent of the time all you were doing was walking. By the time you finished the first day you were reasonably buggered, and you started to switch off, nothing had happened. The next day you got up, you started off again only this time instead of having your rifle up, it's hooked over your pouch. Third, fourth days you just switched off, it was just head down and keep going. Then you get shot at and after that's all over you were back to watching your arse again. Then you go back through the whole process again.

'It didn't matter how well trained or how dedicated you were, you just got to the stage where the heat got to you, the ants got to you and all you were doing was walking, sitting, listening, getting up and walking again.'

We harboured up one night and we could smell a sickly sweet smell. We couldn't work out what it was but we slept there that night. The whole platoon was dog-tired. Moving out the next day about a hundred yards from where we harboured up were half a dozen heads sticking out of the ground with maggots where the eyes used to be and with the noses and lips eaten away. The Kiwis had buried them. They used to bury them that way because the nogs were told that you've got to be buried right or you don't go to heaven.

RON EGLINTON

At forty, he is a truck driver, married, with two children. He lives in Brisbane.

We'd been out in the bush for about sixteen days and we were hungry, dirty and wet and bloody miserable. We eventually came out of the bush onto a road, a dirt road, and there was a man and a child coming along. For some reason we were told to go across and check them out, so away we go, traipsing through the paddies. We were down below road level and there was a culvert between us and this fellow and his little girl, who was four or five years old. The closer we got to them the more they accelerated down towards us and as we got up onto this culvert we sort of met them and foompa, someone triggered a claymore.

It hit a lot of our fellas and the old man, chopped him up badly. It killed Col, one of our section commanders. He was carrying a claymore mine that we'd used in an ambush the previous night and of course when the thing hit him it detonated his too and it blew him literally in half. He just sort of parted. It was total bloody bedlam, because there was a lot of our fellas that had been hit, bits and pieces of Col lying all over the place, and as this thing was detonated the girl's mother came running over the crest of the hill down this road laden with baskets across her shoulders and we thought — because you haven't got much time to think, it all happens pretty smartly — someone thought that she probably had grenades or something in her baskets and she was coming down to do us more damage, and she was shot.

She went down wounded the first time I think but she got up and kept coming again, screaming, and someone else shot her, didn't really want to kill her, but, you know, she had to be stopped. If she had dropped her baskets... but she kept coming with these bloody baskets. And it turned out to be nothing — just vegetables.

BILL DOBELL

There was one incident where I was scared, very scared. I had to bury an enemy soldier. We killed him just on dark and I didn't actually see him until the next morning when I was informed that it would be my duty to bury him.

It wasn't easy. I didn't feel bad about burying it, I felt that was fair, but what worried me was the fact that here was really the first dead man I'd ever seen and now I was going to have to pick him up and carry him over to a grave. I didn't fancy the idea of picking him up. I had to carry him there, twenty yards to a shell scrape, and bury him. It was either that or dig a hole and there was no time to be digging holes.

I didn't know what the body was going to feel like and that scared me, that I was going to have to put my hand on his flesh. I looked for a way not to do it, to use his shirt or something like that, but his shirt was a mess and in the end I decided, well, there's only one way to do this and that's grab him and go. I grabbed him around the wrist. When I picked him up ants ran out of his body up my arms. I broke into a panic. I was hitting myself to get them off. The body had been there at a rough guess twelve or thirteen, maybe fourteen hours. His head had been knocked around and there was a big hole above his left eye. It was just sort of opened up. It was black with congealed blood and God knows what else. That's where the ants came from, there and from up his sleeve.

There was an awful smell too, but you got it everywhere over there. There was that much death in the place. You'd go through an area that had been blown apart, huge holes in the ground full of water, trees are just flattened, all sorts of animal life dead. It smelled of death all the time.

We placed the body in the ground, covered it over and goodbye. There was no ceremony, no nothing. I remember thinking that he must have somebody somewhere who cared. I wondered if they'd ever know. I still cared to that extent.

I believed the enemy would know our movements and would retrieve the body after we were gone.

TREVOR MORRIS

You got a calendar and crossed off day one and six months felt like six years. The days dragged and the closeness went out of people. The food was shithouse. In a way I was glad to get out on operations because at least then we got American rations.

You carried what you could: your ammo and your smokes and a change of clothes because of the ringworms. You'd never get rid of them living on the ground. You'd get them in your crutch and on your legs and the only thing the medics ever had to treat them was pure alcohol and that would bring tears to your eyes. It was a filthy joint. You'd be living in a bloody hole. You could hear the rats crawling around of a night.

VIC

He was a Navy pilot who flew helicopters in Vietnam in 1968–9 with both the Australians and the Americans. He now flies helicopters for an oil company.

One of our blokes had been killed or wounded with the American 135th Assault Helicopter Company at Blackhorse, near Nui Dat, and they wanted another Navy man to go up. I'd already gone up there for a one-week exchange and I thought the work was quite exciting and I said I'd go. It was a bit of a shock really when I realised what I'd volunteered for.

The whole show was covered in mud. You had cold water showers that you walked through mud to get to, if you had time. The food was terrible. Drinking in a shed called the 'Officers' Club' was the only thing to do every night.

We flew extraordinary hours, absolutely extraordinary hours — 13 hours 45 minutes was my best flying for a day. You'd be absolutely exhausted, a nervous wreck, and come back and drink till midnight. Everyone did it all the time — and then get up at five the next morning to do it again.

Blackhorse was on high ground rising into the mountains, and fog would settle over the airfield quite often in the wet season and you'd have to take off in thirty second separations at six in the morning and meet up on top to join up in a formation of ten.

We'd do formation flying combat assaults three days out of four and move two or three units a day. You had to get the troops in so that they could do a day's searching and then pull them out at night. We might deal with two or three different units in the morning, have a break for an hour or two somewhere safe in the helicopter and cook C-rations and then in the afternoon start pulling them out again to put them back in their night positions where they were safe.

I eventually went back to the Australian Airforce in Phuoc Tuy and it was like a training ground. It was a less active, more controlled atmosphere. With the American Army it was a hectic pace, action all the time everywhere. You never knew where you were going and what would happen next. Go there and support the 25th Division, come down here and do the 9th Division, tomorrow morning 199th Light Infantry. New territory, new terrain, new problems all the time. One good thing, you were always in a big formation. The whole unit would go together — more than twenty helicopters — so if you went down someone would get you.

The American troops were disorganised, not as disciplined as the Australians, and they were vicious, absolutely vicious, but with good reason because they were in hotter action.

BOB HOBBS

Our operations were normally four to six weeks in duration and it was a hard slog. My first operation was during the wet season. We were ambushing by day and night for about five days and I hadn't taken my boots off until about the fifth day. When I took my socks off all the skin came off with them. After that I didn't wear socks, or underpants, anymore.

I could never become accustomed to the conditions. Being wet and covered with rashes and leeches all through the wet season and being boiling hot and thirsty and suffering from prickly heat during the dry season. In the dry I carried eight water bottles, some guys carried more, and that was to last four days.

On operations I took every day as it came. I would think about going home and I would think about the next resupply when we could have a break from patrolling. The whole company usually met up for a few hours and often the choppers would bring in a can of soft drink or a bread roll for each man and they would maybe bring us mail from home.

It was good to get back to Nui Dat for a few days after spending a month or so mooching around in the jungle. After you got off the choppers and back into the lines the first thing you did was throw away your greens and head for the showers and then on the first night back we would have what was commonly known as 'a happening'. You'd hit the grog a bit and there was maybe a punch-up or two, just letting off steam. A lot of the guys had bought reel-to-reel tape decks and while we were back at the Dat there would be 'Jumpin' Jack Flash', the Doors, Led Zeppelin, the Rolling Stones, the Beatles and the

Byrds blaring through the lines. I remember one of our cooks had a Vanilla Fudge LP that he liked and he kept playing it and replaying it over and over again.

Conditions at Nui Dat weren't too bad. We were in old four-man tents with corrugated iron and sandbags packed around them for protection in the event of a mortar attack. Inside the tents were duckboard flooring, four camp stretchers and a locker. Some guys had folding chairs and tables but that was the extent of the furniture. The interior of the tents, including the stretchers, were usually pretty grubby, covered either in mud or red dust according to the season.

Compared to living in the jungle it was palatial.

BRIAN GRIFFIN

'One of the things you sussed out very quickly was that the villagers couldn't give a shit. If you weren't there bothering them the other guy would be there bothering them.'

We were moving along the road and someone fired on us from the side of the road so we went chasing off after him through this old guy's rice paddy. It was just prior to harvest and on the way back the old guy was there, going crook about his rice all being flattened. To pacify him we threw him down a few packets of cigarettes. I remember thinking how terrible it was, the troop sergeant throwing down two or three packets of cigarettes. He was crying and waving his arms around and the sergeant threw him down a few more cigarettes. The old guy was still crying and the sergeant said, 'This bastard's just being greedy, I'll shoot the bastard if he keeps this up.' He pulled out his pistol and said, 'Now *didi mau*, bugger off.'

BRUCE POULTON

About nine o'clock at night we came in contact. We'd set up claymores and these gooks tried to creep up and turn them around facing us so that when we opened up we'd shoot ourselves to pieces.

It was a real weird feeling. We could see them. I didn't want to breathe. I'm breathing real shallow, but I'm sure they can hear me. I can hear my own heart beating it's so quiet. They opened up on us and I got hit through the shoulder and Johnno got a bullet through the foot. He's screaming because it's blown half his foot off. We knocked over nine gooks and none of us got killed.

At one stage the skipper had called for artillery and was refused because we were in a rubber plantation. They're the political things. The Australian government had to pay for all the rubber that we damaged so we were refused artillery.

They took us to the hospital and I was feeling really crook and this padre came around selling God. He's standing there saying, 'How are you, son?' really placid and serene and I was out of my head. Johnno was screaming in a stretcher just up from me and I felt bad. I told him to fuck off.

Dr MICHAEL NAUGHTON

He was a surgeon in Vietnam in 1965 and 1970.

You used to see things like a knee joint just ripped open, feet blown off, legs stripped of flesh, and the kids used to know themselves. They would say to you, 'What are you going to do with that foot?' You'd say, 'It looks pretty crook and to be quite honest we don't think we can save it.' I used to fear having to say that to them, but invariably when you did they'd say, 'Yeah, I had a look at it myself, it's bloody ratshit.' Or sometimes I'd say to the medic, 'What's it look like, Steve?' and Steve's job is not to bullshit. Steve would say, 'It's ratshit, mate.' That word, ratshit, used to cover all sins. I think it was born for Vietnam.

LACHLAN IRVINE

I remember that first attack. I can remember sitting in my pit counting the mortars, not for the reason you're supposed to which is to get an idea of how many people there are firing at you, but because it seemed they were covering our position from end to end. From my pit I could hear one land over to my right, then another one would land a bit closer, another one a bit closer and another one even closer and the next one would land over the other side and every time this happened I would count them: one, two, three, the next one's getting closer, four and then it goes over the other side, five, six and I'd start again. One, that's way over there, two, that's a bit closer, three, I could feel the ground shake, four, and I'd hold my breath and think this one is going to be mine, five, over the other side and I'd breathe again.

BOB FREELAND

He was an infantry soldier in Vietnam in 1971.

We were out there for about thirty days in a set ambush, in the same position, eating and shitting. We sat there for thirty days on a well-worn track that they thought some nogs would come up.

It used to be the in thing to have a small radio. Everyone had a radio, had to have one. And the football was on this day, the grand final. I think the signals fellows had the wire up around trees and everything going on their set and we thought well Jesus Christ this is going to be all right so we got a bit of bloody wire and we rigged up our little radios and we sat back there listening to the bloody grand final as it was happening, the VFL grand final from the MCG in 1971. I thought that was incredible, sitting in a combat situation listening to the grand final at home. I thought, Jesus Christ, this is out of this world.

PETER MOLLOY

Out in the bush you just went day by day. You tried to be as hygienic as possible, depending on the season. If you were out in the dry season there was no way in the world you could go using your water for washing or anything like that because it was just too precious. If you could, of a night, you would slip your boots off and try to air them out and fill them with powder, but you were taking a risk if there was any contact during the night. You'd have your daily crap and you might get a bit of paper from time to time, but mostly it was just with grass or shrub, something leafy. It wasn't possibly the best thing to do it with, but that's about all you had.

If we came across a creek or something like that, if we hadn't had any contacts in the area, we might strip our shirts off and have a bit of a scrub, but we never carried soap with us. We only carried the bare necessities: our food, water and ammunition, our groundsheets for sleeping on and maybe a little Instamatic camera. A lot of blokes used to put an extra little pouch on their belt and put their Instamatic in there. When I got over there in '69 it was a fad to carry an Instamatic.

The red ants were mongrels of things and they were every-where. They'd get into your gear, they'd get all over you. Leeches were bad in a lot of the thick jungle and there were bamboo kraits that would change colour with the seasons. We were told to watch out for them because they were poisonous.

MALCOLM McLEAN

We would come back off an operation, probably have one day or less than a day in camp and they'd say, 'Right, you're going out again tonight.' So you'd have time just to replenish every-thing, get your gear together and away you'd go again, com-pletely disorientated, nobody's telling you anything. You're just told to go to a certain area, to a map reference and that was it. Nobody even said whether it was a standard area or a place or a village. You were just part of a machine that was picked up and deposited and told to get on with it.

An Australian soldier drags the body of a dead Viet Cong from the creek where he was killed. Toggle ropes were used in case bodies were booby trapped. (Photograph courtesy of Australian War Memorial.)

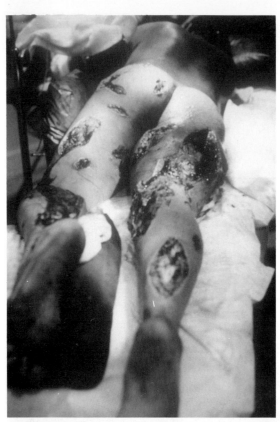

These photographs show some of the injuries inflicted by anti-personnel mines and high-velocity weapons in Vietnam. Death or injury from mine was a constant cause of anxiety for troops on operations.

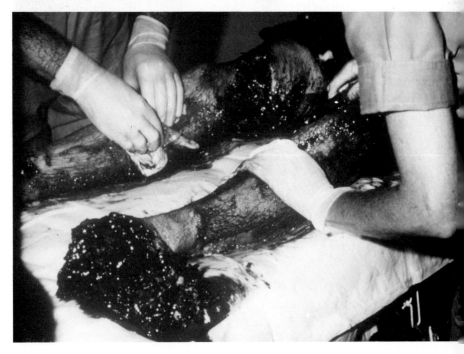

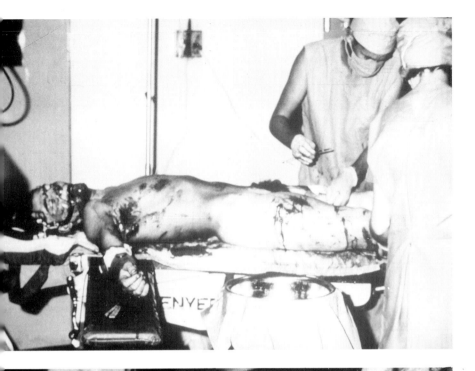

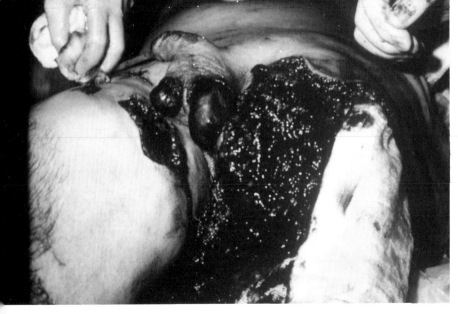

Australian troops move to cover after landing from helicopters to start a search and

A Centurion tank moves onto a road near Nui Dat. (Photograph courtesy of United Press International Inc.)

Australian soldiers collect the bodies of Viet Cong they have killed in a contact near the village of Thua Thic. (Photographs courtesy of Australian War Memorial.)

Children of Xuyen Moc look on as the bodies of Viet Cong are dragged into the village behind Australian armoured personnel carriers. This was intended as a warning to Viet Cong sympathisers. (Photograph courtesy of Australian War Memorial.)

Success in Vietnam was measured not in kilometres, as in other wars, but in body counts and kill ratios. (Photograph courtesy of United Press International Inc.)

MICHAEL SCRASE

He was a despatch driver in Saigon and Vung Tau in 1968.

We were suspicious of the people all the time because you just didn't know who the enemy was. There was a story of a woman with a baby in Vung Tau who blew herself up and the baby in order to kill five Americans who were standing around. She just pulled a pin on a grenade and blew the whole lot up. That was it, that sort of thing was happening.

When I was in Vung Tau and Saigon doing despatch work, one of the fears we had all the time was being blown up in our vehicles. There were so many motorbikes and pushbikes around and we never knew who the enemy was. They didn't have a different uniform on.

It was a big pressure every day, just driving on the street. Whenever we went out in trucks we carried a shotgun in the front and two shotguns at the back because they would ride up behind you and hang explosives on the back of your vehicle. Even in Saigon, at the Free World Building, they blew the second storey out of the Vietnamese university, just next door to us. I saw a doctor assassinated by a sniper in a Saigon street as I was driving past. I took a mate to hospital with two fingers in his throat where he had been shot by a bar owner.

Once I was driving a truck through Saigon and had just gone past a checkpoint guarded by the local Vietnamese police. They blew a whistle when I was almost beside them and pointed at a motorbike in front of me. The two Vietnamese on the motorbike looked around and started to take off. They must have been VC. On the second whistle the police were firing and they shot them in front of me. I went over the top of them in the truck.

FRANK HUNT

The thing that worried me was the booby traps. They really freaked me out, because you didn't know where they were coming from. We had seen a few at the Jungle Training Centre at Canungra, but we hadn't seen anything. There were all sorts of different signs to indicate a minefield, like a leaf with a stick poked through it or a scrub of grass tied around to form a plum, a few rocks together. I mean, you're in half open bush country. To find these signs was... the tension was absolutely unreal.

We had to go out to the foothills of the Long Hais on a search and destroy mission, July 21, 1969. It was around about half past ten in the morning. We were pretty bloody exhausted. We'd had a few light contacts and the tension was there because we knew we were in a mine area.

I'd been carrying the radio, we'd just stopped and formed a circle off the track and the lieutenant and I were going up for a reconnaissance. Jerry, the sarge, was out at point and Doc was looking after the radio. He yelled out, 'Skip, the Yanks have walked on the moon.' 'Fuck the Yanks,' he said. Next thing bang. I always believed Skip had stood on this mine, the jumping jack, but a lot of my mates reckon I stepped on it.

We were there for hours. Shit, it was terrifying, because there were mines all around us. Jerry was hurt bad, and my left boot was up near my knee, my right leg was broken. I was hit in the guts, shoulders, face, arms, upper legs. I'm still picking pieces out of my back today.

I dragged my leg back and I could feel the grating of the bones. My legs were at all different angles and I felt like I was being burnt.

The pain was pretty bloody bad. I crawled back to the radio and tried to give our position but this stupid bloody sergeant-major told me to give the position in code and I yelled, 'You can go and get fucked, Smiley, we've got dead, we've got badly injured.' There were bodies everywhere, injured people, we couldn't move, I wanted air support, I wanted artillery, God knows what.

Johnny Needs came up and took over the radio then. John was brilliant. He made everyone lay down or sit down and he walked around to find out where it was safe. He deserved a

Victoria Cross for what he did that day. He just took complete charge, made sure everyone was right, went to the wounded, risked his own life walking to set up the safe lanes, called in the helicopter, then medevaced everyone.

I can still remember lying there and feeling the blood running down my knee on to my thigh. I immediately thought, 'Oh no,' and stuck my hand down my trousers and felt the old fellow: it was all full of blood. I thought to myself, oh fuck, I might as well be dead. I was more worried about my balls than I was about my legs or whether I was going to die or not, because if they got me in the balls I wanted to be dead.

I was winched up in this bloody helicopter, eighty feet up in a stretcher and this big Negro, holy Jesus he was a brute of a man — it might have been because I was lying down looking up at him, but he had to be six feet seven if he was an inch, and about eighteen stone — is saying, 'Come on you motherfucking son of a bitch, stay awake,' and he's whacking me across the face: 'You motherfucker.'

After I'd been lifted, John and a doctor were carrying another wounded by stretcher into the helicopter and apparently John stepped outside the taped area onto another mine and it killed him instantly. The doctor was blinded. I was nineteen. I'd been in Vietnam seventy-seven days and that was it.

MICHAEL SCRASE

I used to fly all over South Vietnam with the air despatch and we used to pick up the coffins and it got so that I used to sleep on top of them in the plane.

One day I was asleep on one when we landed back at Nui Dat and the tail gate went down on the plane and this officer was standing there and he abused hell out of me because I was sleeping on top of this coffin, that I was desecrating this bloke. I mean, he was dead, I was tired. I was working something like ninety-six hours a week at that stage, literally working around the clock, and I was just tired and it was a flat surface to lay on.

MICK CRAWFORD

We were walking along on patrol not far from the bottom of the Long Hais and a jumping jack mine burst out of the ground in front of me. I don't think I realised I'd tripped it. All I could think was, 'That's it, I'm finished.' You haven't got much more time than that. You're just frozen there waiting for it to explode. You know you're not going to duck it or jump it.

We never did find out why — it must have been corroded or something — but it didn't go off. It just fell on the ground in front of me. I sat down near the side of the track and started to cry. I suppose I cried for more than an hour.

There was talk about bringing in a chopper and taking me out but I knew myself if they'd taken me out then that would have been the finish. I just had to get up and keep going. If you didn't I guess you'd never move again, you'd never take that next step.

DENNIS COLE

We'd dig up graves. You'd follow a blood trail and you'd find a fresh digging and you'd dig it up. It's obviously a grave. That wasn't very nice, to do things like that, especially when they've been there a couple of days. They're pretty smelly.

But following up blood trails was the big thing, because you'd get five guys walk into an ambush and you'd only find one body. With the amount of firepower you'd pour into it, it was incredible how people could get out of it and it gave us satisfaction to find more bodies. It gave you a sense of achievement. It made things more believable.

And then when you've got to bury someone who's as stiff as a board, you'd get guys that would jump on their backs to break them so they'd fit in the grave. It sort of made you feel a bit callous, but you seemed to lose a lot of your human feelings. You became, not an animal, but you became very cold and hard to things.

Most people can't understand how you could do it, but when you don't wash yourself for three weeks, you don't have a shave or change your clothes or your socks or anything for three weeks, I think your whole system of values does drop. When you see people killed, or you're killing people, well, you've got to have completely different values to what people back here had.

RON WITTY

He was a clerk in Vietnam in 1967–8.

Myself and three tankies were sitting in a bar in Saigon, in Tu Do Street, which was the main street in Saigon, and a real old-type grenade lobbed through the window. The windows were French stained glass, with bars over the front of them. Everybody scattered. There were probably another dozen people in the bar, including girls, and the four of us were so drunk that we just sat there and looked at this bloody thing and we started counting simultaneously. I think we got up to about twenty or twenty-five before we started laughing because it was a dud.

RIC

We would come off an operation, hand in our grenades, heavy ammunition and mines and then we would go back to our tents, get a resupply of rations and pack up all our gear for the next operation and then we would wind down. I used to get off on Jimi Hendrix with my mate Tony. We'd roll joints, put on Hendrix and boogie all night. We had a stash of bourbon or Bacardi, too.

Just prior to my going back to Australia we got hold of a ball of opium. I remember there was myself and three other guys and we were sitting around a puddle in our battery area and it was a full moonlit night and the light was shining onto the puddle and this guy was melting down the opium.

But not many Australians were into dope. It was a personal thing. I used to have a buddy who was in SAS and we used to meet between the lines just behind the movie screen and we'd roll a few joints and drink and just talk shit in the dark.

When I was at fire-support bases I used to have a pipe. We used to have stand-to of an evening and I used to fill up my pipe with dope and sit on the gun bund and watch some of the greatest sunsets on earth.

Beer parties and whoring around were never my scene; I was too shit-scared of getting the jack. I just didn't want to whore around or go with the rest of the guys to the suck-fuck parlours and all that sort of shit. Like, I used to come back to the lines at Nui Dat and guys would come back and say, 'Hey, I've got a load.' Hey, fantastic…

I'd prefer to walk up an avenue where frangipani grew in Vung Tau or just walk along the beach by myself. I used to have a favourite little restaurant I used to go to on the front beach at Vungers. I guess it was rationed food which they filched off the Americans in one way or another through the blackmarket, but it was good and it was cheap. It was my buzz. There were a lot of things I loved in that place.

I met a really lovely girl there. Her brother was killed in a car accident in Saigon and she worked at Villa 44, which was the main R&C centre in the heart of Vung Tau. I got to know her really well and she had family in Vung Tau and I ended up going to their place and we had duck and all sorts of strange food which I wasn't used to and it was really neat. I kept in contact with her for quite a while and then it was one of those things. I didn't screw her or anything like that. It was just a friendly arrangement. It was one of my better experiences in Vietnam. It was so pleasant.

But we did some pretty strange things over there. Like, if you did them in Australia you'd get locked up for life. Things like just singling out a nog and just having a good old meat sandwich, fixing him. We heaved a guy out of the Grand Hotel, two storeys up, pissed as farts. He was a little noggy waiter. Heaved him out the window because he short-changed one of us. He landed on concrete. That was pretty rugged. I guess that's coming pretty close to murder.

TOMMY BROWN

I was out at fire-support base Wattle and Mr Lynch, who was the minister responsible for national service at the time, came out to meet the troops. A lot of politicians came over to have a look. He was only there about two minutes and I didn't see him talking to any of the diggers, only to the bosses. It struck me funny. We're sitting out there in dirty greens for five weeks and he jumps out of a chopper in the middle of the jungle wearing a white shirt. I wondered what he was going to say when he got back home.

LAURIE WOODS

He was a member of Australia's swimming team for the 1964 Olympics, but broke his pelvis in training and so was unable to compete. By the next Olympics he was in training for Vietnam, where he was a field engineer. He has a farm at Tambo Upper, Victoria.

We're halfway between Dat Do and Xuyen Moc, doing a road patrol, checking all the vehicles going through. A Lambretta's come through and there's a couple of dozen people in the back of it and one of the women is breast-feeding a baby on her left breast and the right one's just sitting there free. 'Slats' has looked around the side of the Lambretta and seen this breast and he bit on it. He was having a suck before she knew what it was and she says, 'Get away.'

He was a mongrel. He'd come up with all those dirty rotten tricks, but he made the light side of it over there.

ADRIAN BISHOP

'In the period that I was there several momentous things happened, like man landed on the moon, the Chappaquiddick incident with Kennedy, and the students at Kent State University were shot by the National Guard, and Ho Chi Minh died — that had a very big effect on the morale of the VC — and then the My Lai massacre was publicised during that time, and there were anti-war demonstrations at home. It seemed to us that the whole world was going crazy.'

He served with an intelligence signals troop in Vietnam in 1969–70. Today, he works for a federal government department.

You couldn't possibly imagine anything more different than life in Australia to life in Vietnam. I couldn't imagine anybody more different than Ho Chi Minh and Lyndon Johnson for that matter. It was like one was a Martian and the other was an Earth person.

It seemed to me that the Australians and the Americans had absolutely no idea of what the war in Vietnam was all about, what the Viet Cong were all about, or what Ho Chi Minh was all about. They certainly had absolutely no understanding at all of Vietnamese culture. I think they just regarded the Viet-namese as what they used to call them — slope heads or nogs or gooks. I just don't think they gave the Vietnamese credit for having any intelligence or courage or military skills, which was surprising given the history of the Viet Minh and the experi-ence of the French and the Chinese.

Basically speaking, the Vietnamese were already committed, at least in most areas where it counted they were. There weren't as many areas under ARVN and American control as they said there were. There were quite a lot of areas in South Vietnam which were in what they called 'liberated zones', but they were effectively under the control of the Viet Cong right throughout the war and the people knew that. A lot of the people would have two bob each way for their own survival.

We had what we called Civil Affairs and Psychological Operations. We would go in and make a chicken coop and roof a few houses and build a windmill and do their dentistry (which was important because that was one of the worst things they suffered from and we had dental health), but when we'd leave the Viet Cong would come back in.

The Viet Cong made sure though that they never upset anybody, that if they took anything they would pay for it. If they got rice they'd pay, if they took chickens they'd pay. They never ripped the people off, that was one thing. They would kill somebody to make an example of him if he was overtly pro-government, but they would never rip the people off. They would never rape. That was absolutely out of the question. They were too smart for that. No raping, no burning and no pillaging. Pay for what you use or leave a promissory note, and they would honour that too, no question.

The ARVN would go in and they would knock stuff off and, of course, that would cause absolute hatred. When they left they would pinch the rice, the chickens, the eggs — all the things which were in short supply — and that would piss the people off. They would make them natural enemies.

There was such a massive cultural difference between a Vietnamese and a white guy that even if you went in and built a windmill and did their dentistry they would just smile and bow and you could be the man from Mars. They didn't have any idea where Australia was. You were just another person stuffing up their lives as far as they were concerned. They were peasants, very poor people, poorly educated, subsistence farmers. They lived on fish and rice, chickens, coconuts, a bit of cash crop and that's their lot.

PETER VANDENBERG

The Vietnamese in the villages had no idea who we were or why we were there. I remember one time on my first tour we were in a village and the people were giving us food. We had an interpreter with us and I was talking to him later and he said, 'You know, those villagers thought you were the French.' I said, 'What do you mean?' He said, 'Those people thought that you were the French Army come back.'

MARK ROSE

Everyone made a big thing of the bodycount over there. That was what it was all about, bodycounts and kill ratios — the numbers of them that we killed against the number of us who were killed. But the numbers were always suspect. We sprung one ambush when supposedly about sixty guys walked across the front of our company position in the middle of the night. We were in position and according to our last platoon a whole enemy patrol was supposed to be sneaking through on this winding track in our line of fire.

We opened up with the machine-gun and blasted hell out of that patrol, but as far as numbers went there wasn't a body there the next morning. So we got a quick order to invent bodies and go out and find graves somewhere.

We went out looking around and we found two skeletons and they were real good skeletons too. It was like something out of a spook movie, these two skeletons lying around in the bush, dressed in rags. They'd been there for a long time, but we counted them. Two to our side. Blood trails were invented here and drag marks were created there and things like that. I never read the final report. I don't think anyone wanted to read it.

MAX CAMERON

I got in an argument with a bar girl over something. I think she wanted me to buy her a Saigon tea or something and I didn't want to and we started throwing ashtrays at each other. Next thing I know I was fighting with this nog guy and I was beating his head in. An American pulled me off him but when he did the guy jumped up and shot this thing in my face, something women used to protect themselves with and I went down in a screaming heap with a burnt eye. A couple of my mates fixed up that nog guy pretty good.

I went to the hospital at Vung Tau and they flew me straight up to Bien Hoa hospital. I spent about a week there with my eyes covered. I wasn't sure if I could see or not.

While I was in there I used to hear this Vietnamese kid regularly screaming, three times a day. I asked them what was going on and they told me that he'd been burnt with napalm and they had to bath him every few hours and rub him down with some sort of stuff. When I got one of my eyes uncovered I went up and had a look at him. His skin was just burnt straight through to the bone. You could see the white bone in his legs. The kid would have been about ten.

RIC

We didn't get a kill on one operation and our major, in his wisdom, said you don't get hot food sent out to you in the bush while you haven't got a kill. That man was an arsehole.

WAYNE

There was a small orphanage in a village just out of Vung Tau and I used to take medical supplies out there when I could. I went out there this day and the night before the VC had been in there and, the bastards, they'd killed ten Vietnamese waifs, children that were only part Vietnamese; they'd just sliced them straight up the guts. They'd raped the Sisters, who were French, and they'd beheaded the village chief and they had killed these children. There were four girls and six boys. The youngest one was an eighteen-month-old little girl. Now who was she going to hurt? The oldest kid was only five.

They were laid out on a canvas sheet. The girls were cut from their vaginas right up to their throats and the boys were cut from their bellies and they'd had their genitals cut off. Those poor little buggers were waifs and that was the reason they were killed. I guess they were trying to prove a point.

I vomited when I saw it and I was crying and I was so angry. The Mother Superior told me there was nothing I could do and she told me to leave straight away because there were VC still in the village. She just wanted to show me.

I cried right the way back to Vung Tau and I went through the gates and I got myself paralytic pissed that night. I never told anybody what I saw because I wasn't supposed to be giving them medical supplies.

BILL DOBELL

One of the orphanages was built by Australian troops, or most of it, and I remember taking two trucks of kids down to the beach and up around Baria just for a swim and they were great.

We couldn't talk to them. They couldn't understand a word we were saying and the words we knew in their language were of no use to us with kids. They were all right with prostitutes and what have you, but that was about it. I thought it was beautiful. Those kids were rapt. We couldn't talk to them in no way, but they were playing with us on the beach, jumping on our backs. We were piggy-backing them all over the place, tossing them in the water and they were having a ball. That was one of the beautiful things about the place. Kids are the same all over the world I guess.

They could be fair little buggers too, trying to sell their sisters and all sorts of things like that. This one little bloke, he'd come in with his sister in tow. She was only a tiny little thing, a couple of feet high, just a tot I suppose, and he's trying to sell her off to the boys. I'm just not sure what they were up to at the time but mum obviously didn't approve of them coming near the troops. I don't know whether it was just Aussie troops or just troops but she didn't approve and she came along and she grabbed the little bloke. She had him by the arm and she gave him one hell of a whack behind the ears. It nearly took his head off. I still don't know really why she was so upset. I guess we were the aggressor, I suppose. I don't know, it's hard to say.

MORGAN QUINN

He was a spray painter with the RAAF, based at Vung Tau in 1968.

We had to employ a certain number of the indigenous population on the base at Vung Tau. They were an uppity little bunch of bastards too, because once they got a job they were getting thirty or forty dollars a week, which was pretty good money to them. It wasn't hard to dislike them. When we had those early morning rocket attacks you knew when they were on because the locals were always hanging around the bunkers. You thought, 'Hello, there's another one on today.' And I think it was the filth and the way they lived. I just wasn't used to it.

There were a lot of bars just outside our place and there was a bloke who used to come and visit his wife in one of these bars on a Sunday afternoon. She was what they called a taxi girl, working in the bar as a prostitute. That was just a job to them, but to me that was incomprehensible, having your wife work as a whore. I was pretty green I guess. It was an awakening.

GARY VAPP

He is a grey-haired man of forty-two who runs an auto-electrical business in the Victorian city of Maryborough, of which he has been the mayor. He went to Vietnam in 1966.

Hoa Long was always a fairly hot little village and they decided that we were going to surround it so the South Vietnamese could go in and check for draft dodgers and that sort of thing.

It was well into the afternoon and we still had this village cordoned off and a woman came down to where I was. It was hard to get an idea of their age, but I'd say she would have been in her thirties and she indicated she wanted to go to a pool for a bath. At that stage I thought, well, it's only a woman, she'll be all right, so I let her go and I knew she had nothing with her to wash with so I gave her this pink Camay I had. She sort of stopped and she looked at me and I said, 'Go on, off you go.'

She gave me a rather scouring look and off she went. At thirty they're really starting to look old, but I was sitting up on the bank and I watched her while she undid her hair and it fell down to below her bottom and it was beautiful jet black hair.

When she came back she still had her hair down and she sort of stopped and she still had this look on her face, as if to say well what do you want for the soap? I didn't want anything and I just said, 'Go on, back you go,' and she beamed with her smile. She was expecting that she would have to pay for the service. I got the impression she would have been quite happy to do it and probably wouldn't have thought any more of it, because I don't think they were particularly worried by us, or the Americans.

PETER MOLLOY

You put on a front I suppose when you see the effect of throwing a grenade into a bunker, but it's affecting you all the time you're doing it. Shooting at these blokes after they were dead. You've got a hatred there for them because they're killing your mates. You'd hear it when you went back to the Dat, you'd hear D Company lost three or four blokes and Charlie Company lost one bloke and all in all there might have been seven or eight of our blokes dead and possibly thirty wounded or whatever. But just to see the way that those bodies were mutilated... It's not a normal thing to see.

BARRY KELLY

In the villages you treated the women like you'd treat your pet dog, no respect for them. The only time you respected them was when you were on R&C down in Vung Tau and you had a few bob in your pocket. Then they looked pretty good.

I copped the jack twice over there. Out of fifty-four guys in our unit there were only two that didn't. One was the adjutant and the other was a bloke who killed himself just before Christmas in '66. He was the son of a pastor, a national service-man. He wouldn't swear, wouldn't drink, wouldn't do nothing. He'd just sit on the bed and read his Bible. He'd do his job, but it just got too much for him before Christmas; he sat on his stretcher, pulled a pistol out, put it against his chest and blew himself away.

PADDY

I was walking along a track and I turned around to a bloke and I said, 'Guess what?'

He said, 'What?'

'Well, I'm twenty-one today.'

'Yeah, so fuckin' what?'

'Well…'

'Well, keep fuckin' walking.'

RAY PAYNE

Bobby came over and he was talking to me and three Charlie just sort of appeared. Obviously they hadn't heard us, because they came out of the bush and they just had their rifles over their shoulders and they were just walking along. It gave me enough time to say to Bob, quite casually, 'Down mate, they're here.' As they came across I was able to get each and every one of them lined up, the whole lot of them, and I just moved the gun a little and down they went. They were my first kills and I was absolutely overjoyed. I said to Bobby, 'There you are mate, got them on you,' because at that stage he had none.

I had to wait till the clearing patrol went through and I was itching to get out there to make sure that I got all three. The last bloke I was a little bit concerned about because I saw him take his rifle down. I reckoned I'd got him before he'd done anything, but I didn't know whether I'd hit him bad enough.

The intelligence corporal came over and took gear off them, not that they had much, and then we just stuck them in a little shell scrape and covered them over with leaves, the ground was so hard. We left them there. I felt I didn't want to look as I walked towards them, but because the other guys were with me I sort of did. That was just prior to Christmas. I'd been there nearly six months at that stage. They were nothing.

ALLEN MAY

At forty, he is a road ganger with the Brisbane City Council. He was a national serviceman.

Long Tan* was the first big thing we ran into. We'd been in Vietnam a couple of months.

We were just heading along minding our own business and what we thought were two kids came running out of the scrub

---

*Long Tan, a rubber plantation, was the site of the biggest battle Australian troops fought and in which they suffered the greatest number of casualties for the war. Eighteen Australians were killed and two hundred and forty-five NVA and Viet Cong were confirmed dead.

and took off. We gave the enemy sign, brought the lewie up and told him what we saw, then we spread out to see if we could find anything.

We came across five or six Viet Cong sitting around in a little group eating rice and their rifles just laying there in a heap beside them. Doug Fabian and myself both opened up on these people. We wounded two and they took off into the rubber. We went through and followed the blood trails where these guys went.

We went past a plantation house, a two-storey place, and checked that out. There was nobody in it and we went further on and then all hell broke loose. It was just all of a sudden, like fireworks. Doug and I hit the deck and in that initial contact our lieutenant was killed, shot clean through the head, and Bob Buick, our sergeant, took over.

It was eerie. The VC weren't running and diving behind trees like you'd expect them to. They were just walking toward us like zombies and every one you knocked down there were two to take his place. It was like shooting ducks in a bloody shooting gallery. I would have killed at least forty blokes that day.

One bloke, he was just walking towards me firing, and I could see the bullets coming, like in slow motion, across the ground towards me. I hit him with a round of tracer and he just stood there screaming and scratching at his chest, like he was trying to put the fire out.

Bob Buick came up almost directly behind me and Bluey Moore and Doug Fabian and said, 'Right, we're going to retreat; when I give the word every man for himself,' and then there was a big 'go, go, go' and everybody ducked.

Well there was so much fire activity going then that I never moved. Brian Halls, he was about three rubber trees away, never moved, and Dougie Fabian got hit.

I was about to go when he yelled out. He had a bullet through his elbow. I wasn't brave, but I wasn't going to leave him there, so I stayed with him. When the shooting died down we got up and started running and the next minute a bullet hit my pack. It was just like getting hit in the back with a ten-ton truck. I was bent backwards and skidded about fifty yards in the mud.

The funny thing was that we had been through the same area about four days previous, through a whole patrol, and there had been nothing there whatsoever and yet three or four days later there was an estimated two thousand Viet Cong dug in.

I didn't sleep that night. There was no way. We didn't know who was where, we didn't know how many we'd lost. I was looking for a mate of mine, Victor. I went around looking for him everywhere. Next morning we found him. He was dead.

When I was checking through the bodies I found another good friend of mine. He had been laying down in the firing position and a mortar had landed between his outstretched arms and his head... it just took the top portion of his body completely away.

We had to pick up any pieces we found and wrap them in a plastic groundsheet to send back to camp. I had to collect his scalp, which was hanging in a rubber tree. That just about killed me.

People went off their brains because of what they found when we went back there. The corporal in charge of my platoon, a very fine little bloke, completely snapped his brain. He picked up one of the dead Viet Cong by the feet and just swung him around and smashed his head open against a tree.

We buried the Viet Cong, but three months after we went back to that place and you could hear the pigs at night time, you could hear all the wild pigs digging up the bodies.

PADDY

The leadership over there was a heap of shit. You probably hear that in any war, even the World Wars, but I just couldn't believe it. They were sending over young blokes with brand new commissions and putting them in charge of guys who had been there and they didn't know anything.

DUNCAN McINTOSH

He drove a tank in Vietnam in 1968. He lives in Corio, Victoria.

We were scrambled one day and I was driving the lieutenant's tank in 3 Troop.

We jumped in and he said, 'We're off to war.' He was a career soldier. We took off up the road and I'm flying along in fourth or fifth gear and I put it down to a lower gear to make a turn but it slewed off sideways into a rice paddy and bogged. The lieutenant, he jumps off and he throws the headphones down and says, 'You bastard, you meant that, didn't you?' He abused buggery out of me. Then he saw Bravo tank coming down and he jumps into the middle of the road and waves it down, gets on it and says, 'I'm off to war,' and away he went, left me high and dry.

COLIN NICOLE

We had a major who had a grenade thrown in his tent. I didn't have much sympathy for him. Most of us had a fair idea who the soldier was. I lost count of the number of officers in our company who were dismissed for incompetence or who were killed or who left early. We had four or five corporals who were either killed, shot themselves or were removed for incompetence.

JOHN ATKINS

He was a tank commander in Vietnam in 1968–9.

Some of our officers were real weirdos.

We had one guy who was only in the Army to get his grandmother's inheritance. He didn't even look like a soldier. He was a little fat guy, a spoiled kid, and his grandmother apparently had a lot of money and she said to him if you can hold down a job for six years you'll get the inheritance. So he joined the Army and they made him an officer. In Vietnam he used to carry a big pearl-handled pistol that he'd bought off a Yank.

We were at this place down near the mountains and we were told that there were noggies everywhere. We had infantry there and they had everything ready, just in case we got hit. We were scared.

Next day an infantry patrol had gone out and been hit and they told us to get down there and lend a bit of weight and get them back. So this officer took us out and he reckons the stouch is going to be over before we get there, so he pulled us up in a rubber plantation, formed a circle and he started shooting the rubber trees. Because they had nothing to do, guys were throwing their bayonets into the rubber trees and hacking them with machetes. That officer, he didn't want to go out, no way. He didn't want to get shot.

GEOFF COLLINS

I saw a lot of stupidity from junior officers. The guys out of Scheyville, they just had no training at all. There was one lieutenant, he walked his platoon into a minefield.

We came down out of the Warbies and surrounded the village of Hoa Long to do a cordon and search. About two o'clock we hear explosions and my mate and I are called up and there he is, this lieutenant's got himself and about ten others in a minefield.

We spent about four hours down on our hands and knees in the dark using whatever we could to get the guys who were still alive. One of the guys that was dead he just had no head at all. I had to prod all the way around him; his head had just been blown right off.

I was in there for about an hour before I got to him, because the minefield would have been a hundred yards long and the lieutenant had got within thirty or forty feet from the end of it before he got hit. He was dead.

He killed himself and two others. There were some wounded I didn't hear much about because just as we finished my mate walked out of our safe zone and stood on a little anti-personnel mine and blew the front part off one of his feet.

In the morning I was ratshit, just a bundle of nerves. Four hours we were in the minefield, just with a torch and a knife feeling our way around, putting the safety pins back in any mines we could find, trying to get the live guys out and then seeing my mate blow half his foot off. That's when I really fell to pieces. I know that I was howling in the morning.

DAVID COWDREY

We went into an ambush position and I took my pack off and leaned it against a tree. I put my hand into the pack and this spider falls on my hand. It covered the whole palm of my hand and it was digging into my first finger with its fangs, so I screamed out, 'Fucking hell!' This bloke said, 'Shh, we're in an ambush position.' I'll never forget that, it was the first thing he said: 'We're in an ambush position.' I said, 'Look at fucking this,' right, I'm dead, you know. I've collapsed and I'm dead because no-one's told me about the spiders there, what they're like. I'd already seen a cobra, which I didn't fancy. So there's this thing hooking into my hand, I've collapsed, I'm ratshit, the medic comes over. When they get me around he's poured this stuff on it, fuck knows what it was. Jesus did it sting.

I've got a mark going halfway up my arm soon, so they call in a chopper. Not for me, for the fuckin' spider! They took that spider in for identification. The message came back and it said, 'It's not poisonous, but if the mark goes up past his elbow bring him in,' and I said, 'You're fucking kidding, I'm dying. Why send the spider, why not send me?' The reply was: 'No, you're needed.'

Another time, it was the battalion's birthday and we were in an ambush position, no-one's supposed to know we're there, everything's cool, everyone's waiting. Next minute over came the chopper, big megaphone: 'Happy Birthday, today is One Battalion's birthday, Happy Birthday from the CO.' They had helicopters going out to the blokes on Christmas Day playing 'Jingle Bells' and everything like that. That's what a lot of young blokes couldn't understand, the incompetence.

We were at base camp and we got a new officer sent to us to take over mortar platoon. He took us out on a TAOR patrol, and we came across a flat bit of land that had a little bit of a hill on it facing us. He put us down in the grass in a straight line and called his mortars in on this hill to see how good they were and when they stopped he said, 'There's enemy still there and we're going to do a bayonet charge on the hill.'

He got us to fix bayonets, but no-one had them, only him and the sergeant, so then he passed the order down to the sixteen guys that we were to pretend we had bayonets and we advanced on the hill. Me and my mate really acted the part and we were going in, out, en garde, like we'd been trained at infantry centre on imaginary enemy. When it was all over he came up and congratulated me and my mate for doing such a good job in bayonet fighting, and we didn't even have a fucking bayonet. Now what was he doing in Vietnam?

CHRIS LUCAS

I stopped one bloke from shooting our lieutenant. He was a reinforcement, only been in the jungle about a month and a half. We were walking Indian file and I saw him lift his rifle and sight up on the lewie. I could see what he was doing. I stuck my rifle barrel on his neck and said, 'You can shoot him if you like, but you're next.' He decided not to and I never said anything about it. He just cracked, that's all. Some people did.

I remember we were ambushed and we had a bloke who broke down five minutes after it was all over. He was all right while it was on, but afterwards he was just a screaming mess on the ground. He sat down and went into hysterics. He never went back in the jungle again.

We had blokes do it in the middle of the night, just suddenly start screaming. I saw one bloke go into a fit from tension — scream and thrash around on the ground, then he got up and was all right. I saw an officer standing behind his desk in Vung Tau just bawling his eyes out and I bet he couldn't tell you why.

I was a batman for a lieutenant colonel for a while, Second World War veteran. His way of dropping his bundle was getting drunk. I'd wake him up and he'd be that drunk he wouldn't know where he was. I remember he asked me what time it was and I said, 'Seven o'clock,' and he said, 'Night or day?'

GIL SCOLYER

We had a bloke with us by the name of Mukowski and he was straight. He'd joined as a reg and he was a good soldier. He was good in the field, he knew what he was doing, but he never smoked, never drank, he didn't fuck, and all he used to do was sit in his space every night and just read the fucking Bible. Here in Australia he used to carry it in his ammo pouch and he took it bush with him in Vietnam for about the first three months.

Another rifle company knew they had three kills but they couldn't find them so we were called in. We got tracked in and then spread out and went through the same area where the contact was and we found these bodies. They were just dug about six inches in the ground and then just covered over still as they were. Well, we were digging them up and Mukowski thought he'd struck a root with his entrenching tool, but it wasn't no root. It went straight into this gook's head and the head just splattered. He had his entrenching tool at an angle and he just pulled out this nog's fucking brains and it just splattered all over him and that was that. He took off and went straight into the river and he washed and soaped but you could still smell him. He was foul.

He went right off after that. We went down into Vungers and he came back with a load of the jack, and he drank piss and he gave up reading the Bible. That was Mukowski.

LACHLAN IRVINE

February '68 we were at a fire-support base called Anderson on Operation Coburg and a bloke I knew was killed there. He had been very badly wounded by mortars and he knew he was dying. A group of his mates were gathered around him and he was sort of cradled in their arms. They knew he was dying. The last words he said were, 'Help me, help me,' and you knew, being there, that he wasn't saying help me to live and help me with my wounds. He knew that he was facing something that nobody could help him with; he knew he was going to die and he just didn't know how to handle it. It brought home to me the loneliness of death.

That day I was given a book, *Catch 22*, by a friend of mine and I sat down and started reading it. Throughout that book there's a laugh on every page yet there's somebody getting killed on almost every page. Somehow that book seemed to help me to deal with the situation at that time and I kept that book with me, almost like a Bible, for the rest of the year. I'd pull it out and read a bit of it every now and then, and even though it was a work of fiction and it was about a different war and a black comedy it seemed to say a lot about what Vietnam was about. There was excitement, there was boredom, there was fun, there was laughter and there was a lot of people getting killed. That was what was happening. That was what it was all about.

TED COWELL

He was a field engineer in Vietnam in 1966. 'I was a regular Army soldier so I never had any real choice about going to Vietnam. I'd signed up for twelve years in 1958. I wanted to be a digger. Jobs were pretty hard to come by and soldiering at that time, while it didn't carry much money, did carry a bit of respect.'

Because I was a dumb, skinny, silly-looking bastard that could fit down these little rat holes like a bloody pull-through on a rifle I was volunteered to go on this tunnel team. I wasn't too keen about the whole idea; as a matter of fact I turned pale when they told me about it, but I couldn't see myself making it out of the joint anyway, I was resolved to dying there, so I thought one way is as good as another.

I never liked going into those complexes at all. They had some charming little traps. First of all you had to find them. The entrance could be a hollowed-out stump, something that's been blown off by artillery; if the Yanks had hit the joint then it was ideal for them and it just looked so bloody innocent. You had to get the blokes to lower you in by your feet because usually on the floor they'd have some sort of a spring trap. You'd find they employed a hell of a lot of spring-loaded spears so that once you set the pressure plate off, if you stood on it or anything, it's done you an injustice. You got past that lot by getting the blokes to hold you above the line of fire while you gave the pressure plate a bang with a hunk of wood or something.

From the moment you went through the entrance you were into the dark and it was pretty tight. The Vietnamese are pretty small characters and they could move like little lizards through there, but we were bumbling, stupid bastards. Although we stripped our shirts off and we took our boots off we still had to carry a 9mm Browning, a prodder for booby traps, a bloody sharp knife, and two lights strapped together, one shining up and one shining down.

You'd be crawling down on an angle and you'd come to a blank wall and a puddle of water, so you'd get your prodder and you'd feel around inside and you can feel the bamboo spikes under the water and you've got to go around every spike to make sure there's no wires on the bastards. You'd do the floor, then you'd do the walls, looking for little bits of piano wire, little bits of anything that looked out of place. So, you've cleared it of any sort of trip, then you've got to find the widest part of the spikes and go through there under water — that was the most harassing part because you didn't know how long you were going to have to be under water or what was waiting for you out the other side.

Sometimes you'd find they'd have about six snakes, bamboo kraits, hanging there waiting for you. The first I knew about them snakes was when the order came down that we had to go to the Q-store and get a plastic bag and a pair of scissors, which I thought was bloody ridiculous because I wondered what the hell we were supposed to do with the bastards. I went back and saw my boss and he said, 'It's to cut the heads off snakes that the blokes have been finding in the tunnels.'

'Jesus, you've got to be whackers mate; I'm not going in no bloody tunnel with them poofters in it.'

'Oh, they're only little snakes.'

'Well, what sort are they?'

'Bamboo kraits.'

'You've lost me, that's it, finished, I'm signing out of this mob.'

They were deadly. They wanted the heads to get the venom to produce an antivenene.

The worst tunnels I went into were the ones out the back of the Long Hais. They were like Gorgonzola cheese. They even had an underground hospital there.

We were called in just after Long Tan, when we knew that they had a hell of a lot of wounded and the artillery couldn't close them down. They belted hell out of it and they brought in B52s and the B52s absolutely flattened it. Five o'clock the afternoon before, it was a complete jungle range and the next morning it just looked like barren red desert, blown to hell. And then they shot us in.

The infantry located the entrances and then we had to go in after them, see what the hell was in them and try to get them out. We got a few out. Some that were too bad we wasted. One poor bastard I found was the local schoolteacher, from Hoa Long.

He'd disappeared about two months beforehand, and been replaced by a young girl schoolteacher who was a Viet Cong sympathiser. He could hardly talk and he was bleeding, pusy and gangrenous. His wife and two children were there, but they were dead. He was wired up by his arms and testicles and he'd had his eyes put out. The rats had been chewing on him too. He was sort of making hoarse sounds out of his throat. It wasn't a mouth even; it was just a hole. Most of it was eaten away. I don't know how he was alive. He was just sort of making sounds. I cut his throat, put him out of his misery. I felt guilty about killing him for a long time. He wasn't enemy, he wasn't Cong. He was just trying to be a teacher, you know.

I saw too much of that sort of thing, far too much, and you never ever forgot it. I still have nightmares about it eighteen years later. That's the trouble, you see. You never forget it.

JOHN

He served in Vietnam in 1969.

We had a Yank with us one time as a forward observer, a big Negro. We shot a couple of nogs in an ambush and I always remember him afterwards kicking one of the bodies and screaming out 'stupid'. He's just screaming 'stupid' and he's kicking the dead nog. He was upset that we had shot this bloke and I think he was just saying that this was madness.

I looked at him and I thought, 'You might be right.'

RAY PAYNE

We went into a house and these people were in fear and were praying. One of the guys hit all their Buddhist idols onto the floor with the butt of his rifle. I'm not a religious person really, but that was something I never touched and I said, 'How would you feel if someone came into your house and did that?' He said, 'They're only shit anyway.'

RAY ORCHARD

We heard a lot about people blaming us in Australia, people on strike and everything, people like the wharfies not sending over our Christmas supplies. I never worried about that. After six months there I didn't give a stuff about anybody else. You got that way where you just thought about yourself and how to survive. I was the main item.

ROSS MATHIESON

He flew helicopters in Vietnam in 1967–8.
'When I first went there I mainly thought of it as an adventure and I believed in the Domino Theory. I felt we were doing the right thing by going.'

All the pilots monitored the guard frequency, 243 MHz, so if anyone had an emergency they called up their mayday on that. People used to make unauthorised comments too. First thing of a morning someone would call, 'Good morning Vietnam' and someone else would say, 'Vietnam sucks.'

4

Sour Rain

'You can kill ten of my men for every one I kill of yours. But even at those odds, you will lose and I will win.

Ho Chi Minh

PHIL JOHNSTONE

We meet nine hundred feet underground in a coal-mine at Wallerawang, New South Wales, where he works as a mine electrician. He is bearded, stocky. We have been brought together by another veteran who works in the mine and the three of us stand in a dark corridor of this labyrinthine pit. Our faces are black and the air is rank and we talk about Vietnam where he was a medic.

I worked with the mortician. I used to assist him on the body runs, picking up bodies or helping to move anybody who had very bad head injuries to the American hospital at Long Binh. That's when I saw quite a few things that I really wasn't ready for.

We had I think it was five guys go up in an APC. They came back in one bodybag. You know, one bodybag for five guys and you've got a finger, a hand and a foot, a head and there's not five guys there.

Around the Tet, we picked up seven guys who'd been wrapped up in their hoochies and left in the bush for three or four days and they were pretty ripe by the time we got them. We put them on a stainless steel bench and hosed them down. I had six masks over my face.

I think the thing that really got me the worst was when we had this one fellow come in. I related very much to him. I put myself in his position.

We had him on the bench and we were cleaning him up. He'd got an RPG in the shoulder which took out half his neck. His heart was just hanging out, his arm was gone. There was a dazed look in his eyes. He was obviously killed instantly. I lifted all his gear off and went out to burn it while the sergeant was cleaning him down and I happened to look at his field message pad. I'd opened it up, ripping off the pages to throw into the fire, and he'd written a letter to his wife. And then in the back of the field message pad was a letter from his wife. She had a young child and I very much related. The things she said in the letter were what my wife said to me, like their kid needed shoes and stuff like that. I should never have read the letter.

With the bodies that I have moved and done I've always had the dread of coming across somebody who says, 'I had a brother overseas, he was killed.' Should I tell him that I hosed him down or that I put his head in a bag and sent a couple of sandbags home for you to bury just to make up the weight? That always worries me.

The grunts, they had their problems, but when their mate had been choppered out to the hospital or when he was killed they never had to worry about him, they'd never see him again. They had fond memories of their mate but they had to worry about themselves. They never saw them after that, when they were lying on the slab and I've got them. A lot of those memories stay because you know exactly what injuries, what horrific bloody things they had. It's a bloody waste.

RAY PAYNE

'We would go along through a village in the APCs and kids would be standing along the side of the road with their hands out and we would throw these tins of white bread, ham and lima beans in front of the APC so that the kids would have to run out and pick them up. How none of those kids ever got run over I don't know. But you know how sick we were? We used to save up our white bread and lima beans for the next village.'

We had an operation in the Ho Bo woods. We went in with choppers to an area where we were going to be stopgap for the Yanks who were going to do a big sweep to the north and to the west of us.

As soon as we hit the place we copped shit, right from the bloody start. I came in on the fourth or fifth stick of choppers and as I came off the chopper they were carting wounded out past me. I couldn't believe it. We were stopgap, you know. What the bloody hell are we doing?

Everywhere around us there's shooting going on and I'm thinking this is bloody crazy. I can remember thinking what the stuffing hell have we got ourselves into? We moved in down a well-worn track. There's a dead buffalo on the side that the blokes had mowed down, everywhere you looked there were chooks running around, there were pigs, domesticated animals and I couldn't figure it. There were communication trenches that looked like they had been smooth trowelled, they were so immaculate.

We moved into position and they gave me this spot on the edge of a communication trench and I sat there while a clearing patrol went out.

Keith Mills, a sapper, came over. We sat down there and we were talking. It was Keith who spotted movement along the trench. I didn't take much notice because I'd been told the clearing patrol was going to come back through my gun and I thought it was them coming in.

They kept coming along the trench. We could only see their hats and then I realised that they were noggies. At that stage they hadn't seen me because they seemed to be looking the other way, further down, towards where there was a lot of shooting going on. One guy was probably no more than a yard in front of me, that's all, because I remember I emptied about twenty or thirty rounds into his head. The machine-gun was holding him up. The top of his head was just sort of lifting. The rounds hitting him were stopping him from falling.

He was about seventeen I suppose. He was wearing a pair of black shorts and a black top and he had a belt around him with three grenades on either side and an AK-47. They reckon that his gun had a round jammed in it, but I don't think he even saw me until it was too late. I remember the look on his face as he turned and saw. The only thing he did see was the machine-gun barrel pointing right at his face. He was about seventeen. I was nineteen.

I had to wait for my number two, Harry, to clip another belt on the gun and then I zapped off after another bloke that was running down the trench. I got him but he disappeared around the corner. I reckon I got him and the guy in front of him.

We followed the blood trail a good klick down through the scrub then they just disappeared into one of the tunnels. We counted it as two possibles and left it at that.

When we got back we set the gun up in the same spot. We pushed dirt over the top of the dead noggie and we stayed there the night.

That was the worst part, the fact that he was down there all night. I looked over at him in the afternoon a couple of times. I can remember coming up to the edge and it was like the feeling you get when you look over a very long drop and you're standing right on the edge, wanting to step back.

That was a really bad night. That was the night we had Penny killed. That's a hard thing. Penny was shot by one of our own blokes moving between pits and he was lying out there, screaming for his mother and the nogs were out there with their lights trying to draw our fire to find out where the machine-gun positions were.

They'd get a candle and put it on the end of a long stick, like the old cowboy-and-the-hat trick, and try to draw fire. We were under instructions not to fire and that was frustrating.

Penny was out the front and he was screaming out for his mum and I'm thinking to myself, 'Why doesn't he shut up, why doesn't he be a man? I wouldn't yell out like that if it was me, I wouldn't yell out like that.' I can remember holding my hands over my ears and thinking 'For fuck sake stop yelling out, Penny, the bastards will know where we are.' I didn't want Charlie to know that we screamed out like that. I didn't want them to know that we were as vulnerable as that, that we weren't invincible.

We moved off that position on patrol and we came on this place where there was a whole pen full of pigs, and I just opened up with the machine-gun and killed the whole bloody lot of them and thought it was good fun because I was firing single bursts with the machine-gun going blat, blat, blat. I really felt proud of myself, I did. Those pigs were food for the Viet Cong.

COLIN NICOLE

When the contact broke out there were two people killed, and one was a woman. This bloke went up and just shot all her face away. He went gaga after that and raced off to the padre. I went up and had a look at this woman lying on the ground. She was only a tiny little thing, no face, nothing at all. You'd seen so many operations at that stage that you tended to get used to it. It didn't affect me so much as when a bloke in the platoon picked off all her jewellery. I think there was a twenty-four carat gold bracelet and a necklace. I couldn't touch it. There was no way in a million years I could touch that body.

BOB GIBSON

It was about one o'clock that night when the first rockets and mortars started coming in.

I can remember there was nothing up — no barbed wire, no nothing — and I was laying on my back and it was just like a sky-rocket, the tail of a sky-rocket, went over and I thought, 'Holy shit.'

I hadn't been mortared or rocketed before, but I knew what the bloody hell it was when it lobbed right in the middle of us. All hell broke loose then, mortars and rockets and Christ knows what.

My number two on the machine-gun, he'd only just come to us. He hadn't fired a shot, hadn't seen nothing, and he said to me, 'Jesus Christ, I'm scared.' I said, 'You're not the only one.'

It was drizzling rain and he said, 'I don't know whether I'm cold from the rain or I'm cold from being scared, but I've just pissed myself.'

I said, 'Hang on, you'll be right, just play it cool, you'll be right.'

After the rockets everything went dead silent. You could not hear anything. I mean, if you wanted to hear absolute silence, total silence, not even a bug, that was it.

Then the lewie called around to the four of us and said, 'Ground assault'. Well, I mean, he didn't have to do that. It was pretty obvious it was going to be on.

Then you could hear the cracking of the sticks, a lot of people walking on dead sticks and grass and stuff and then all of a sudden the flares went up, flares started going off everywhere and you could see shadows down through the grass.

They'd had us cased. They knew exactly where everything was in that fire-support base. They knew where the mortars were, where the infantry was set up, where the machine-guns were, they knew where to hit and when to hit.

They'd circled right around the main force and they'd gone right bang straight through in amongst the mortars.

There was screaming, there was hollering, there was bellowing. It was like nothing I've ever experienced before in my life. It was just noise, like you could never believe that there could be so much noise, with the rockets and the mortars and the machine-guns and the guys screaming and bellowing. Then the choppers came out, the gunships, and Puff the Magic

Dragon, which was the plane with the Gatling guns. I think there were six or eight choppers plus the Puff, and I mean the fire just rained down like lava coming out of a volcano.

That went on till daylight and I lay there and it was the longest night that I've ever spent in my life. I thought, 'I'm never going to see the sun, the sun is never ever going to come up,' and I was praying for the sun to come up because then you could get into them.

It was about seven a.m. when they got the last of them out of the bunkers. There was just a whole mass of bodies, about thirteen pairs of boots underneath ground sheets. It's something that I've never forgotten.

There were some blokes brought in later that had been wounded, from the perimeters, and some North Vietnamese. The doctor was there trying to patch a few up and one guy rolled over to go for a rifle and the doctor just pulled out a gun and shot him.

There was a dead guy out the front of my machine-gun pit, a couple of hundred yards away, and we went and got him. He was sort of stiff from the cold. He was a guy about sixteen, maybe twenty years old, you couldn't tell with a lot of them. I didn't think about it over there, it meant nothing to me there, but we threw him up in the air, kicking him when he was coming down. We were just throwing him around and laughing and joking and carrying on.

I felt a bit crook about it after a while and somebody said we had better bury the poor bastard. So we threw him in a hole. They threw some lime about because there was a fair few dead.

It wasn't until a couple of years ago when the POW issue came out in America, that there's so many Americans unaccounted for, that I thought about that one particular guy, and that his family would never know where he was. He was just buried in some hole somewhere in Bien Hoa Province that would never be found.

BRIAN GRIFFIN

The way people treated bodies, that's something that sticks in my mind. I can remember people going out and standing over bodies and having their photo taken — the great white hunter. Other bad things: being in contact and seeing a bloke zap away at a body lying on the ground, just blowing it to pieces; seeing people disintegrate. They get hit with a .50 calibre machine-gun and there's none of this slowly-sink-to-the-ground-clutching-their-side like you see in the old cowboy movies. They spin in the air and bounce around and bits fly off them. It jerks them and convulses them. I often have recollections of that. I've seen bodies jerk and jump about.

I can remember hitting a bloke at one stage with twin .30s and watching him spin.

We were near the village of Thai Thien with some American advisers. We went up this fire trail and all of a sudden these guys just came up from the side. I was firing as I brought the guns around. I had a lot of tracer in them and I started spraying them all around this bloke. It was just like I was hosing him, you know, boogying him around.

I was on a complete high. Everything was in slow motion, my back was aching from the adrenalin. It's a high you'd never experience again.

We got to buggery out of there pretty quick. We had South Vietnamese with us who went to ground and wouldn't go forward and there was one suicidal Yank. He was a medic of all things, Steve the medic, a real Audie Murphy. He ran forward to get his Vietnamese out, these fellows he'd been training, but they were stunned and they weren't going to move for anybody. He was hollering at them, 'Get up, get up and go after the bastards,' but they just wouldn't move. They'd just lay there and look up and shake their heads. So this guy went running forward by himself, firing an Armalite off one hip and changing magazines as he went with these rounds jumping behind him. I'll never forget that.

GRAHAM WALKER

He lives alone in bushland near Bermagui, on the south coast of New South Wales. He was a major in Vietnam in 1969-70 and retired from the Army in 1980 as a lieutenant-colonel.

The greatest propagators of the illusion of what was happening in Vietnam were the American advisers. Every province chief had a district adviser and each district chief had an American major or captain who was his adviser. These guys were only there for a short period of time — six to twelve months — and each one was desperate to make a name for himself. He had to succeed. And to succeed he had to show that the district or province was in better shape when he left it than when he arrived.

Every few months these advisers had to fill out a great big form showing how their district or province was going. Every village had to be categorised from VC-controlled right through the spectrum to completely loyal to the Saigon government. When one of these district advisers arrived he knew that the villages in his district were categorised in a certain way. What he wanted to do was to be able to upgrade them before he left, yet I think it was highly likely that when he arrived, particularly as the war went on, he would have arrived to find that the supposed categories for these villages were a lot of crap. In fact, the villages were nothing like the forms said they were.

There was this creeping lie, if you like, because they had to appear to be successful. If a guy arrived in a district, looked around and said, 'These reports are a lot of crap' and wrote a report saying that they were different, he would have had all hell break loose around him. He would have brigadiers and generals down there asking him what the fuck he was doing and what had he done? That wasn't the way to do it. The way to do it was just to hang on for a year and try and inch up a bit here and there.

If you can imagine it, every three months all those forms went in to a computer in Saigon to show an upward graph — that there was light at the end of the tunnel. But it was a lie, a complete and utter lie.

The Vietnamese themselves were often much more realistic. I remember talking with a Vietnamese major, the district chief of Binh Ba district. He was a very experienced soldier. He had been in the French Army fighting against the Viet Minh. At that stage it had been announced that 8RAR was not going to be replaced — that was the start of the pull out.

I said to this major, 'I don't want to be rude, but my personal view is that as we start pulling out, the Viet Cong and North Vietnamese units will slowly start to move back into the jungle areas in the north-east and they will start to reoccupy all the bunker systems and so on and slowly they will get control of the province.' He looked at me and said, 'Slowly! The security of this province will fold like the card house. I have air tickets to France. I and my family are going to France.'

MICK CRAWFORD

We all went out on tanks one time and we had a Kit Carson scout with us, a North Vietnamese turned good guy. Hai was his name. We stopped for lunch and Hai stepped off the track and stood on a mine. One of our guys lost his right eye from flying stone and stuff and one of the tankies was pretty knocked around, but all we picked up of Hai was his head and shoulder. The rest of him was nowhere to be found. I don't think anyone cared. He wasn't a bad guy, but you could never really get involved with defectors and I don't think we ever really trusted them.

Only a few minutes before he copped it he told us that his job before he defected was to run down the Ho Chi Minh trail every second night carrying two rocket propelled grenades on his back in bamboo canisters. They would give him a handful of rice and he'd have to be back in two days to get another two. He did that for a month, just carrying these two shells down the track every second night.

Lieutenant-Colonel MICHAEL McDERMOTT

He did two tours of Vietnam, as a platoon commander in 1969-70 and as an adviser to the South Vietnamese in 1971.

We had a chieu hoi captain called Ky with us for a while. He had been posted from a very good North Vietnamese regiment to a group of Chau Ducs* and he had found they were all drug addicts, outlaws from the local community and so he defected. The next thing he did was take us back to the area where the Chau Ducs were and we set up a claymore ambush and hit a fellow and a girl carrying a Chicom sub-machine-gun. The commander of the platoon that got them said, 'Bring in Ky and see if he recognises them.' When Ky came in he was suddenly confronted with the bodies of people who he was probably living with only a week before. Suddenly here they were dead, his nationality. They probably weren't bad people as far as he was concerned, they weren't immoral. He stood there looking at these people who were just laying out dead on the ground and he started to cry. You couldn't talk to him after that. The next day I was in Sydney. I walked out of that and I flew into Sydney on my R&R and I was with my eight-month pregnant wife at a little motel in Coogee Bay Road in Sydney.

MORGAN QUINN

I came back to Australia on R&R to see the wife. I'd done just over six months, it was early January, '69. I didn't fit, even then. Everybody asked me, 'What's it like over there?' I said, 'Oh, it's hot and wet, I don't look like getting killed. It's all right.'

I had three or four days at home. My oldest boy, Brad, he was just on two, he sort of knew it was his father that was home, but that was all. The youngest one didn't know me. It was like meeting my wife again for the first time. I was afraid to have sex with her.

An ethnic minority in Vietnam.

When I got back to Vietnam blokes said to me, 'Bad luck you had to come back again.' I went along with it, 'Yeah, bastard of a place to come back to.' But I more or less felt that I was back with the people that I fitted with, with my mates.

GEOFF

He was an infantry soldier in Vietnam in 1969.

I didn't get any R&R because I was wounded halfway through my tour and medevaced home, but I got a week in Saigon on what they called a Saigon guard. I really won the lottery there.

While I was in Saigon I screwed a young girl. She wouldn't have been any more than fourteen, working in one of the bars. She was only a little thing and she didn't really know what to do. She just lay there while I did it. It was a crazy place, Vietnam. Kids grew up pretty quick over there, I guess.

MICK CRAWFORD

I was asleep when they came through the first time and, of course, you get the tap on the shoulder and instantly you're awake and you know what's going on and you can see them coming down the road. There's heaps of them, you couldn't help but hear them coming. The sergeant said, 'All be quiet, no firing, we'll let them go through.'

There were eight of us and we estimated there were a hundred and fifty of them, half were women and about one in five were carrying weapons. They weren't loaded down, they were fresh and they were going to fight, so we just lay there and let them go through. I don't know how long it took for them to go through. It seemed like hours, but it was probably a few minutes and I reckon we all held our breath for that whole time.

After they went through the sergeant said, 'We're going to move' and I think all of us thought, 'Beauty, they're going to come back out the way they came in and we're not going to be there.' What it was though, the sergeant reckoned we didn't have a good enough killing ground.

When they came back out they were loaded down with supplies. It was about one o'clock in the morning. I was sitting on the machine-gun and all of a sudden I hear this noise coming down the track. It was surprising how much noise they were making. You could hear them all talking. I tapped the sergeant on the shoulder and said, 'Is that them coming or am I hearing noises?' He just said, 'No more talk.' I was so scared. I mean, you could see them coming down the road, you could actually watch them coming down the road, and you knew you were going to have to do something about it. And you think, 'Crikey, they're really only human, what have they done to me?' See, I wasn't long in Vietnam. I suppose I'd been there three months at most, never been in a contact before that, and all you could think of was, 'They don't look much different to me walking down the road in the moonlight, am I going to be able to pull the trigger or am I going to freeze up?'

When the time came I was quite prepared to lay there and bury my head and hope to hell they wouldn't see me, stop breathing if necessary. My guts had just turned into one big knot.

The sergeant pushed the claymore mines when he reckoned it was the right time and as soon as we hit them the radio man behind me is yelling 'Contact' into the radio.

As soon as we hit them we called for the APCs and choppers and everything we could think of because we knew it was too many to handle. They brought flares in from the artillery to light up the whole area, which was frightening because all of a sudden you could see what was going on and see that these women were trying to roll us up on the flank. As soon as the APCs got there and cleared the area around us we were straight onto the APCs, going along on the tracks with searchlights going looking for any dead and wounded and any more that were hiding. We get along the track a bit and there's this sheila, crawling along on her hands and knees with half her foot blown off and she's yelling *'Chieu hoi, chieu hoi'*, open arms surrender, and the guy with the .50 calibre machine-gun on top of the APC just said 'Chew lead, bitch' and that was the end of her, stitched her right up the middle, no problems.

ALLEN MAY

The one that hit me came over with an ear-piercing scream. Graeme Dawson, Dougie Fabian, and myself were standing there in a little group and they hit the deck behind this big rubber tree and I said, 'Come on you pair of weak bastards, what's wrong with you, they're not going to hit us.' The next thing there was a big blue and orange and black flash.

When I opened my eyes I couldn't see — it was just all red. I cleared the blood off my face, and all my shirt and trousers were just covered in blood. I looked up and Dougie Fabian says, 'But fuck me, you're dead.' 'No I'm not, I'm all right,' I said. But my head was just so sore. I got my hand up and put it on top of my head, but with my hair completely full of blood it was just like a big mush. So, with the pain in my head I thought there was a big hole in my head and the first thing I did then instinctively was to grab my plastic camouflage hat and put it on because I thought with a big hole there all my brains would fall out.

Apparently I was out for quite a few hours and I woke up on the operating table as they were scraping all the fragments out of my head.

They sent a telegram home to mum stating that I'd been critically wounded in Vietnam with a head wound, that I wasn't expected to live through the night and if I did I'd be a vegetable.

A colonel delivered that telegram and spoke to mum at home at Wynnum and she literally punched him, scratched him and abused him. She had a nervous breakdown. Then he went and told dad on the job and my dad went white overnight. He was a healthy black-haired man but the next morning his hair was white. He just completely washed out.

TED COWELL

When Jose got his foot blown off and we couldn't do nothing about it, I actually cried that time. He stood on one of them chicom jumpers, the type that would punch straight up once you let the pressure off; once you hear the click you know you've had it.

I tried to get a bayonet under his boot and hold the pin down while he pissed off, but it wouldn't work, I wouldn't have been able to hold the pressure on. The blokes were busy trying to fill up sandbags and packs and Christ knows what to try and hold the bayonet down and keep pressure on it, but it wouldn't have worked because once he lifted his foot the pressure-release spring would have been too great, it would have just punched up in the air.

So he just told us to piss off, get out of his way, you know. We sandbagged his foot so he wouldn't lose his families and then once we were out and behind trees he lifted it and it blew his foot off. It blew the front part of his foot off, but they didn't bring him home straight away and gangrene set in, so they cut if off a bit higher and then flew him home. Now he's lost it up to his knee. The gangrene had set in and then come up the bone so they had to cut the whole bloody thing off. He had a lot of guts too, Jose. We were pretty close, real good mates.

The truth, I was swearing, I was cursing the world. See, he knew it and I knew it. I didn't want to accept it, but he already had because he'd stood on it. I couldn't accept it. I told all the blokes, every bastard, I said I'll shoot any bastard who ever says anything about any of this, I'll kill you on the spot. Jesus, I was wild, I was wild with the world. I threw the anger at them.

Shorty was something else. Shorty and I had formed a hell of a relationship, the way a lot of blokes do in a war when you're fighting and one life depends on the other. It's not just camaraderie; it's more, it goes deeper. Shorty and I were like brothers.

When we came back from our R&R in Taipei the boss said to me, 'Righto you pair of bastards, you've had a real good bludge, you're straight out in the paddock because there's an operation going on.' The crunchies had found a tunnel complex and instead of pissing off they wanted to investigate it. I don't know why they kept telling us about it. By that time I was worn out. I wouldn't admit it but I was had it, I was a real nutso case. That was why they gave us the break. We were both going off our heads.

I had this funny feeling that if I went in I wouldn't come out. Call it a sixth sense, call it whatever you like, but I knew if I went in I'd be dead. Shorty could see I hesitated and he said, 'Piss off, this one's mine.' Well, I rolled it over a bit because I had already done the last three before that and left him seconds, so I said, 'Yeah, righto mate, take it easy, eh, I'll follow up.' And in he went.

I was talking to him on the radio for a while, listening to him, and then it went dead.

I ended up dragging him out by his feet because he got it, he was killed, and they done a good job of it too. That was the end of me. I went back in and I was down there for seventeen hours going through the complex, unhooking little booby traps and in general killing any bastard I got my hands on.

But it's a real slow job. It might take you anything up to an hour to move one foot, or if you're lucky two feet. Sometimes you know they're there, you sense it, and you're really keyed, you're hyped up. I think one of the worst things, more than even finding a track or a snake or anything like that, is to hear a bloke breathing; if you can hear a bastard breathing you know he's pretty close and you say, righto, you've got a fight on your hands and you're wondering whether he's doing it on purpose trying to lure you in.

In actual hand to hand combat I killed three in the complex, and then the next morning I got a bloke by the river. That was a bit sadistic, but I had great joy in doing it. He came down in the morning and the mist was just on the creek and we were sitting over the other side and he didn't know we were there. He drove a stake into the side of the creek and he was having a crap. I could see him sitting there through the starlight scope on my Armalite. I could have shot him in the back of the head I suppose, but I didn't. I dropped the scope and blew his family jewels off and he ran himself out of blood.

Before I went away I never thought that I could do that and now I wonder how I could have done it, but Vietnam changed you.

Contacts were bad, picking up mines was bad, going out with the SAS was bad. It's hard to say which was the worst. I think the hardest was when Binky got killed because I'd known him since I was five and he was seven.

We'd harboured up for the night and I'd gone out and placed claymores all the way around the perimeter. Binky had already finished tea and he said, 'Look, give me another claymore, I'll put it out.' It was just on dark, might have been six o'clock.

He walked over the side of the paddy bund and on to a tank track, pushed in the claymore and he's pushed it on top of an M-60 mine. A couple of pound of explosive and there's nothing much left of you.

As soon as I heard the bang I knew that Binky had gone.

I've gone over the top of the paddy bund and they're trying to drag me back and the tears were crying in my eyes.

We went out with torches and mine detectors to pick up the body. I remember picking up the torso of him and then finding an arm and a leg. He was still minus a leg when he was bagged to come home. He was blown to the shithouse. He was eight days away from going home.

The chopper came in that night and took the bag away. I worried about it for a little while and then I realised that I had to look after myself. I became hard towards it.

An Australian soldier guards one of only three prisoners captured after the battle of
ng Tan, August, 1966. The Vietnam war was one in which prisoners were rarely
en by either side. (Photograph courtesy of Australian War Memorial.)

A Viet Cong prisoner is taken for interrogation at Australian Task Force Headquarters at Nui Dat. Women, just as much as men, fought with the Viet Cong. (Photograph courtesy of Gabe Carpay.)

An Australian medic examines a peasant child (top). Civil and medical aid projects (bottom) were undertaken to win the 'hearts and minds' of the South Vietnamese people. Villagers often welcomed help but sympathised with the Viet Cong. (Photographs courtesy of Australian Army.)

Villagers at Binh Ba wait behind barbed wire as Australian troops conduct a cordon and search operation. The heavy-handed style of these operations often further alienated the local population. (Photograph courtesy of 5/7 Battalion, Holsworthy.)

This propaganda photograph shows a Viet Cong receiving his cash reward for defecting. Vast sums of money were offered by the Americans to defectors or informants. (Photograph courtesy of Michael Currie.)

concert party for Australian troops at Nui Dat.

On 6 June, 1969, Australian troops clashed with North Vietnamese and Viet Cong forces in the village of Binh Ba, barely six kilometres from the Australian base at Nui Dat. At least ninety-one Vietnamese were killed, with one Australian casualty. (Photographs courtesy of Australian War Memorial.)

The Australian soldier who shot this Viet Cong soldier also took the photograph.

MICK RAINEY

Westmoreland* flew in after all the fighting had finished. He just had a pair of fatigues on but they were fairly clean and fairly well pressed, the ones with the big pockets that hang out on the outside, and a baseball cap with silver stars on it.

He came up and we were working on the vehicles, all just in green trousers and GP boots. He said, 'God damn, you guys repulsed the enemy. God damn fine job to stop all those gooks from getting into Saigon.' I mean, the tanks weren't even there when the main stuff was on. He hadn't been briefed very well because the blokes he was talking to weren't even there.

He walked around and then got back on the choppers and was gone. It struck you how ludicrous it was.

BRIAN THOMPSON

He was an Airforce supply officer in Vietnam in 1969.

When I flew up to Vietnam, a navigator who was posted to Two Squadron flew with me and I got to know him on the aeroplane. I went to Phan Rang after I had been there six weeks and there was an alert and we were rocketed and mortared. We went down to the bunker and I sat across from this bloke.

He was wearing shorty pyjamas, a flak jacket and a helmet and he's staring straight ahead. I said, 'G'day.' He didn't look up. 'How are you?' He looked up, barely recognised me, and sat back. I thought, this bloke is really ratshit. Later on I asked the pilot who flew with him what was wrong with him? It turned out that he was a bombardier in the Canberras and he just refused to fly.

He hadn't been there long when he refused to bomb because he didn't like what they were doing and then he refused to fly. And yet that was the squadron that had the best bombing record of any unit in Vietnam. He was sent home about a month later.

General William Westmoreland was the supreme commander of all allied forces in Vietnam.

GEORGE BOSTOCK

He is Aboriginal. He spent twenty years in the Army and went to Vietnam in 1968. He now works as a warehouse storeman.

One thing happened that upset me, it was murder and I never reported it.

I was coming back from my R&C leave and there was a group of us all in the back of a truck. You've got your weapons and grenades and everything that you've got to carry from Vungers to the Dat and I saw a Kiwi just casually pull his grenade out and drop it over the side in all this traffic. We all hit the deck in the back of the truck and, boom, up it went. 'Contact,' somebody yelled out. 'Ambush.'

This guy had killed a couple of people and it was all made out it was an error.

BOB RYDER

Originally from Maryborough in Queensland, he left school at twelve and afterwards joined the Airforce. He was among the first pilots to train on helicopters. He had always wanted to fly. Today he is a Squadron Leader.

The first day of Tet, when things started happening, we flew up to a little place called Trang Bom, just to the east of Bien Hoa. The Australians had been put there as a blocking force for Saigon and when we arrived in the morning our blokes had been mortared. Everyone was digging in like you wouldn't believe. We had to go into Saigon to pick up our OC at the Free World Headquarters so we flew in along Route 1 over Bien Hoa and Long Binh. As we got towards Bien Hoa, we could see there were tanks firing as they rolled down the road and there were houses burning and all this sort of stuff. We couldn't believe this, we had never seen a really big stouch. Normally most of the shooting was done on a very small scale, man to man in the bush or gunships or fighters bombing or whatever.

We were doing the odd orbit here and there to see what

they were shooting at, because we thought it was most intriguing. Being typical Australians and seeing Yanks in action we sort of thought, 'Oh, what are the Yanks on about now?'

Down the road a bit further soldiers were wandering off, shooting at things and lying down every now and again. The next minute there were a couple of gunships rolling in, giving them some help so we got out of their way. By that stage we were getting close to Bien Hoa and there were F100s taking off from the airbase, climbing up, taking formation, and then napalming and bombing, within a klick of the end of the runway. We thought, 'These pricks have gone crazy.'

Approaching Saigon we called up the control tower for Heliport 3 at Tan Son Nhut and told them we were going to Free World Headquarters. When we arrived there this Yank came out in a flak jacket and helmet and said, 'I wouldn't stay here sir, we're expecting to be mortared.'

We sent one of the crewies in to find the boss, couldn't find him anywhere, so we flew up to Heli 3 and they said, 'Make your approach at not less than fifteen hundred feet because we're under heavy machine-gun fire.' I said, 'Come on, this is the middle of Saigon for goodness sake.'

We landed, sent the crewie off looking for the boss again and as we were sitting in the chopper on the ground next minute a whole heap of tracer comes howling across and shatters the tower. We hear over the radio: 'Heli 3 is going off the air,' and the two blokes in the tower came down the steps flat as a rat.

RAY STOCK

He volunteered for national service and went to Vietnam in 1967–8.
'I had read a book by Bernard Fall called Street without joy *and I thought that possibly it was like the stories that I'd read in the book and that the south was being invaded by the north. I didn't believe in the domino theory, but I did believe the communists were trying to take over.'*

The one time where I really started looking at my attitude to the war was after the Tet Offensive. We were allowed back out of camp and I travelled up through Baria, which was the provincial capital and passed a church there and it had all these big holes in it. I was told by an American that the local Viet Cong, when they took Baria over, herded a lot of the locals into this church to use as hostages and that the gunships just hovered outside the church and fired rockets through the walls and killed both the hostages and the Viet Cong. I thought, 'That can't be true,' but as the year went on you realised that it was, because to the Americans especially, those people were all just bodies and the bodycount was everything.

BOB WALKER

I was at Binh Ba* on 6 June, '69. Yeah, it was a massacre. What can you do against tanks, for Christ's sake, when you haven't got air support or anti-tank weapons? A lot of their soldiers just got hit at point-blank range with our canister rounds, 500 ball-bearings, and it was just like mincemeat. Where you hit two or three together you were hard pressed to see how many were actually there. It was a massacre.

We went through a complete bomb load, all main armour. That would have been near on sixty shells of all types, mostly canister, high explosives, and most of the small arms and the .50 calibre. We virtually got rid of the whole bomb load. All four tanks did. At the end of the day I was that tired I couldn't put my fingers together to hold a cigarette.

I remember a couple of ridiculous minutes where one tank officer and one grunt officer were arguing over who had killed this poor shapeless mess. These two clowns, virtually off their face with adrenalin, really on a high, arguing, 'That's ours, that's ours.' Who gave a shit? I couldn't believe it. I'd never seen so many bodies in my life.

*The village of Binh Ba was the site of a major battle between Australian troops and NVA and Viet Cong forces. At least ninety-one Vietnamese were killed for one Australian killed.

There were quite a few people in that village who should never have been killed. They should have had the chance to get out. There were a couple of people cowering in the back of some stables and they just got brassed. There was one celebrated moment when our gunner shot a woman's foot off and he said, 'Have a look at this.' The sights were mostly dusty, but I could just make out this old woman. She'd been taking ammunition from one house to another and Paul took her foot off with the .50 cal. I was asked to load canister just after that so I assume he got part and parcel of her.

But gunners are a funny lot. All of the gunners that day were nashos and it's funny, I've seen all of them since and I asked them about that day and all of them can't remember a damned thing.

BRIAN LONDON

The room is filled with trophies, the tusks of wild boar. He did two tours of Vietnam, in 1965 and 1969, the second time as a platoon sergeant, and would have gone back a third time.

'I never wanted to leave a place so much in all my life as the last trip and yet when I got back home there was something missing. Everything was pretend, everything was artificial.'

He was awarded a Distinguished Conduct Medal after Binh Ba.

We pulled up outside Binh Ba and the tracks turned in towards the village. I was sitting up in one of the APCs and as soon as we pulled up they started firing RPGs at us. And then there were mortars coming down.

I could see people running around, scurrying and hurrying. One of the corporals in the APC wanted to open fire and I wouldn't let him because I didn't know who they were. They could have been our own people for all I knew; I didn't know who was there and who wasn't there.

I had two APCs and one tank in support and we'd only moved a short way when I lost one bloke straight away. A bloke stepped out of a doorway and he was shot through the neck. He'd only been with me about a fortnight too.

After that we stepped back a bit and I thought we'd better do it some other way. We broke up into small groups and we searched house by house in three-man teams.

The first house where I lost a bloke I called the tank up. I told the commander to fire a high explosive shell into the house. It blew the walls over, took the roof off, and then we went in and picked up the body. The situation was like that all the way through.

The ground was absolutely strewn with enemy weapons. There were mortars, ammunition, there were machine-guns and rifles, there was all sorts of military equipment that they had abandoned.

We did find some civilian bodies, but that was from when the gunships went through and strafed the village. That was the only thing that could have done it because these bodies were so mutilated.

I went into one house and pulled back a curtain and there was a magnificent double bed, still made, big quilt over it and I looked at this bed and I thought, 'I wonder if there's anything underneath it?' I turned it over and there were two people staring me in the eye, two enemy soldiers. I fired and they threw a hand-grenade. Next thing I remember I was on my ear outside the door. I remember then I said goodbye to Marie and I said goodbye to my kid and I went back into this house because I didn't know if I'd killed them or not. I went back in and threw a hand-grenade under the bed and then I brassed up the house. They were dead, of course. They hadn't long been dead because they were pretty well cut about and the organs were still pumping. I dragged them out by their feet and went on.

These places had a lot of little air-raid shelters that the civilians had made. They'd dig a hole underneath their house and put a bit of covering over the top of it. We didn't go down them because they were too small. We just dropped grenades down and waited till the smoke cleared.

We got one bloke out of a hole. I escorted him to a waiting APC and the body of our bloke who'd been shot in the neck was already in the back. This nog looked at me rather strangely because he could see the Australian's body on the deck. He looked at me as if to say, 'Are you going to do that to me too?' Of course it didn't happen, I never shot him. That's one thing my platoon never did. We always made sure that we kept our sanity. If you started killing people indiscriminately, then you'd lose all sense of what the thing was about.

It went on for two days. We'd go through one end of the village, take up defensive positions for the night and then sweep back through it again at first light the next day. We'd got most of them that were in there. They were identified as a North Vietnamese regiment. The bodycount for my platoon was about twenty.

I only found one dead civilian. I saw an old woman who was down in a little shelter. It was open, blown apart at one end. It obviously had received a direct hit by some heavy-calibre weapon.

I told her to come out, that we weren't going to hurt her. I couldn't speak Vietnamese, only the essential words that I needed to know, but I eventually coaxed her out and she was quite distraught. There was a body — a child's body — still in the bunker. It was only half there. I don't know whether it was a boy or a girl. It looked like a girl to me, from the hair, and she was blown in half. That's why the old woman was so upset. We got the body out and wrapped it up and I reported to my commanding officer that we had found a civilian's body.

There has been some talk of a lot of civilians being killed there. I saw no evidence of that. I only saw one, and that was the child.

BARRY ROE

A regular soldier who went to Vietnam when he was nineteen. He lives in Cranbourne, Victoria.

Alan and I were sitting having a beer and the plant sergeant came to the flap of the tent and said, 'We've got a job on, we want you to go up to Binh Ba.'

We said, 'Oh yeah, what for?'

He said, 'You've got to bury some bodies and I want you up there straight away, no details.'

We got the vehicles and took off up the Binh Ba road and as we got into the plantation we could see smoke and a hell of a lot of grunts moving around with tanks, APCs, the whole box and dice. One of the grunts came up to us and said, 'We want you to dig a slot; we've got a few bodies we want to put in.'

He took us up to the plantation manager's residence, which was an old brick place with a big driveway and all the front from the road back to the house was nice green lawn. I dropped the blade and started ripping into the ground and I dug a slot about two or three feet deep, came back out of the slot and parked on the side and I thought that would do. A grunt came up to me and said, 'You want to dig that a lot deeper.'

I said, 'How many have you got?'

'There's a lot.'

I suppose I dug down until the top of the canopy was just level with the ground, which would be ten or fifteen feet, then this guy came up and said, 'Righto, we're going round to pick the bodies up.'

We drove down through the rubber and then we started seeing what had happened. I'd been through Binh Ba before and seen what it used to look like. Now all the rubber trees had splintex sticking out of them, and where there had been huts there was nothing. You could see where the walls had been and just nothing.

As we got down further we could see a dozen or so bodies scattered around. There were bits and pieces of flesh hanging out of trees. It was just frightening. We could see more of the grunts then who had been in it. It was funny, some of them were laughing and joking and others were just sitting there grey in the face.

Then it was just a matter of running around where they told us and picking up bodies and the bits and pieces of them, hunks of flesh, arms, legs, and chucking them in the bucket.

We'd have half a bucket full of bodies and I'd be standing on the teeth of the bucket leaning across looking at them and they're just wobbling like jelly. I'd jump off as we'd get to the slot and Alan would tip them in and as they'd hit the others they'd just all flop like jelly. It was just like a big bloody mass of jelly, just moving. I don't know what the final bodycount was. We reckoned it was about one hundred and twenty. I think it took us three or four hours to get them all in. I kind of switched off after a couple of hours because I thought to myself, 'If I think about it too much I'm going to go around the corner.'

RIC

What I remember about Binh Ba is we'd just come off an operation and we'd put all our stuff back in the store and were just sort of winding down. We'd just got off this damn op and, boing, here we go again, straight to Binh Ba.

We'd been told there was Viet Cong and elements of NVA there and that the people were told to get the hell out of the place and they were allocated a certain area and told it was a safe place to be at.

It was a massacre, it really was. But those people were warned; they were told to get out, but they wouldn't leave. It was house to house. You'd throw in a couple of grenades, give it a burst with the machine-gun, then you'd look for trapdoors and, again, it was just blat with the gun.

I cracked up after then, just dropped everything, I was that frightened of losing my life. Some hundred and twenty nogs were killed there. It was pretty heavy stuff. But we had armour backing us up. Tanks would roll up to a hut, poom, goodbye hut. When I say I dropped my bundle, I lost control of my situation. My section commander grabbed my headphone and started relaying fire orders and commands like that to the guns because I was out of control. I just couldn't cope, there was too much going on. I just couldn't hack the pace. There was so much involved. You had APCs, Centurion tanks and they were all talking cross key. I was running, running. It lost all sense of reality.

There were quite a lot of villagers killed. They weren't all VC, or 'the enemy'. There were a lot of innocent people killed at Binh Ba. I saw an old lady blown away by a tank round of canister, for nothing, wasted. She was carrying one of those yokes. I think the only thing that was left of her was a bit of her hand and a foot and a couple of pieces of the yoke — that was all.

I shot a kid in Binh Ba and it was the worst experience I ever had. The kid was still alive and I blew him away. I had a lot of hate on, you know, sort of confusion. I'd wounded him first up. He was running. It was like a Tom Mix thing, from the waist. I saw him go down and I kept going and then I thought, 'Fuck this,' and I went back and emptied a magazine into his head. He was maybe sixteen, only a young kid. He had an AK so it was valid, but you just didn't know. Binh Ba was really fucked up.

It was fascinating, I guess, watching a human face turn to pulp in front of your eyes. But I saw the whole thing as a Charlie Chaplin movie, I really did. It was just like a Charlie Chaplin movie.

I stopped after that. I didn't talk to anyone for a long time and just isolated myself really. I see the face of the kid. It still haunts me today; just the eyes, just to see the kid looking at me and I said, 'Fuck you.'

JACK MORRISON

One of Australia's most decorated soldiers, he saw action during the Second World War and in Korea. He went to Vietnam as an adviser in 1964–5 and 1968–9.

I never saw the South Vietnamese ill-treat one NVA wounded prisoner. They couldn't get a chopper in quick enough to get them out, because they were regular soldiers from the north and they had respect for them. But the VC, their own people from the south, I saw them beaten across the face with a bayonet to make them talk. They would take them up in choppers and drop them out over their villages from a thousand feet: 'You go back and see your relations.'

BOB PRIDE

We used to get a Sunday off a month and we'd go down to Vungers either by truck or by helicopter. Vung Tau was about twenty or thirty kilometres down the road, which was about a half-hour boozy ride. Blokes would be falling out of the trucks left, right and centre and you'd have to pull up and throw them back on.

I used to like drinking at the Grand, which was the main boozer. The bargirls there used to wear these big numbers, like Number 10, so if you wanted a bird to sit with you you'd say, 'Number 10, come over here,' and she'd sit there and you'd be paying your five or six bucks for a Saigon tea for her. You'd get to the stage where you'd be that drunk you wouldn't know what you were doing. You'd be throwing money on the table and these birds would be picking it up. Then if you wouldn't buy them a Saigon tea you'd be the cheapest bloke in the world. *Uc Dai Loi* would be number ''welve'. 'You are number 'welve tonight, you are number 'welve.' That was as low as you could go. There was a song they used to sing to the music of 'This old man'. It went: Uc Dai Loi, cheap Charlie, he no buy me Saigon tea, Saigon tea cost many, many pee, Uc Dai Loi, he cheap Charlie.

MARK ROSE

R&C usually meant you went into town, got rolling drunk and bought some girl. I fell in love the first time.

Her story was, and I think it was pretty true, that she was a fairly educated girl, an ex-student of a Saigon university and her father had been killed in the ARVN.

She went to a place called Bien Cat for a bit, that was half-way between Saigon and Vung Tau, working as a secretary for the Yanks, then she must have wised up to the fact that there was more money for a pretty girl in other places and ended up down in the Wiupi Bar in Vung Tau. That's where I met her, just after being wounded.

I liked her, she liked me, so I paid mama san to get her out of the bar. We had a bit of a relationship and then she started to develop other pretty boyfriends. I suppose before the end of the tour of duty I was fairly battle weary and she was getting hardened to the game. I'm not trying to be moralistic here, that's just the way it was.

She was one of the reasons I went back to Vietnam just before the fall, just wondering how she was and to make sure she hadn't had a baby to me. I saw her, but she had changed a hell of a lot, into a pretty professional girl.

DENNIS COLE

You'd go into Vung Tau and kids as little as my youngest would rip the watch out of your hand, or cut the pockets out of your pants and take your wallet. I had no sympathy at all for the local people and I could quite easily believe they were VC sympathisers.

It was a strange war. It was a war where no-one was not involved. They were involved one way or another and many were involved both ways, like on our side today and the other side of a night. I mean, that was the big thing, you could never trust anyone.

The Reverend RICHARD BROWN

He is four feet eleven and a half inches tall. 'They told me I had no chance of being accepted for the Army because you had to be five feet two inches. When I got called up my local doctor asked if I really wanted to go. I said, "Yeah." "How tall are you?" "Five feet two inches." She wrote it down and no-one really worried about it.'

He became a minister of religion several years after returning from Vietnam, where he served two tours as an infantry soldier.

I never worried about birds until I went into the Army and went overseas and then I was in and out of brothels like a yoyo. The very day that I was supposed to go on leave I realised I had gonorrhoea. I didn't tell anybody and went down there and I just had a great time. It was so painful I couldn't do anything the last time.

JEFF SCULLEY

We were having dinner and the platoon commander decided to go on a recce forward, just to see what was about, with a section of blokes. They'd only gone about three minutes when there was a bang and screaming.

Being the platoon medic, I grabbed my bag and started to go, everybody wanted to run up forward, but the sergeant said there might be more mines so we had to prod our way up with a bayonet. We could hear them moaning and screaming out for help. I don't know how long it took us to prod our way up to them — it seemed to take us hours — but the first thing I saw when we got there was the platoon commander laying on the deck and he's got the side of his face blown out. He put his thumb up, trying to give me like, 'She's right mate, just hang in there, don't worry about me.' Like I say, he's got the hole out the side of his face, all his cheek was gone, it was just a big hole, you could see right into his mouth cavity. He was a top platoon commander, a Duntroon graduate, a really top bloke.

My mate, Snow, was lying there. Just two minutes before he left I'd taken a big splinter out of the top of his head and now he's laying there with the top of his head lifted off. Brizzo was alongside him all brassed up the leg and young Graham, he'd only just turned twenty, he was laying on his back, one leg was completely off and the other leg held on by an inch of skin. The company medic had to cut it off with a pocket knife. He just picked up his boot, held the leg out, cut it off and just chucked it to the side.

Another fellow there saved Graham's life by taking his boot-laces off and tying them around his stumps in a tourniquet to stop him from bleeding to death. He got an MID for it.

I went over to Brizzo, who was still alive at this time. He was laying down and he had no wounds from his knackers up, but every square inch of his legs was just hole. He kept on trying to sit up, but I had to keep him down because I didn't want him to see his legs.

'You've got to lay down mate.'

'I want to sit up; for fuck's sake, let me sit up.'

'No, you've got to lay down.' Then he died.

Snow, the bloke that had the top of his head lifted off, he lived for a while. They revived him three or four times on the operating table so I've been told, but he ended up dying, which is just as well, poor bugger. He probably would have been a vegetable.

That was the day I think all the blokes who were there could say they became men. I really do believe that. There's not too many people could point to a day and say that's when they became a man, but by Christ, I never felt so old and so drained of everything.

We used to have a scoreboard — them and us. It was all right while it was them being killed, but I can remember when we got back to camp one of the blokes grabbed that sign and just smashed it up and chucked it away. He was Snow's mate.

BOB HOBBS

I decided to come home for my R&R. My mum had been ill.

The first night home I went along to hear my old band play at one of the popular nightspots and that's when the cracks started. Things like, 'How many women and kids have you killed?' I was alarmed by their attitude and angry.

When I left Vietnam all our blokes were dug in around the village of Thai Thien and the VC were trying to get to the rice caches. We'd crawled around until we found their tracks down around our perimeter and we were armed to the teeth because we were expecting VC to come in and take the rice. So here I am, twenty-four hours out of the jungle, thousands of miles away surrounded by people who didn't want to know about it and who couldn't have cared if we lived or died. I could see myself two years earlier not caring about what was going on. They weren't aware and I thought to myself, 'I don't belong here, I belong with the guys in the platoon.'

PETER MOLLOY

I remember the thing going off. I remember hurtling through the air and coming down on a branch of a tree and I was winded. I couldn't breathe and I couldn't feel anything. I couldn't feel my legs, I couldn't feel any pain at all, not the same as what I got later.

There were blokes screaming their heads off and then the pain started and it got that bad I was screaming my brains out too. It was that bad I just couldn't stand it. I couldn't move my legs and then the medic, Wayne Herbert, came around and he was down trying to bite through my jungle greens to give me an injection of morphine in the top of my right leg. He said, 'I can only give you a little bit.' I think he only had about two ampules and he had to share it with a lot of blokes. He'd got a piece of shrapnel in his eye too and he was going around treating us, in the night, in a minefield.

We'd come under fire from Viet Cong as soon as the mine went off. I remember lying there and the fire coming from the mountains. The bullets were going everywhere. I didn't have a clue where my rifle was, I wasn't interested in where it was. As far as I was concerned that was it. I didn't think I'd make it. A couple of blokes came around and put a sweat cloth around my leg and got a stick and turned it around and told me to hang onto it. I hung onto that thing like grim death.

I couldn't say for sure how long it was before the choppers came to pick us up. Maybe half an hour. I could hear the chopper coming and I could see the red light inside it. They put myself and Hans and Peter on the floor of the chopper. All the other guys were standing around. I was told that Les was dead — they reckoned he set off the mine and it killed him outright — and I was told that Hans wasn't far off it. There were blokes wounded everywhere.

When we got up into the air the pain in my legs was driving me crazy. An Airforce bloke took his jacket off and put it over my legs. I remember him taking it off and putting it over my legs.

When they got us to the hospital at Vung Tau they laid us on benches and asked us questions and then the priest gave me my last rites. I distinctly remember them telling me that my right leg would have to come off and the other one may have to come off, but they would do their best. I said, 'No, I don't want my legs off, leave my legs.' I can still recall that.

MICHAEL SCRASE

I worked in the signals centre, in the cipher room, and we used to get all the signals through on anything that happened to do with atrocities, or actions. We knew what was going on before a lot of others did. As soon as anything happened that involved an American or an Australian it was all over the papers and yet you hardly ever heard about the atrocities that the Viet Cong and the North Vietnamese did to the South Vietnamese. They'd go in and just butcher whole bloody villages; butcher the elders in front of the kids and all this sort of thing. We used to hear about it all the time. That used to annoy me, the way the headlines used to build it up in Australia at that time. We often used to get the paper and just look at the front page, because it would be splattered over the first or second page, and just throw it straight in the bin.

LACHLAN IRVINE

There was one occasion when we set up an ambush and we killed one man and wounded one woman and discovered later that they were unarmed. It was a genuine ambush. It was a free-fire zone and they knew that if they were in that area at night they were going to be regarded as enemy. We found out later by questioning people in the local village that they were the parents of a Viet Cong guerrilla who was up in the hills and they were on their way up with baskets filled with fish and fruit and vegetables when they walked into our ambush.

When we discovered they were unarmed our platoon commander told us to put some grenades in the basket along with the fish and the vegetables and we reported on the radio that they were carrying grenades. Nobody enjoyed lying about that, but as far as we were concerned they were the enemy.

But then one of our blokes — and I mean he was mad — came over to me and asked if he could borrow my bayonet. I said sure. Later, when I went over to get it back from him I found him posing for photos sticking my bayonet into the stomach of the body. He had my bayonet on the end of his rifle and he was standing with a foot on the body and my bayonet sticking into the stomach, posing for photos.

I thought it was a strange thing to do, but there were some guys like that. There were some guys who were disturbed about killing and some guys who thought it was fun and some who didn't think much about it at all. I think I fitted into the third category.

TERRY LOFTUS

He served two tours in Vietnam, in 1965 and 1968.

The American mortuary platoon had a list of about twenty things they had to do to bodies, such as cut fingernails, give them a shave, clean their teeth, and if part of the head was shot away reshape it. They were professional morticians, all draftees, and that was their job.

In this particular week the Americans had lost five hundred killed in Vietnam and everybody was coming through this one morgue. There were Australians, New Zealanders, Thais, Filipinos and what have you and it was just like an assembly line. I had to identify three people that day, and no matter which way you looked there were bodies and they were terribly young fellows. Some of them looked like they were just asleep and someone had made a mistake.

While I was there they had one bloke who had only just come in. He had multiple wounds to his legs, he had nothing on, and rigor mortis had set in and there was an orderly either side of him and it looked like they were taking him for a waltz down the hospital ward. I thought I'm not coming back to this place ever again. There would have been at any one time probably fifty, sixty, a hundred bodies there.

The American sergeant came out and said, 'How many bodies are we shipping off to Clark?' Someone answered, 'I think we've got twenty-eight.' He said, 'I don't want to think, I want exact figures.'

I couldn't get out of that place quick enough. Because that's the end result. That's the end of the assembly line and the pantomime is still going on.

KEV O'NEIL

He was an Airforce engineer in Vietnam in 1970–1.

The Americans operated in Vietnam as a big machine. Where we were they had a helicopter servicing base, a pretty big one, and if you wanted anything you just rang up. We wanted an empty engine case and we rang up and about five minutes later this bloke roars up with this big steel canister and says, 'Where do you want it buddy?' I said, 'Just over the back of the shed there.' So he puts it over the back of our section and roars off again.

A couple of weeks later we thought we'd better send all these unserviceable engines back, so we go to the back and lift the top off this case and it's not empty, it's got a brand new engine sitting in it. This is what used to go on. The bloke dropped off what was supposedly an empty case and there was a brand new jet engine in it which was worth probably quarter of a million dollars in those days.

JOHN ATKINS

About two weeks before I came home I was down at the regimental aid post at Nui Dat and a dust-off came in with a couple of Yanks. One was dead and this other little Yank he was crying and screaming and saying, 'They shot us up the ass, they shot us up the ass.' I went over and sat down and lit the guy a fag and he just kept yelling 'They shot us up the ass.' I found out they were walking up the middle of a track listening to radios.

MICHAEL CURRIE

He was a propagandist in Vietnam in 1968–9, seconded to the CIA-run Joint United States Public Affairs Organisation. His principal job was the Chieu Hoi defection program. He was also involved in the notorious Phoenix campaign which aimed to 'neutralise' the political infrastructure of the Viet Cong by assassinating many thousands of targeted individuals.

In my last few months my priority task was to help the Phoenix campaign by passing intelligence to the Province Reconnaissance Units.

Initially, the PRUs were officered by contract employees of the CIA. Mercenaries if you like, albeit American ones. They were good. I had a lot of faith in them and they were very brave men. Knowledgeable and good officers.

Our Province Reconnaissance Unit used to operate out in the Rung Sat special zone. That's mangrove swamps. And between the PRU and the province chief's personal reconaissance platoon more kills were racked up per week than by the whole of the Australian Taskforce put together.

Later on all the contract officers were sacked. The career men from the CIA took over and they fragmented the PRUs into small district and village cells of five or less and put them out in the villages across the province, the theory being they were supposed to keep tabs on who were Viet Cong infrastructure and eliminate them.

I know that some of them turned into petty hoodlums and stand-over men, holding up restaurants, cafes and the like around the province.

Phoenix had an aura about it. It was the CIA and they used to get around and bump people off. But what people tend to forget is that we were fighting a war and the Viet Cong were bad bastards.

I'm not saying it was morally justifiable — for one, I think it would have been better to have tried to get them to defect rather than 'neutralising' them — but it was all fair.

While I was there two leaders of a Viet Cong assassination squad blew up a group of school kids. They planted two jumping jack mines, one by the side of the road and one by a well and arranged them so that they would be triggered by an old man who used to draw water from the well at the same time that the children walked up the street.

I've never seen such a mess in all my born days and even nurses and the doctors were crying while operating. I assume the intention was to punish the people of those hamlets for allowing people like myself to spread the government's word, only it backfired because it turned the people against them not only in those hamlets but around the province.

I spent something like three months running photographs of the two assassination squad leaders. One of them was accidentally caught in an ambush by the taskforce and killed. I believe Charlie probably took care of the other one themselves. He was not heard of again. It was the only time I published posters around the province with a photograph saying: Wanted dead or alive.

On another occasion, the Viet Cong disembowelled the pregnant wife of a village chief, made him look on and then beat him to death. That happened in Duc Tho, a little farming district.

It was hard to get people volunteering to be hamlet or village chiefs so we would often have to appoint them and almost as soon as they were appointed they were assassinated. Day in, day out assassinations went on. The prime targets were village officials, teachers, anyone with a modicum of nursing instruction, people of that ilk. I lost count of the number of assassinations that took place at Suoi Nghe, the artificial village we Australians built, God help us.

I think the Viet Cong understood the importance of propaganda better than we did.

Although I've said it was the least of my priorities, a good deal of my money was eaten up getting the printing presses of the province going again so that there was not only a province newspaper, but there were district and in some cases village newspapers putting out the 'true' message as we saw it.

We ran a Vietnamese Information Service where people were trained in how to conduct a reading-room, what publications were available, how to make up leaflets, that type of thing.

There was one woman we trained. We armed her with books and newspapers and bought a suitable building for her and sent her off into Xuyen Moc. She was caught by the Viet Cong motoring in from Xuyen Moc to Baria. There was a taxation point run by the Viet Cong and they identified her as being an employee of the Vietnamese Information Service and they shot her, chopped out her tongue and stuffed it up her vagina. That type of incident to me was the whole thing in a nutshell. I interpreted that action to be a graphic visual symbol that our propaganda was non-productive.

One of the things we did to encourage defections amongst the VC was drop leaflets and play tape recorded messages at night. We had a chopper fitted with banks of speakers and chutes for leaflets.

We used to play funeral music. We used a tape called the 'Wandering Soul', which I got in '69 from an American friend of mine from 6 Psy Op Battalion. It was the story of a VC soldier who was killed somewhere out in the jungle and never properly buried. The Vietnamese believe that unless they received a proper funeral their soul will wander forever. It was eerie. When I first played the tape I tested it on my own compound and all the sentries deserted their post and begged me to turn it off.

FAY LEWIS

I think I was a pretty cool-headed person most times, but I think that it eventually got to us, because they were all young people that were coming in with their legs off, multiple wounds, and you were sending home week after week, planes full of young, mutilated people.

Most people see amputated limbs as nice rounded finished-off stumps. We didn't get that. We had the ragged ends.

JOHN SKINNER

Warwick, Queensland. He sits hunched in a chair with a dust-covered photograph album across his knee. The tears roll down his face. 'I tried to avoid remembering it for a long time. I didn't want to. It's something I'd prefer to forget. When you talk about it it doesn't seem all that bad, it all sort of blurs in looking back, but it was so horrible...' He went to Vietnam in 1969.

'Sluggo' was a thick, heavy, solid sort of a guy, a typical regular soldier; not too much interest in anything but doing what he was told to do. He was one of those guys that always had to prove to everyone that he was tougher than everybody else, that he could handle this situation far better than anyone else.

There was one situation where we killed a man and a woman and we dug a grave for them and they wouldn't quite fit. 'Sluggo' was the one who went up and broke this guy's legs to fit him in the grave. He just put his foot on one leg and broke it but that was a bit hard so he hit the other one with a rifle butt. I couldn't watch. That was the sort of thing I couldn't stand.

I kept in contact with him for a long time afterwards, but I believe he is probably in an asylum now, if you could ever find him. He went back to South Australia somewhere and the last I heard of him he had been committed, because of what happened to him in Vietnam. He just let what happened over there affect his mind.

I can remember a couple of years afterwards he would start telling us stories about what happened over there and he just exaggerated things all out of proportion, things that I was actually involved in. I mean, we laid side by side on a number of occasions, and where there had been only two people suddenly there were twenty people in his mind. It just played on his mind so much. Well, the last I heard of him I think he was right on the edge of madness.

SIMON

I went into a bar in Vung Tau. There was no actual prostitution on the premises as far as I could see. You had to book a girl out and she would take you to her private room and then you had to pay the mama san on the way out. Well, being a Vietnamese linguist it was very difficult for me to do things like that because once you started talking with them in Vietnamese there was a sort of relationship immediately built up. You wouldn't want to break that type of thing by getting involved in something as sordid as prostitution.

I was speaking to a girl while there was not much business doing and the old mama san said, 'Why don't you take him around for a meal?' So she took me upstairs, round the back alleys to the only genuine French restaurant I ever saw in Vietnam. There were Vietnamese waiters and a couple of half-caste French. It was very enjoyable; I had a good meal and a good chat. The girl turned out to be quite well-educated. She was a product of a private school in Saigon, her family was living in Saigon and she was making money in Vung Tau. At the end of the meal, she said 'Come round and meet a few friends of mine.' I was a little bit worried because we were warned not to go alone with people because of the dangers of being assassinated or kidnapped. Anyway, I decided I would go with her. She took me through a couple more winding alleys and knocked on the back door of a double-storey Chinese shop-like building. A young lad of about eighteen opened the door and when we walked in there was a whole row of about forty hairdressing machines, each with a Vietnamese girl underneath having a hair-do. They were all prostitutes having their hair done for the evening shift. It was quite amazing, like a huge smorgasbord.

I had a very interesting hour or so there. They offered me beer and were quite friendly. Many of them wanted to show me photographs of their relatives and some wanted me to write to the Australian government to see if I could arrange to have their family migrated to Australia. Even at that time it was quite clear that there was a sort of bush telegraph view that the VC were going to win. That was 1970.

BILL

He was an adviser, working with the South Vietnamese and the Americans close to the demilitarised zone.

I saw the South Vietnamese do something once that bothered me. It was only the once.

We came across a village, moved in there about eight o'clock in the morning. We'd come under small arms fire and we went into this village and it was definitely Viet Cong because we recovered a Viet Cong flag, photographs of Ho Chi Minh, and they wouldn't tell us where the tunnels were — we knew they'd got out by tunnel. Eventually they told us, but what the ARVN did to this girl...

She was a very attractive-looking girl, about eighteen, nineteen. They cut her hair off — Vietnamese women are very proud of their hair — and then they hung her from the rafters in this hut, just off the ground, and lit a fire under her on the earth floor and burnt her feet. After they cut her down they made her walk all the way to the compound. My boss, the senior adviser, protested about it to the ARVN battalion commander. I kept right out of it.

I was told to keep quiet about torture. They were my orders when I went there, and if I saw any to keep away from it because we didn't want to be involved. What happened that night I prefer not to know. It was a savage bloody war, there's no worries about that.

MICK RAINEY

I watched the South Vietnamese interrogators work. We were in our vehicles at a cordon and search of a village. They had the villagers divided into three groups, sectioned off with white tape and steel pickets in the ground. All the blokes of fighting age were in one group, kids a bit younger in the second group and mothers and babies and old people were in the third group.

A Dodge pick-up arrived with a South Vietnamese major and

four or five blokes in the back. They started yelling and went to the compound where the young men were and grabbed eight or nine of these blokes and made them squat on the ground with their knees apart. They stood in front of them with big sticks and asked them questions, and when they weren't satisfied with the answer they would whack them between the legs and ask the question again.

This went on for half an hour and they really let them have it. The blokes that were being interrogated wouldn't fall over unless they were kicked over, and then they were quick to get back up because they knew that if they didn't they were going to get more of the same.

Finally they put four of these blokes in the back of the Dodge and some of the women in the compound started screaming, a typical type of Asian scream they make when they know that their husband is not coming back. They were screaming and rolling around on the ground. No way were they ever going to be coming back home.

JOHN PRINTZ

He served in Vietnam in 1965.

I made some good friendships with Americans and one of these guys I was very friendly with was a crew chief on one of the big choppers. He was one of the Americans who I really respected.

On one of my days off I arranged to go on a flight as a gunner for something to do, unofficial. We went out and we picked up a spotter aircraft that had been shot down, we picked up a landing craft that had been shot up in an ambush down the Mekong Delta and we picked up a helicopter that had been shot down. We were flying back over the Mekong Delta to Tan Son Nhut where they were based and the next thing I get over the headset, 'Boat on the starboard side — open fire.' There it was, on my side. I opened up with a twin M-60 and shot shit out of it. I vividly remember seeing the bullets hitting the water like you see in the movies, and a couple of people going over the side. Then the chopper did a turn and the other gunner did his bit and that was it, the thing was sunk and we went back to the depot.

I went back to the NCOs mess with this American and we sat down and we were having a couple of beers. After a while I said, 'How did you know that was a VC?' He said, 'I don't think it was.' He was one of the few American guys who I really had respect for, yet to me that was murder.

ROSS MATHIESON

People that were captured were normally turned over to ARVN troops for questioning, but I landed once to pick up some Kiwis. Usually whenever you landed people would sprint over and be aboard in seconds, but this time there was just one bloke sitting there and no-one seemed to be taking much notice. I waved him over and said, 'Where are the guys; are they ready to go?' He was a big Maori, looked very fierce with a green band around his head. He said, 'They're just doing some converting.' I said, 'What are they converting?' He said, 'WIAs to KIAs.' I presumed from what he said that his mates were slitting the throats of some VC that they had wounded. I didn't ask any more questions and after a while they came out of the bush.

JIM CHALLENGER

He was an adviser to the South Vietnamese in 1967–8.

We'd been in a contact and the South Vietnamese I was with called in an air strike. They were dug in around the village. I was laying there with a camera, a very small one, and when the air strike was going on I was kind of in limbo, just waiting.

Then I saw these civilians coming out with napalm burns, all little kids and that. It was sickening. I think that's why I got so hard and so callous. I seen that much of it.

MICHAEL

You'd been told a little bit about the history of the country as part of your training. You were told about their customs, how they're supposed to act, how they expect people to act, what you're supposed to do and not do, like patting them on the head. It was a centuries old culture. Then when you got there, in a situation where you didn't trust anyone, your values changed. You didn't see too much of what you expected to see. You saw the black market, the begging, the prostitution, the fact that you didn't know whose side they were on. I guess that would rock anybody's outlook on a supposedly ancient culture.

By daytime those people would sit there and watch you going past and at night time they would be ferrying ammunition, or they'd be out laying ambushes. That was happening. They had immunity because there were in civilian access areas, friendly zones supposedly. But if you start working in an area which you're told is a friendly area and you keep running into ambushes and you keep getting in the shit then obviously you start putting two and two together and you say, what's happening?

We were getting fire in the general area of this village all the time. I mean, we always seemed to be running into it, and there was just no way that the people in that village were not the reason for it. It was obvious someone was feeding information as to where we were and what we were doing. So we selected people from the village and took them out into the scrub. It was to set an example.

There were two platoons of us working together, maybe twenty blokes. All of us were young. We took upwards of a dozen people out of that village — old men, women and young kids as well. The kids would have been ten, eleven, twelve I suppose. They weren't very big. We took 'potentials', ones that we thought likely to be VC and we said we'll take them and we'll take a few others as well and hope to hell that will set an example along the same lines as the VC used, when they wanted allegiance in the villages.

We had an interpreter there and we had a bit of a try at finding out some information but they weren't going to tell us anything and then we had a bit of a yippee shoot and wasted them. They 'walked into an ambush'.

The women were raped. It's a bit hard to pass up a bit of pussy like that, isn't it, although it might be hard to believe in a situation like that. But not all the slopes were bad-looking. Some of them were quite attractive in their own way and, I don't know, it's just a bit of the animal comes out. About half the blokes were involved in it. I didn't participate in that. I was a bit yellow I suppose. I thought there was a fair chance they would have had the jack. I had my fun later with the machine-gun.

One bloke in the platoon screwed one who was already dead. I couldn't take that in a fit. That revolted quite a lot of blokes. They reckoned he was an outright bloody animal after that. You know, to me, using a pair of secateurs and taking a bloke's finger off to get a ring which you could use for bartering later on was not the same as that.

When it was over, we used a couple of grenades to disperse bits and pieces around a little bit. If you've ever seen what concentrated fire does to a body there isn't a hell of a lot there and we knew it was going to decompose pretty quickly. There wasn't much chance of anything being found and the people in the village weren't likely to report anything. Who would they report it to and who would believe them?

It was wrong, but the way I looked at it, if we hadn't got them there we might have got them the next day or the day after. Who's to say they wouldn't have done the same thing in that situation? It was a matter of cutting down the odds. The end result was that there were a few more dead gooks.

I'm not saying that I enjoyed it all, but nobody twisted my arm. We were all in it. There was no point in trying to stop it. I mean, for a start your mates wouldn't have thought much of you anyway and you had exactly the same reason to hate the gooks as they did. We were there and we were getting hurt too.

RAY CALDWELL

A New Zealander, he served in Vietnam as a field engineer in 1968.

We were getting near the end of our duty, sitting playing cards on this track, when three VC appeared further down. This Kiwi guy with us lurched over and in the one action brought the machine-gun up and blasted them and I said to him, 'One of those is a sheila.' He said, 'It's not!' He's dropped the machine-gun and he's down the track and he was taking her gear off and he was going to screw it before she went cold. The bullet had gone in under her shoulder blade and blew a neat tit right off, but he didn't care. He had her by the knees and he's saying, 'I'm going to hump this harlot dead or alive.' The lieutenant came down and he saw what was happening and he went off his brain and this guy just stood up and stared and that lieutenant was close to dying. The Kiwi was going to screw that sheila right or wrong. His father was a priest and he'd come up through the church all his life and that was just something that he did.

BOB GIBSON

You could see the fear in the faces of the old people. You'd kick a door down and there would be an old man and an old lady huddled up in the corner and, I mean, you felt like saying I don't want to hurt you, that if I could talk to you and if I had time I'd fix your door. But you couldn't. I couldn't speak Vietnamese other than to tell them to stop or to get going, or to swear at them. I think the fear, the look of the old people, of just sheer terror and confusion is what I remember most and wondering why, why they looked like that when we were there to help them. That will always stick in my mind.

5

Short time

'Vietnam could prove a turning point in our history. It could make us into a grown-up nation.

For us, this will be the only compensation for the unnecessary loss of hundreds of thousands of Vietnamese lives.'

Jim Cairns

BERNARD SZAPIEL

Two weeks before coming home we were patrolling an area which we knew was infested by North Vietnamese. Our section went out to do a recce patrol around where the company had settled down for the night and we came out into this open area, beautiful and green, so peaceful and serene. We thought, well, there's nothing here, so we threw down our rifles, lit up a smoke, laughed and carried on. After having a cigarette the section commander said, 'Okay, let's get back into camp.'

The perimeter of the company was very dense jungle and as we were coming in I said, 'Look, you better radio in and tell them that we're coming.' He said, 'It's all right, don't worry about it.' I thought, okay, and I started plodding in and as I came through the perimeter, there's my mate with his finger on the trigger of an M-60, just white. He said, 'I was going to shoot you because I saw those bushes rustling, except the guy next to me said, "Just wait until they come right out into the open, let's just see them."' That guy practically fainted because he'd nearly killed me.

Next morning, up at dawn, first platoon goes out and my mate says to me, 'Thirteen and a wakey to go.' I said, 'Terrific.'

We were just finishing our coffee and all of a sudden just all hell broke loose. Over the wireless we get back that two have been seriously hit and six or seven or eight have been hurt.

I led out and we got to their position and it was the same area we'd stopped the day before and looked around and smoked and laughed. What we didn't realise was that we were right on the perimeter of a North Vietnamese camp.

The first sight I saw when I got to them was my best mate, white as a sheet and just bloated. I don't know what happens, but he was just bloated in the face and totally white.

He'd been hit with an RPG. His face wasn't affected, he must have been hit in the side, the side that was away from me. He was still alive, for a while, and then he went. He was totally unconscious. He just twitched and quivered and that was it.

They had the medico there and when they died he yelled out, 'Number one gone, number two gone,' and I thought, 'Why yell that out?'

I had no feeling of anger, I had no feeling of revenge or remorse. There wasn't any passion. There was just a total disassociation from everything, no feeling of anything, nothing. We were close friends and I felt nothing.

DES

He served in Vietnam in 1970.

There was a contact about a week before the platoon was due to come back. Eleven VC walked into an ambush; six of them were killed, five were wounded.

After a contact you'd go out and get the weapons off them. One woman there was wounded and she threw a hand-grenade in and we got three wounded and one killed out of it, which was a bit of a bummer with a week to go.

When the VC were all brought together the platoon lieutenant said that the count was wrong. It wasn't six dead and five wounded, it was eleven dead. And that's what it was.

The woman was shot. The fellow that did it was telling me about it. I can't remember exactly how many times he said he shot her, but it was quite a few times. He said she just refused to die. It was just madness at times, you know. Just total madness.

BRIAN THOMPSON

I found it hard to write letters home sometimes. What was I going to write about? Was I going to say for the three hundredth time that I missed my wife and kids, was I going to tell Bev what the latest bodycount was, or that we were losing the war, or that we sent home eight dead bodies and thirty-two wounded yesterday? What for?

In the end I communicated simple things, just trying to reach into their lives back home again and saying that I'd be home soon. The words 'I'll be home soon' cropped up in almost every letter, especially in the last three months.

COLIN NICOLE

The day before Christmas we got these two prisoners, which was quite rare because you just didn't see them in the bush. Like, it was kill or be killed, you pour out six or seven hundred rounds of ammunition and then you go see what the results are.

We caught these two prisoners and I can remember I stood outside myself, really. It was an incredible feeling. I saw how well trained, but how young I was.

This bloke looked across at me and smiled; the other bloke had one ankle missing and he was blind. I was just thinking, 'This is ridiculous. I don't hate these guys, I don't hate this person.' I offered him a cigarette, which he took. I noticed that the officer didn't feel the same feeling towards him, you know. Everyone was shoving him around a bit.

They choppered out these two prisoners and the story came back later that one of them got thrown out, which wouldn't surprise me in the slightest. I thought. 'God, I don't hate these folk. What am I doing here, what am I doing here?'

LAURIE WOODS

One of our last ops we were down near the beach and we walked into a bunker system. The forward scout called us up and he said, 'Well, what is it?' I had a look at the signs and I said, 'We're coming into a bunker system, but I think it's a big bunker system. Just keep down until we've worked it out.' One of the blokes near me stood up and said, 'Oh, there's nothing around here,' and as he turned around he wore a bullet straight between the eyes and I remember I spewed all over him.

We brought in Spooky and the gunships that night and they plastered the joint and then the next day they came in and defoliated until everything there was stark and the trees had no foliage on them at all. We were called back about a kilometre but we were covered in whatever it was that they sprayed. It was like a shower of rain. We didn't know what it was. We were expecting napalm. Three days later we walked through with flame throwers and burnt everything.

BOB STEPHENS

It was late in the afternoon and we were called up into the Long Hais, a treacherous part of the province. We had to pick up some wounded, some South Vietnamese troops with some Australian advisers.

We came into the position. They threw us smoke so we knew where they were but couldn't land because of the rough terrain.

We went in, hovering about twenty feet above the ground, everything was going all right, and I sent a winch down. I could see wounded and bodies lying there. The first bloke they put into the litter was a fellow that had both legs blown off at the knees, a South Vietnamese, and I remember he had a piece of bone about three or four inches protruding from one knee.

I'd just started to winch this guy up when we were shot down by automatic weapons fire. You could hear the rounds hitting the aircraft and they must have hit the engine because the next thing there was no noise.

We hit the rocks, the aircraft rolled over onto its right side. As it was rolling I was looking out the door and I could see the fellow in the litter, who thought that the aircraft was rolling onto him. He didn't scream, but just the look of despair on his face...

I dived in behind the back of the pilot's seat for safety and the aircraft shook itself to pieces until the the rotor broke itself off and the aircraft stopped. Straight away there was a lot of smoke, there was screaming. The aircraft was on its side and I was standing in the opening on the ground realising that I was still alive. The gunner and then the co-pilot brushed past me and went up through the opening. I watched the co-pilot slide to the ground alongside the aircraft and I watched him rolling down the hill. Then the Army medic, who had taken my machine-gun while I was on the winch, yelled out 'Help me, I'm stuck, I'm stuck.' Something had rolled forward onto the back of his legs and he was sort of kneeling. I put my arms under his armpits to lift him out but I couldn't move him.

I could hear screams coming from the front somewhere and I didn't know whether it was the pilot or some of the men who had been underneath the aircraft when we crashed. I thought I would get out and smash the windscreen in but I couldn't climb out and I thought, 'I'm caught, I'm going to be the next one.' Then I realised that I still had on my safety harness, which stops you from falling out of the aircraft. I got outside and I was about to knock the windscreen in when the aircraft captain, who had already got out, yelled to me to get away before it blew up. He was down behind a large boulder.

I started to run to where he was and I saw the body of one of the Australian advisers who had been assisting in putting that wounded fellow in the litter. He was killed.

It wasn't long after that you could hear the aircraft burning and the ammunition was going off. Once I heard that I knew that I couldn't have gone back even if I had wanted to.

A helicopter came in to get us out just on dusk. There was a wounded South Vietnamese fellow who had taken shrapnel wounds to the head. He was bandaged up, but he was standing underneath the aircraft to be winched up and the downwash from the rotor blades was just swirling his blood everywhere. You could see it going against all the rocks and everything.

When I got on, there was wounded and dead everywhere. Normally they probably would have had a couple of aircraft to remove that many people, but it was right on dark and I suppose if they didn't get us out then they wouldn't have been able to get us out.

I went around and I sat next to the gunner and I just broke down and cried. I was relieved to be getting out of that place and I thought of what had happened and I just broke down and cried. The gunner put his arm around my shoulders and tried to comfort me. I just felt exhausted, as though all my strength and energy had been drained right out of me.

We landed on the pad at the hospital at Vung Tau and the place was all packed with people ready to tend the wounded and the dead and I just stepped straight off and sort of ambled over. I still had my pistol at that stage and I was trying to get the magazine out and an Army fellow quickly snatched that off me in case something happened there. I was just sort of lost. I felt I was nowhere.

BOB WALKER

I only saw a couple of Australians killed. It was devastating. I saw Jimmy Kerr dead in '69. He was a driver and the steel drainage plug in the driver's compartment had come up through him when his tank hit a mine. He just got put in a plastic bag.

Jimmy and I had been fairly close because we played football together and we were both in B Squadron. He'd been overseas for about a month and he was busting his neck to get out and drive and the second day he was out that was him finished. He was nineteen. He was a lovely little fellow. I was stunned; I couldn't believe it. I looked, then I turned away and I could taste the bile in my mouth. It virtually disintegrated the centre of him.

The other Australian I saw dead was a grunt. He was just a rifleman I think and he stepped on a mine. We had him on the back of a tank for a while and that was probably the worst memory I've got. His legs weren't fully together. I think the term the whalers use is 'flensed', like the flesh taken off the bone. I know he'd copped a hell of a lot of metal in the body; there was a huge amount of blood.

Once they're inside the plastic sheets it becomes rather impersonal, but you can't take your eyes off. You've got that almost compelling urge to go over and lift the bloody sheet to see if what you saw was real, to see if what you saw was correct, could really have been done to someone. I was like that for Kerr too. I mean, I didn't go over, but I had that urge to say, 'I want another look at Jimmy...'

CHRIS LUCAS

We got ambushed, but we got ambushed because we asked for it. We were ordered to follow a telephone cable through the bush and they set up the mortars on us. We got to a certain spot and they opened up and we got pounded with it. Blokes got bits and pieces ripped out of them. There were seventeen wounded out of twenty-five in about half a minute.

I got blown through the air by a mortar. We could hear it whistling coming down and I was going around and around in a circle wondering where to go. I was looking at a little bit of a dip in the ground I was going to dive in, but the artillery forward observer we had with us said 'get down' so I just hit the ground where I was and the mortar landed where I was going to dive. It would have landed right in the middle of my back.

As it was it landed just a few metres away. It just picked me up and stood me on my chin and I just came crashing down again. Never got a mark on me.

The blokes that were beside me got shrapnel all up and down their legs and up their backs. I had a rattled brain for I don't know how long. Didn't know whether I was Arthur or Martha for about three weeks.

At that point the blokes were getting so they didn't care whether they lived or died. When they opened up, when the bullets were flying, one of the blokes was just putting his finger up above his head and bringing it down, just being funny. He was just putting his finger up as the bullets were flying past and we were laughing at him.

I thought we were ratshit. We were just waiting for them to come straight over the top of us because they were ready for us, but it just didn't happen. The Yanks saved us. They could hear over the radio what was happening because we were in contact with the company commander who was bawling his eyes out that he'd sent us in. He should have got his arse kicked for the whole thing because he got us into that trouble.

We couldn't refuse to go in and we knew it was wrong, all of us did. We found out later there were three hundred and fifty of them in a bunker system, not fifty yards away. We knew we were walking into something bad.

LES MYERS

They made a stretcher and carried me to a point to be picked up by the APCs. It was only about a hundred metres away. Jack Lockley was sitting on the ground leaning against a tree, blood all over his left leg and foot. Lloyd Harmsworth was there, with his right arm in a sling and blood all over his shoulder, arm and chest. Allan Lloyd was there on a stretcher, blood everywhere, over his arms, legs, chest, stomach. I guess I knew then that he was buggered.

They took us on the APCs to a clearing where a medevac chopper took us out. Lockley and Harmsworth were strapped one each side of the chopper in the gunner's seat, I was put in next facing the back and Allan Lloyd was put in behind me.

On the way to the hospital no-one tried to speak. I don't know if it was the noise of the chopper, or just the shock of the whole bloody thing. I was just lying there thinking and listening and watching that rotor go around and around. It was a strange feeling. It all came to an end so quick.

Allan Lloyd was a bit of a rough type. He would never allow himself to get closely involved with anyone. I guess he was a bit of a loner. I had my back to him when I felt him put his hand across my side. I was surprised. It wasn't like him to do that, at any time. I felt bloody shithouse and I knew he felt the same and I held that hand, but something felt wrong. When I had a look I saw that half his hand was gone, clean as anything, no blood, no bone, just gone. I held that hand until the chopper landed and I know I haven't felt so close to anyone before or since and I think he felt the same. I hope so anyway. That was the last time I saw Allan alive.

When I first saw his hand I've never felt such anger as I did then. It went over and over in my mind: 'Bloody bastards, what have they done to us?'

ALLEN MAY

After I got hit I was in hospital twenty-two, twenty-three days and when I got out it was arranged for me to take over in the canteen because I told them I didn't think I could go out again.

The thing that really cracked me up was the day before we left to come home they took me out of the canteen where I had been for three months and stuck me out front as forward scout on one last patrol. And where we went was the very same place where the battle was at Long Tan.

I went the whole patrol with my gun at my shoulder because I was fucked three months, you know, seeing my mates go out every day and hoping they'd all come back. I was really scared shitless and I think that last patrol is what really got down deep into my body.

RAY CALDWELL

We were clearing mines and we had one left that we couldn't find. We'd been all day on it. There was myself and another Kiwi and four Aussies and one was a sergeant, last day in the country, he'd done his time. We must have found well over thirty mines that day. We had them marked down on a piece of toilet paper but we couldn't find this last bastard. Our mine detector was a bit on the blink so we went and had a cup of tea to relax and the sergeant came down. He said, 'You Kiwi bastards, haven't you found that last mine yet?' I said, 'No, I think the mine detector's on the blink.' He says, 'Fucking lazy bastards.' He grabbed the mine detector, went down there with the map, boom, that was it. It got two of them, last day in the country.

We had to go down and put him in a bag and I mean a little bag, I don't mean a bloody flour sack. That's what you can fit a body in when it's hanging in the trees. They've got no friends, them mines. It's just all bits here and there. I think part of his boot was about the biggest.

BOB GIBSON

We were all sitting on top of an APC, coming back from Operation Coburg. My best mate was in front of me. It was a straight road and there was a hut on the left-hand side and an old tree on the right-hand side and I remember thinking if there was going to be an ambush it would come from around that hut or from over near that paddy and that old tree.

I could see this truck coming down the road towards us. I was just sort of looking at the hut and I looked at the tree and I was holding Doug around the front. Next thing, this truck came straight for us, swerved in at the APC and rammed us up the side and with that Doug was thrown out of my arms. The corporal in front of Doug and the sergeant was thrown in between the truck and the APC, and I was the only guy on the right-hand side who was thrown the other way. I went down the back way.

I looked back and Doug had been cut in half and the corporal and the sergeant were laying on the ground with their legs busted. My rifle was about twenty or thirty yards away. I grabbed it, I ran to where parts of Doug were. I remember screaming. It was like I screamed for five minutes but it must have only been a couple of seconds and I felt like I was going to explode from within, that everything was just going to burst. I raced to the truck and thought, 'I'll kill this noggy bastard, I'll empty this whole magazine on this bastard,' but he wasn't there, he was gone.

An American jeep came along behind us and one bloke jumped out with a camera and started taking some photographs. I said, 'If you don't put that camera down I'll shoot you, you bastard.' The other bloke said, 'Calm down, calm down.' One of them said, 'Well, this bloke's gone.' I can remember everything was just like it was a bad dream. I mean, Doug was thirteen days from going home.

TED WARNER

He served in Vietnam in 1965.

I did about eight weeks all told on the edge of Bien Hoa airfield and I used to smell this strange smell. I thought it was the smell of death or something. It would almost make you sick at times, you'd actually feel ill. I never knew what that was. I know now that they used to spray cacadylic acid, arsenic, or Agent Blue there.

The part that I noticed mainly was between Bien Hoa and Saigon. When we first went driving up there it was like any other South-East Asian country that I'd been in. It was lush paddy fields and tropical growth. The last time I drove up the Saigon–Bien Hoa road it was a desert, completely bare. It was unbelievable. The area was completely defoliated.

ZEV BEN-AVI

A war orphan who was born somewhere near Paris in September 1940. In 1945, he was taken to what was then British Palestine where he grew up in a children's kibutz. He emigrated to Australia and served in Vietnam as an APC crew commander in 1969–70. Today, he lives in Brisbane.

We went on patrols every morning before they would let the plant equipment or any transports through, because the engineers were rebuilding the road and, of course, the theory was the bad guys would slip in at night time and lay mines on the newly made pieces of road.

It was done with a section of carriers and either two or a mini-team section from engineers with a mine detector. They'd be out there with a carpet sweeper and a bayonet. Mostly it was visual, on top of the lead carrier. This had been going for six weeks and it was boring because you had to be out there before sparrow fart.

This particular village of Ngai Giao, which is where we had to clear to, the Civil Aid crowd had been in there and they had put in a Southern Cross windmill, wells, all sorts of other village improvements. And just to relieve the monotony, rather than go back to the engineers' night defensive position we used to stay in this village and we became very friendly with this one guy. He'd lost his wife, two sons and a daughter and he had two daughters left. He lived on the edge of the village in a little hut made out of flattened Coca Cola tins, the usual scene.

There was an ARVN outpost on the edge of the village and the bad guys used to come through at night time and this guy had had his hut brassed up, this is how he had lost what he had of his family, so we stole a bale of sandbags from the Yanks and piles of C-rations and made a sandbag revetment to put around his little hut so they had some cover.

And these two little girls made a string of love beads for each guy in our troop and presented it to us, and we were quite sort of touched. We more or less fostered these two little girls.

We were off that job and we finished up at the other end of the province for about five or six weeks and when we got back we found that in the interim period the Viet Cong had come into that village, got this family with the two little girls and cut their throats. It was an object lesson for the rest of the village not to accept anything from Australian soldiers. That was on 24 April, 1970.

You can't imagine how we felt. Shock, grief, anger all in one. They had been buried some time before we arrived back there and having been told what had happened we went to see this father. I thought, this guy is going to hate my guts but he didn't! I felt worse, you know. I thought, for Christ's sake, hate me, take it out on me. He had every right to hate me.

I felt personally responsible because I thought I was the one who put this idea forward to the rest of my troops and sort of encouraged my section to do this thing for these people. I felt personally responsible, that if I had left it alone it would never have happened. And let's face it, I think we were all a little bit troppo after you've been there for a while. Anyway, all we wanted was revenge. Didn't matter how we got it, that's all we wanted.

On 4 July we were in the Courtenay rubber plantation and we got onto some NVA and we chased them. I tracked them down and we crossed into Long Khanh Province, where we weren't supposed to be, and we finally nailed them in a rubber plantation. It was an unused rubber plantation where the undergrowth was probably about four or five feet high and we started chasing these guys, this NVA group, through the rubber and we were so full of this revenge bit that all we wanted to do was to nail some bastard.

I had a flex .30 calibre on top of the turret and we nailed a few of them and then we went in and started running over people with the carriers. My driver, Roger, who was a national serviceman, a sort of peaceful, home-loving man, he was standing up and just right stick, left stick, screwing these people into the deck with the left track — and I'm encouraging him.

We just went crazy. We nailed them first and then we just went and systematically screwed them into the ground, in a lot of cases while they were trying to crawl and run away. I can remember laughing, probably hysterically. As it turned out I got a tremendous pat on the back because the lead guy was an NVA intelligence major and he was carrying a great wad of paper on him that was incredible intelligence material.

We finished up screwing eight of them into the deck with the tracks, and that didn't improve my situation at all. On top of having this massive guilt complex about those two little girls and now having screwed those blokes into the ground...it sickened me, but it didn't.

About ten days later we were in roughly the same area and one of the drivers in my section, a Maori who had enlisted in Australia, took a shovel and went off into the bush by himself. When he came back he was carrying a sandbag. Nobody took much notice and for about a week or more we couldn't work out what this putrid smell was coming out of Ike's carrier. What he'd done was go out and dig up one of these bodies, cut its head off with the shovel and take the head back in the sandbag.

When I saw it, all I saw was a skull with this cap of hair on the top and a few chunks of meat on it, wired through the chinbone on the front of his carrier. I knew straight away who it was, what it was, where he'd got it.

Every time he'd got a spare moment he'd skulk off somewhere and get his bayonet out and scrape all the meat and brains, what have you, just to get a skull. At that stage of the game I was getting closer and closer, looking back at it, to being pushed over the edge.

Not long after that we were in Xuan Loc, up in Long Khanh Province. While we were there, two Buddhist monks came into the centre of the city, sat down and just calmly poured petrol over themselves, hit the Zippo and up they went, right in the middle of the place. All the locals knew it was going to happen; we didn't. The first half of the tour comparatively little happened. Just the odd contact, fairly routine. And to see that, that was pretty horrific.

A couple of weeks later I hit a mine and that sent me home.

MICHAEL

I had a couple of ears for a little while that I had taken off bodies after ambushes. I had them on a piece of green twine and I wore them around my neck with my dog tags and crucifix. In the end they started to smell so I sold them to someone who wanted a souvenir of Vietnam.

RAY ORCHARD

We were sweeping through a village, cordon and search, looking for weapons, supplies, ordering people everywhere. We seen one person go, run. This woman, she ran to a cellar. We heard their voices coming up. We were going to throw a grenade down. Then this child came up out of there. I had my machine-gun. I seen the terror in his eyes. I let him go by. Other people came out then. Even though I sighted him I had to still be a good soldier and to watch for the next person. We were aware that they used to send children up and I was ready for the next person. I couldn't hug that child to say I'm sorry because I had to be ready for the next person. He wouldn't have been more than five, six years old, but instead of hugging him when he went past me, crying. I said, 'Go on, get by.' You had to say that because there could have been somebody else coming behind, using him, and you always had to be aware of that. That was the way.

RON EGLINTON

We were moving along a track and we saw a Vietnamese across to the left through the trees, just one fellow in black pyjamas. The company commander, for some reason known only to himself, called in artillery. There had been no shots fired, no-one hurt and he called in artillery.

They initially put a couple of rounds out just to make sure their bearing was right but they were off a bit. I can remember hearing him correct and next minute about twelve rounds came out, nowhere near this fellow, who would have been long gone, but landing right down the track we were moving along. We threw our packs up over the back of our heads trying to protect ourselves. There was nothing you could do with artillery. It was all over in a few seconds and there's been fellows killed, there's been blokes wounded.

Jack Kirby, who had been decorated for his actions at Long Tan, was killed. He was a big, gruff, heavy man, a real father figure to us all and he was dead. No reason.

We secured the area and called in a dust-off. I can remember when we were taking his body out to the chopper on the stretcher the wind from the rotors blew the poncho off him and I can remember someone screaming, 'Cover him up'. No-one wanted to see him dead. It was just so bloody pointless.

LAURIE WOODS

We were up near Bien Hoa and we'd picked up four North Vietnamese. There was a major and a lewie and their two batmen and one of the batmen was shot pretty bad, he wasn't going to make it. We called in the Yanks to pick them up and a chopper came down and the Yankee gunner off the chopper got out, took one look at the guy that was pretty crook, pulled out his pistol and went bang. He said, 'He wasn't going anywhere anyway.' They put the other three on the chopper and took off and they were probably up at about two thousand feet and all of a sudden we could see this little nog doing cartwheels out of the chopper. He was the other batman. He wasn't going back either.

JEFF SCULLEY

One night down in Vungers we were in the Grand Hotel. There was a floor show going on and when it stopped a guy who was in our platoon just walked up and sat down on the stage and he just started crying his eyes out, he just started bawling. He was pretty pissed. The MPs came in and asked him to get off the stage. They wouldn't have known what he was bawling about, those Vung Tau warriors. We knew, because we had been there.

PETER VANDENBERG

'You wait until the medevac choppers arrive and in the cases of the dead people there's nothing left. I mean, they're stripped of everything, all dignity. You just throw them in the bag, and if there's no bag you just throw them in the chopper and if there's more than two or three you just stack them on top of one another. There's no dignity whatsoever, there's nothing left.'

The company I was with got dropped in second and it was supposedly a secure landing zone, there was to be no hassle when we arrived, but when we came towards the area something was amiss; you could feel it.

I remember this big Yank Negro sitting next to me in the chopper. He was one of the machine-gunners, and he started firing as we were coming into the landing zone. I shook him on the shoulder and I said, 'What's the matter, where's the enemy, what are you firing at?' He said, 'The place is full of slopes.' I couldn't see anything, I couldn't see a bloody thing, I couldn't see anybody except our own people who were already on the ground. He grabbed me by the arm and pointed back towards his head and I looked around and a bullet of some sort had passed right between our heads.

I was shaking, there was no way I was going to get off, and when we were hovering just off the ground he grabbed hold of me and just threw me off into a rice paddy full of water. Amongst a lot of shouting and carrying on the choppers took off but they'd put us down on the wrong landing zone. They'd put us down only about five or six hundred metres away from the underground village we were looking for and so while the choppers were coming in we were under mortar attack. Everything was utter chaos. A lot of our ammunition and mortars caught fire on the ground and started going off. We pulled out of that area with maybe twenty or thirty per cent of our allocated ammunition.

There was a village with a big row of bamboo on the right, an open field on the left-hand side which was the village graveyard and on the right-hand side in from the bamboo there was a washaway, a dry creek. We had to clear into the washaway.

The forward scout got about halfway along and he just died on the spot, he just crumpled and that was it. We didn't see anything, we didn't hear anything, he just crumpled. They yelled out for the medic but I couldn't move because we were pinned down by fire coming across the graveyard. A very good friend of mine, he went out to try to fix him up and he only got to the stage where he was bending over him, he didn't even get a chance to undo his medical bag, he just got shot straight through the heart, from one side to the other. Another one of our medics got there and he got shot just straight through the head. We couldn't see anything, you know, nothing.

That particular engagement lasted for something like two and a half hours, and when we ultimately went through we found that in the side of the washaway was a hole, and it was completely hollow inside and there was a bloke with a machine-gun and he was just simply waiting. They had arranged it in such a way that the only place anyone could go was through the washaway. They had it sown up.

They made me bag them up in the green bags and I can still remember my friend's face. He was smiling. I'd known him since 1961, so I guess by the time of his death that would have been five years, and we often used to sit at night after operations were finished and talk about what we would do once we got back home. He was a married chap with four kids I think. At that time, to me it seemed so unfair because, sure, I was married, but I had no kids, and maybe it should have been me that had gone out there.

That same day I was asked to treat two male villagers. In the second case, an old man had got caught up in the firefight and he'd got hit by a claymore. He'd been hit hours before and he was just sort of laying there on the ground, all full of holes. There was no hope for him and yet I tried to patch him up, knowing full well he was going to die. The younger chap, I'm ashamed to say it, but I felt like God. It was up to me to decide whether that bloke was going to live or whether he wasn't going to live and I decided that because of what had happened to my mates there was no way he was going to live. I just simply turned around and I said that I didn't have anything to treat him with, which was a lie. I just didn't want to.

WAYNE

Because I was a non-combatant, I was posted to Vung Tau, and the first day I just couldn't handle it. I came in on the bus and I saw all the poverty of the place and the children and it really, really upset me.

Vung Tau was the sort of place where every night we could go out and have a fuck if we wanted to, or get onto the piss.

I wasn't into that and I got to know a couple of Yanks who said that they did some voluntary work in the local orphanage, so I used to go there. It was run by the Mother Superior.

The first time I went there it really screwed me up because I saw people, kids, with no legs and terrible napalm burns. Have you ever seen anyone with third-degree burns? The first little kid I saw, his hand was just... They had to amputate it. It was just burnt to cinders. We had oil baths for them, but when I say bath it would be an old tub we'd find or something. All the medical stuff was done under the cuff; we traded beer for medical supplies.

I had a mate who worked in stores at the Department of Motor Transport in Victoria who knocked off pencils and paper for me because the nuns used to teach them how to write. I wrote to the RSL and I got boxes of toys sent over so that every kid had a toy at Christmas and all this type of thing.

Most of the kids were waifs — the children of the occupation forces — and they weren't wanted. You'd get two hundred and fifty kids up to Danang where they could get treatment for their burns and the next day there would be another two hundred and fifty kids come up and you don't know where they've come from.

I got to know this little blond-headed kid in the orphanage at Baria. She'd have to have been an Australian because this orphanage was in our province. She was a beautiful little thing. She had the slanty eyes, but she had blond hair. She had terrible burn scars on her, she had one leg and she had one arm and I used to take dolls and things to her.

I wanted to get her an artificial leg and an artificial arm. I took her up to Saigon on the wallaby transport plane unbeknown to my boss, who always used to be pissed. I got a mate to take her to the plane, gave the load master ten bucks to get the kid on and then got a Pan Am flight from Saigon to Danang. Danang was a fucking big place. It had a population of about 300,000 US personnel and the hospital was the size of all the hospitals in Melbourne put together.

I had a jeep lined up to take me to see an orthopaedic surgeon. He got her a bed and she spent three months up there. She got an artificial leg and an artificial arm and she learned to use them.

She came back to Baria just before I was posted to Saigon and oh, she was really beautiful. I'll always remember I bought her this beautiful pink dress. She was five and I bought her these white fluffy panty-type things that five-year-olds wear. I gave a Yank lieutenant up at Danang, a nurse, fifty bucks and said buy her a doll or buy her dresses or buy her anything you like and she came back with a pink dress on and white shoes. She looked really nice. She was a beautiful little girl.

I promised her, I wish to Christ I'd never, I promised her that I'd take her home, I'd get her home to Australia, but that fell through. I can't think of her name. It's funny. Doctors tell me I don't want it to surface, I just want to forget it.

ADRIAN

He served in Vietnam in 1965–6, when he was nineteen.

On my last patrol we shot a woman and her kids on a river-bank. They had come down to wash some clothes. That was the sort of savages we had become.

STUART DALGLEISH

He flew a helicopter gunship in 1970. 'Most of the time we were flying over the top supporting troop movements, we'd be brassing up the sides of paddies to frighten off or kill any baddies that were there so that they could land safely. But you never saw anybody, you were shooting trees. That was the joke: "Let's go out and shoot some trees."

The one time I heard people shooting back at me I really felt angry. How dare they shoot back at me! It just seemed totally unreal, until one day we actually saw some people.

They didn't have a lot of cover. They were in an area they definitely weren't supposed to be in and our guys were close by, so we tried to and did shoot them.

We hit them with everything we had at our disposal. We had twin mini-guns — they fire six thousand rounds a minute — plus rockets.

I guess the thing that I find most difficult to handle about it all is that at the time it was incredibly exciting. It was an absolute utter high. I didn't feel like that was me, because I couldn't believe that I was so stirred up about killing people.

Later on, when you had time to think about it, you could see the one-sidedness of it, because nobody shot back at us. We didn't even know for sure that they were enemy. I still don't.

We rationalised it by saying that they had to be bad guys or they wouldn't have been there.

As the time went on I became more and more concerned about the war and less and less interested, so that by the time I finally went on R&R I didn't want to go back, certainly not back on the gunships. There were quite a few pilots in the squadron who really just wanted to get onto medevacs and work at saving people instead of killing them. I took as many medevacs then as I possibly could and flew as little as I could. I really just totally lost interest in the whole thing and just wanted to get out of it.

I put a peace symbol on my helmet and was told by the group captain to get it off because he thought I was joking but really I was serious. There were a few of us by then who didn't want to have a bar of the violent side of the war.

It was probably a combination of the things I had seen and experienced and read in the papers, knowing that the war was unpopular at home, and a growing feeling that we were wasting our time over there.

It was the only war I've seen so I don't know how I would have felt if it had been like the Second World War, but it wasn't what I had expected it to be.

BARRY KELLY

'There were things that happened in Vietnam that I'd blocked out, that I didn't remember being involved in. When I went into the repatriation hospital, part of the psychiatric treatment was to bring a whole lot back to you. They fed you sodium pentathol and video-taped you. We blew up a woman and four kids with a rocket launcher and I didn't remember that, but that was me on the film and that was me talking.'

We'd go out with infantry and they'd surround a village and do a field of fire, blow the joint apart so there was nothing there, then we engineers would go in and look for trip wires or hand-grenades or whatever the nogs had set up for you.

We'd gone into this village with the infantry backing us up, and just as we were about to go into a hut a body emerged in the front door and we went zappa with a rocket grenade. It hit this thing and blew it to bits, but we threw another two grenades in to make sure there was no other bastard kicking around in there. When we got in there the one we'd hit first had the chest bone blown right through the back — it was a woman and inside were four kids, all under five years of age.

One guy got sent back to Australia. He went off his head on the spot. He was a national serviceman. He just went to bits, threw his weapon away and just wouldn't have anything to do with the war. They threatened to charge him and he said, 'Well bloody shoot me, I don't care.' He didn't care. He just wanted out, that was it. He said, 'Hey, come on, they're kids.'

Me, I blocked that off. I said, well, that hasn't happened and I pushed on and it never worried me all the time I was there. We never mentioned it and that was it.

TOMMY BROWN

Bobby was my platoon commander in Sydney. He was young and probably inexperienced. When he took me through corps training he was a nice bloke; I used to get on all right with him. He used to drive me home sometimes on leave. I didn't see him for about twelve months, until I was in Vietnam when he came over as a reinforcement. He came to mortars for a couple of weeks with us and he was all right, good as gold with us in mortars.

Two days before the battalion was coming home one of our blokes dropped a grenade in bed with him and blew him all over the tent.

That bloke was charged with murder, or manslaughter, I'm not sure. He finished up doing about seven years. That was two days before the battalion was due to come home. I was home. I read about it in the paper. But, you know, that's how blokes changed over there, even murdering one another.

HOLT McMINN

'I think the whole bloody place was mad, all the commanders, every-body. It was like having a concession ticket to Disneyland. The whole place was just absolutely, totally unreal. The machinery, life, death, there was no reality about anything. You'd come back after a patrol and you had movies, jukeboxes, pool tables, all this sort of thing, and life went on all around you in a weird sort of light. There's people dying, you would see dead people on the side of the road and you just paid no attention to it after a while; you were just so blasé about it, you just didn't give a stuff. All the children were mad, everybody was mad.'

In Vietnam, he served with the SAS. Today, he lives in Canberra.

This particular ambush there was one man left alive. He was a Viet Cong officer and I went down and knelt beside his head and I looked at him briefly and he looked at me. He was in a grotesque shape: I think he'd lost a leg, the other leg had disappeared somewhere up his back, one arm was mangled; his face looked all right.

I went to grab his pistol and he grabbed me by the wrist with his good hand. I had to kick him a couple of times to get rid of his hand. Maybe he wanted to stay alive, I don't know, but he was going to die, whether I killed him or not he was going to die a horrible bloody death. He may have lived another two minutes, he may have lived another half an hour, but nothing on God's earth could have saved him. So I shot him through the head.

I can remember him dying, I can remember the sound of him and I can remember him watching himself going to be shot, knowing that this was the end.

I didn't feel anything when I killed him, no emotion at all. It was like having a glass of water. I think you just got so conditioned that it didn't bother you. I think I was twenty at the time.

JACK

He served in Vietnam in 1965–6.

We dragged two young boys out of a pit in a house. They would have been fourteen, fifteen I suppose. We found them hiding in a sort of makeshift air-raid shelter. We were trying to get information out of these two young kids, just our platoon, and one of the blokes said, 'There's only one way to make them talk, that's do what the Yanks do, shoot one of them.' One of the guys walked up and he just shot one of these kids, just standing there. He walked up and he went bang and shot him through the head. His brains just went all over the ground and the Vietnamese interpreter we had with us pushed the other kid down onto his brains and pushed his face into it.

If anything out of Vietnam worried me it was that, that we as human beings could do that. That was pretty close to us coming home.

LACHLAN IRVINE

The last two months or so in Vietnam, when I was getting short, I had a completely different attitude to the war. I arrived over there feeling pretty gung ho, let-me-at-them sort of thing. I didn't place much value on my life and each operation I went out on I was quite prepared to be killed. In my mind I was already written off. But when I was getting short I went out there with the purpose of surviving. I didn't want to meet any Viet Cong, I didn't want to shoot anybody, I didn't want to be shot at. I just wanted to survive.

BERNARD SZAPIEL

Until the plane actually took off, until the wheels had left the tarmac at Tan Son Nhut, I didn't believe that we were getting out of there alive. When the wheels came up and we were a few hundred feet in the air the cheers that rang out through the plane were just phenomenal.

We'd been told not to bring whiskey on the plane but we all had the bottles out and we were just, you know, quite stupid.

TREVOR MORRIS

I couldn't wait to get out of the joint. In fact I was that nervous the day I left I just couldn't wait to get on that plane.

In Saigon, waiting to go, things go through your mind: surely they won't rocket the joint now, I'm not going to get zapped now am I, when I'm in my last day? I looked across the tarmac and there were hundreds and hundreds of bodybags lying there. They were loading planes with bodybags, the Yanks. I thought, 'Will I ever get out of this rotten joint?'

When that plane took off from that tarmac one big loud cheer went up. We just couldn't believe it.

BOB GIBSON

As the back of the cargo plane came up I was looking back at the Dat where all my mates who hadn't finished their three hundred and sixty-five days still were. You fought the calendar, you fought nothing more than three hundred and sixty-five days which you marked off after every operation and every day that you were back in camp. The guys who hadn't got up to their three hundred and sixty-five days were still back there, and I thought it's not over yet, what's happened, what's this year been for? There was a feeling of emptiness and sadness and wondering what was going to happen to them. You were going home but it wasn't over, it was still going on.

6

Homecoming

'Australia went to South Vietnam as a political gesture. It has stayed in the country as a political gesture and it will withdraw at a rate which is also a political gesture.'

Brigadier Ted Serong (who led the first advisers to Vietnam)

BARRY ROE

I remember landing at Melbourne, and it hit me that I was home when I came out of the plane and saw my mum and dad and my sister and a couple of mates. They had a big sign up: 'Welcome home Barry'. I came down the walkway and put my feet on the ground and I thought, 'Well beauty, I'm home.'

I walked across the tarmac and came inside Essendon airport and I think I gave my mother a kiss and I think I shook hands with my old man. I remember him saying, 'Come on, we'll jump in the car and we'll go home now.' It sounded funny, 'jump in the car'. I couldn't kind of get it through my head that I was home and I was safe and all I had to do was get in a car and drive home.

I remember driving down Mt Alexander Road in Moonee Ponds and I thought, 'Jesus, this isn't happening this is not happening,' because eighteen or nineteen hours ago I was in Vietnam. It still didn't click.

We got home and there was a big party organised and I still couldn't believe it. There were uncles and aunties there, I just got bombed out of my brain and stayed that way for three or four weeks.

MICHAEL SCRASE

One minute I was in Vietnam and the next minute I was home, and I was totally lost. Cars backfiring scared the shit out of you, you were on edge the whole time for weeks afterwards. There was no debriefing, no time to melt back in. I know my mum and dad found it very hard to handle me. In fact, they told me quite plainly that I wasn't the same person any more. I was prone to get violent, punch walls, get into rages very quickly. I've never slept right since the day I came home.

BOB PRIDE

I suppose I had this idea of coming home to a brass band and ticker-tape processions and women falling at your feet and guys coming up and shaking your hand and all that sort of stuff — the way it was for the Anzacs and the Second World War guys.

I think we landed at Sydney airport about ten or eleven o'clock at night, went through customs, and got our pay. When the doors opened up there were these people waving placards and someone was holding up a page out of a newspaper about women and children being killed.

JEFF SCULLEY

I found it very hard when I came home. I came back to Ballarat and straight away people were asking: 'How many did you kill, mate?' Stupid questions like that.

There was nobody I could relate to. All the mates I had before I went seemed so childish when I got home, the things they were doing were just so dumb.

TREVOR MORRIS

We landed in Sydney about ten o'clock at night, freezing cold. Customs pulled everything out looking for drugs or souvenirs. That went over like a lead balloon. I had friends from Sydney and I went back to their place, had a few Scotches, just couldn't believe I was home. I was on cloud nine.

I couldn't wait to get to Melbourne. They put on a special flight to take the blokes to Melbourne, Adelaide and Perth about three o'clock in the morning. We landed in Melbourne about half past four in the morning and I got home about six in the morning. I went around and saw my fiancée first, then I walked home and it was a great feeling to be home. It was just like Vietnam had been a bad dream, that it never happened.

The next day a reporter from the *Sun* came out and I spoke to him for about an hour, told him really what the whole game was all about. Of course they didn't print it. They printed all the bullshit, but nothing about how we were losing, how we were wasting our bloody time over there and how the blokes shouldn't be over there. They probably thought I was a treasonable bastard. It was a joke. People weren't interested.

When I landed I'd shared a cab from the airport with a bloke who lived in Kensington. He was on his R&R. The last thing I said to him was, 'You're not going back there are you?'

He said, 'What do you reckon?'

I said, 'You'd be bloody mad.'

LACHLAN IRVINE

Arrived at Sydney airport, met the family, went home, spent the next couple of weeks going around seeing old friends, having parties. At this stage I was twenty years old and my old school friends and people that I'd known before Vietnam just seemed like kids, which of course they were and which of course I should have been. But it was as if we were living in different worlds.

JOHN SKINNER

What was left of the battalion were lined up on the deck of the *HMAS Sydney*, looking spick and span with polished boots, all ready to go and do this march through Sydney, and all of us nervous with excitement waiting to meet our families. I remember Colin Khan, the battalion commander. He marched out, very brusque, like on the parade ground, and he looked around at us and said, 'For twelve months you've been carrying this pack on your back and you're all bent and stooped and you're weary, but today you're walking through this town and I want you to throw that pack off your back and march because you are the Tiger Battalion.' It was, I guess, you'd call it gung ho stuff now, but it made us all feel good and proud.

We spent about two hours with our families and then we marched through Sydney. I felt ten feet tall, I really felt good. They had ticker-tape and there were people in the street, but what I didn't realise was that most people were only curious. They weren't cheering us home. They were just lined up to see something.

BOB SAILLARD

He served in Vietnam as an infantry soldier in 1968–9.

'The day we left to come home we were taken by truck to Vung Tau and we passed by the blokes who were just arriving to replace us. It was strange. There were none of the usual comments like "Good on you mate", or "You'll be sorry". We just sat there. We couldn't believe we were getting out.' He lives in Canberra.

We marched through the city of Adelaide and it was unreal. The only people watching us were lunchtime shoppers about two deep on the sidewalk, not doing any cheering or anything. There was just no welcome home at all.

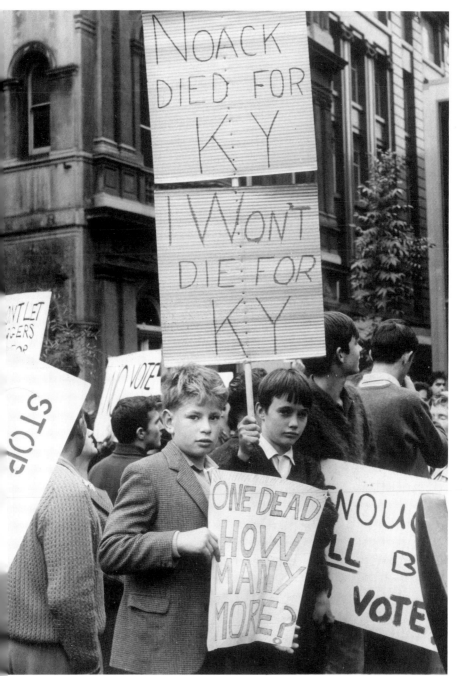

An early anti-Vietnam war and conscription rally was held in Melbourne after the death of the first conscript in Vietnam, Errol Wayne Noack, on 24 May, 1966. (Photograph courtesy of the Age.)

The sign that moved a generation. Here students from the Australian National University in Canberra demonstrate for an end to the war, May, 1971. (Photograph courtesy of Canberra Times.)

A conscientious objector burns his draft card during an anti-war demonstration. Conscription, which was initially supported by a majority of Australians, became the lynch-pin of the protest movement. By 1971, an estimated 11,000 Australians had failed to register for national service. (Photograph courtesy of Herald and Weekly Times.)

By late 1969, public opinion in Australia had turned against the war and tens of thousands of people took to the streets in protest. (Photograph courtesy of Herald and Weekly Times.)

Dr Jim Cairns, a leading anti-war activist, addresses moratorium marchers outside the Melbourne Town Hall, June, 1971. (Photograph courtesy of the Age.)

Peter Molloy and Les Pettit, both aged twenty-one. Molloy lost his right leg and Pettit was killed.

Members of the 7th Battalion crouch in readiness to be lifted to another batt[le] area in Phuoc Tuy Province. Australian soldiers rarely knew where they were being sent or who they woul[d] be fighting. (Photograph courtesy of Australian War Memorial.)

Australian soldiers near the end of their tour of duty in Vietnam. (Photograph courtesy of the Age.)

For many of Australia's war veterans the joy of coming home often turned bitter in the face of public antipathy for their involvement in the war. (Photograph courtesy of John Fairfax and Sons.)

Returning Australian troops often flew back into Sydney's Mascot airport after dark to avoid demonstrators. (Photograph courtesy of John Fairfax and Sons.)

A flight of four US Air Force C-123s spray jungle near Saigon with a defoliant. The effect of these chemicals in Vietnam has become the subject of bitter debate since the war. (Photograph courtesy of United Press International Inc.)

A battalion marches through Sydney on its return to Australia. Ticker tape parades were common but little jubilation welcomed the men home. (Photograph courtesy

BILL DOBELL

They flew me into Laverton and I was taken from there to the Heidelberg Repatriation Hospital. My mum was there and my grandfather. It was great to see them again, but I was feeling pretty crook. I was also a bit scared. How do you come to your mum just after going to war? I was more worried about what she might think or what she might say. But the first question she asked me was did I see any enemy soldiers? I wasn't sure I knew what the answer was she wanted. Did she want me to tell her just that I'd seen enemy soldiers and that's all there was to it, or did she want me to tell her that I'd actually got into combat with them, or killed, or whatever? To what extent? What did she want to know? I think I just said yes and left it at that.

I looked at my grandfather and he sort of looked at me and then looked away. He had served in the First World War, in the Light Horse. He was wounded, and he's never told me much about it but from what I can gather he saw quite a bit of action. I think I looked at him as if to say, 'Well, what should I do? You ought to know.' But then he wouldn't know any better than I do. He just looked at me and then sort of let it go.

RAY STOCK

I came back from Vietnam just before Christmas in 1968 and my girlfriend was having a Christmas party at her office and I was invited to go along. She was very upset because I wore civilian clothes. I didn't want to wear my uniform any more.

My conflict was that I didn't know whether Vietnam was winnable or not, because I didn't know enough about the warfare there to answer that, but from what I had seen I knew it was corrupt and I knew that it was a war that was futile because we were going back into the same places all the time. At the end of my tour we were going back into the same areas and doing the same things we were doing eight months before.

The moratorium movement was starting up at the time and I thought, yeah, I'm against the Vietnam war. I'd never marched in anything in my life, never demonstrated against anything. I was working class, I'd left school at fifteen, but I believed the war was wrong and that it should be stopped so less of my mates would die.

That was a very lonely march for me because most of the people demonstrating were university students who had kept on courses so they wouldn't have to go into the Army if they got called up. And there were even younger people there who didn't really understand the issues and were shouting about Australian soldiers being war criminals and I didn't agree with that and the people they were siding with were communists and I didn't agree with that either.

I just thought the war was futile and corrupt and dishonest.

RAY ORCHARD

We marched through Sydney and everybody said hooray. At Garden Island I said goodbye to all my mates. In my own mind I was thinking that I would see them again, but a lot of the fellas were going to Western Australia and that. It never crossed my mind until the next day when I woke up in a hotel and thought, 'Shit, this is it, I'll never see those fellas again, all them fellas I've lived with for over twelve months, they're gone.'

I went home to Bundaberg. I arrived there at four o'clock in the morning. I jumped in a cab and drove up McKenzie Road where I lived, and I said, 'Blow the horn, cabbie, I'm going to wake them up.' It was just starting to break daylight: 'Wake them up.' I jumped out and the whole street must have seen me jump out. I had my gear on and kids were coming from everywhere to look at it. I felt like a big hero.

Later in the day, after we'd sat around in the shed at home and had a couple of beers, I said, 'What'll we do today?' They said, 'Let's go down to the Railway Hotel. There's pool tables and a dart board.'

There was six of us. My uncle, two cousins, a brother, myself and somebody else. We went in there and I walked up to the bar to get a round of drinks and the owner said, 'No, I can't serve you fellas.' I said, 'Hold on, I've just come back from Vietnam.'

He said, 'I couldn't care less. When you mob get together you create a problem.'

He was talking about Aboriginals. Back in my own town, the thing that I'd dreamed of, that had kept me alive all the time, the thing that I had focused on.

I always think it must have just been one fool, but that's not the way to come back home.

DAVID BEAHAN

He served in Vietnam in 1966.

My homecoming was great. I was met about two mile out of town by probably a hundred and sixty people, my friends, out on the highway and they followed us into town. There were parties every night for a week afterwards. I was treated like a king. I was the first guy from Armidale to go into national service, the first one to go to Vietnam and the first one to return from Vietnam.

ADRIAN HINCHEY

He had both his legs and his left arm blown off in Vietnam in 1969.

I remember waking up on the plane and this nursing sister asked me how I felt and I said I felt all right and sort of looked around in the plane. It was stacked with other blokes on stretchers and I think there were a couple of coffins on it and heaps of gear. Next minute she gave me a jab and I was out again.

I was pretty much asleep for five days and then when I got back to Concord Hospital that's when it started to wear off, that's when the pain started and all the silly nightmares: choppers up the walls and Cong under the bed.

My mate Peter said I screamed a lot when I was awake. I was in hospital for seven months and hospitals are unreal. You're in there and everything is happening on the outside. I wanted to get out and get started. I was wondering what was going to happen to me because no-one had told me what was going to happen when my rehabilitation was finished.

MALCOLM McLEAN

What really hit home, when we got to Richmond in the morning, was they were supposed to have a police escort to get us out to Ingleburn, to the 2 Mil Hospital there. It was early December, it was a really hot day. There were five ambulances I think lined up near the hospital gate ready to go. They had us loaded on the ambulances. We waited in those bloody things for well over an hour and a half and they wouldn't back them into the shade, they wouldn't do anything, and we just sweated in those bloody tin boxes.

A lot of the blokes were in plaster. I was in a spiker cast from the neck to my bloody waist and at that stage an infection had already set in and the wound was starting to weep, it was all starting to run down inside the bloody plaster across my chest and it was unbearable. The stink was like gangrene. More than an hour and a half we stayed there and just out of the blue it hit me: 'Well, shit, is this reality? This is what your country thinks of you.'

In the hospital we were treated like freaks with interesting injuries. At that stage the government had just about washed its hands of us because they knew they'd made an error getting involved in Vietnam, and that made it so much worse for us — we realised we were washed up has-beens that shouldn't have been over there. I was six and a half months in hospital and I chewed this over in my mind time and time again to come to terms with it but I couldn't because it came to the point where nobody wanted to talk about it. I wanted to talk to somebody about it, what we'd experienced, but it wasn't there.

BOB WALKER

I copped some flak in my home town. A woman who taught me at school spat at me. She was in the Save Our Sons. Yeah, spat at me and I adored that woman. The best teacher I'd ever had I thought. You remember one or two teachers in your life and she was a magnificent woman. I didn't think any less of her; she had her axe to grind. It was just surprising more than anything else.

RON EGLINTON

We got down to Bishop Island at the mouth of the Brisbane River and coves just chucked everything overboard: rifles and webbing and uniforms and boots, just straight over the sides of the ship. We came up the river and I can remember the water-side workers turning their backs on us, because they didn't support things up there.

And I can remember the colour. We hadn't seen colour for so long. Everything in Vietnam was sort of black and green and white. We got back to Brisbane in June, winter time, and the people on the wharf were wearing jumpers of reds and blues and yellow.

We grouped in town and marched through the city. It was subdued.

The first year I got back I took my medals into a big department store in town to get them set up, and I bumped into a fellow who had also been at Long Tan and he was there obviously doing the same thing. We exchanged pleasantries, but that was about it. I was a bit embarrassed and he was a bit embarrassed. He pretended to be buying a suit and I pretended to be there getting a haircut. It was terrible.

GEOFF COLLINS

It was mainly what my mates were doing when I came back that was the biggest change. I went over there just before the psychedelic age came in. I came back after two years and all my mates are sitting around smoking pot and I was straight. The music scene had changed a lot. The Thumpin' Tum in the city and Catcher in the Rye were the places to go when I got back. This is when the first of the strobe lights came out and they were illegal. All we got in Vietnam was the American Armed Forces Radio and mostly what they played was Glenn Campbell type of music. You came back from that to Janis Joplin.

PHIL JOHNSTONE

When I first came home I had a bit of a breakdown. They said I'd cracked, bashed the hell out of my father's car. Just snapped. My wife, Kim, was scared of me and she wouldn't stay with me for three or four months and then she'd only come back if I went to see a psychiatrist.

So I went to a psychiatrist in Parramatta, had a yarn to him, and he said, 'Your problem is your mother. Your mother is too domineering.' Oh godfather, I just didn't want to hear this sort of bullshit. My poor mum: I wasn't game to tell her that she was the root of all my problems.

Before I left I was playing football with Parramatta and I had a lot of mates and we had a good time and everything was good, but when I came home I couldn't relate to them, I couldn't talk to them again.

I left when I was playing under-twenty football. I'd just got into fourth grade in Parramatta. I was playing back man and most of my mates were playing second row. I tried to join back in with them but I was out of it. They'd met other girls, and a couple were married. It was just...I was alienated. You just didn't fit back in again.

PETER MOLLOY

After I came back to Concord Hospital I had a nervous break-down. They put me in a room by myself and that was like torture. I couldn't stand it of a night. When a nurse would come into the room I'd plead with her to stay with me and just talk to me. I was frightened.

I had two years in Concord, something like twenty oper-ations: bone grafts, skin grafts, numerous operations trying to get rid of rotten flesh, grafting bones where they had been shattered, trying to get them to knit. Every time they'd come and tell me that I had to have another operation I'd burst into tears because I just couldn't handle pain anymore.

Then I had osteomyelitis bad in my right leg and the infec-tion just wouldn't heal up so they took it off after about twelve months. I can remember when they brought me back from theatre and it still felt like the leg was there. They had the cradle over my leg to keep the weight of the blankets off it and I looked down and saw it was gone and I burst into tears. I was sort of right after that. I knew it was gone.

And then getting addicted to the drugs: morphine, Fortrial, pills. We were asking for pills when we really didn't have pain. It was all in your mind. We used to do a lot of drinking in hospital, under the blankets.

There was no counselling when you were discharged from hospital. It was just, 'That's it, see you later.' I went back to Merriwa, but the blokes back there were just cold. They sort of said hello, but there was not the comradeship there that you had with your other mates, your Vietnam mates. They just didn't seem to accept you back.

I don't think they'd changed. I think it must have been us Vietnam blokes that had changed, but there was nobody to tell us these things.

DAVID COWDREY

We stopped at Butterworth on the way back and they looked after us pretty well there, then the plane took off and landed at Richmond. I was with a guy from Revesby who'd copped a claymore in the hand. I was still really limping bad.

We got put into our beds at the Army hospital in the afternoon and we were woken up at five o'clock in the morning because it was our roster to make toast and a cup of tea for everyone. My mate was in the heebie-jeebies, his hand was all bandaged and everything, and up came this big patient who told me he was a sergeant and our names were scheduled because of the beds we were sleeping in, which I politely told him was a bag of shit: 'I've just got home and I don't feel good.'

They told us that standing orders at the time were we get out of bed and make the coffee and the tea, so I immediately dropped thirty-five plates and seventy-six cups. Me and my mate were taken off that duty pretty quick.

I told them I couldn't stand on my leg because it hurt too much. I kept on complaining to them, something's wrong with my ankle. They said I didn't get hurt in the ankle. I said, 'Look, it swells, it pains, something's wrong with it.' They said, 'Okay, we'll put you in for an exploration at Concord Hospital.'

I let them do everything. I've let them cut into it, I've let them shove big needles in it, I've let them put electrodes onto it for the dead toes that I complained about. This doctor operated on it and he called me a malingerer and said nothing was wrong with it. They moved me into another ward. They said they'd like me to go down there and talk to this psychiatrist about the nightmares I was having.

I became quite friendly with a very old First World War pilot. I woke up one morning about two o'clock and a guy was going through the old man's drawers and I said, 'What are you doing?' He was a wardsman and the old bloke used to leave money and his watch and ring just lying around so I think this guy's having a dip so I kinged him — jumped out of bed and hit him. Next minute another bloke was there and I was in a straitjacket and I was in the illustrious Ward 32. Well, that was the living dream of being a soldier, to have been in overseas service and come back and go into the nut ward.

They had all the old Second World War soldiers there who had cracked, all the drunkards sobering up. I met Sir Francis

Drake, I met a man that had the fear of God in him so when my wife came to visit me someone put a crown of thorns around his head and put roses in his hand and made him lie on the bed so all the visitors could see JC was come back.

They decided I needed occupational therapy. I went down to this little house and everything's cool, I sit down at the table and this lady came out and said, 'Twelve nuts in this plastic bag and twelve bolts in this plastic bag, stamp them "Nock and Kirby's".' Nock and Kirby's was a big company that used to do little packets of things.

I said, 'Why am I doing this?'

She said, 'That's occupational therapy.'

I said, 'I'm a war veteran.'

Up went the table, three thousand nuts and bolts everywhere. In comes a huge warden, Mario, into the jacket again, back to my bed. Bad man this fellow.

Hardly anyone came down to Ward 32. The Red Cross lady was wary, so the sister gave me a job there to keep me occupied. I had to pick up the flowers to bring down to the ward. I always had a morbid fear of funerals and especially cremations and I found out that these flowers were given to them from funerals, so I told them I wasn't going to do it no more.

They said 'You will,' so I ate the flowers and I told them I'd keep eating them. Then they wouldn't let me do it no more, all they'd get back was the stems because I ate the flowers.

They got me to talk to the psychoanalyst and they gave me that ink-spot test. I sat there with this young girl and I opened up the first page, a big black spot, and she said, 'What do you see there?'

I said, 'A big black spot.'

We go to the next one and she said, 'You must have some imagination.' I looked, I can't see nothing there and she says, 'No, you've got to.'

So I turn the page and I start going on about dead bodies and this sheila went crazy with the pen. The next page, all black and green and red: 'This is a man that's been shot close.' The next one: 'Two women arguing over food.' This sheila is having an orgasm about what I've told her and I couldn't see nothing. I got embarrassed because she kept on saying to me, 'You've got to see something, there is something there, look harder,' so I thought, 'Fuck it, all right, I'll tell you what you want to know, I'll play your game.' When I got the report back it said 'raving nut'.

NORMIE ROWE

A teen idol in the sixties, he was conscripted in 1967 and served as an APC driver in Vietnam.

When I came back I did one concert, realised that it was all wrong — I looked around, felt uncomfortable, like I was on a different planet. I didn't know what to do on stage. That was on 1 February, 1970. It was all wrong, so I didn't work again for almost another year. I'd lost two years and it was another four or five years before I really felt confident on stage again.

I just went down to the beach, took my dog and a couple of bottles of Bacardi, and just sat around and beach-bummed for six or eight months. The thing that really woke me up was that I'd committed myself to a house three or four months before I went into the Army and I didn't have any money left. Sooner or later I was going to have to go to work and what else did I know?

For a long time I didn't want to think about Vietnam, because the rest of the population of Australia didn't want to think about it. I said, 'That was two years out of my life, I don't want to know about it any more.'

I hid some things from myself — and I didn't even realise I was doing it. I subconsciously put aside memories of two guys who were close friends of mine who were killed when I was in Vietnam. I put it aside and never thought about it or talked about them.

BERNARD SZAPIEL

When I came back the first reaction my parents had was that here was a man that has no feeling, cold, totally cold. When I'd left I was a really affectionate, home-loving person. I love my parents, I love my sisters — I used to remember their birthdays, special days, gifts, kisses and cuddles — but when they came to pick me up at the airport I just stood there. I didn't want to know. I had no tears, I had no feeling. It was 'I'm here' and that was it.

CHRIS LUCAS

I had changed a bit, like I was nine and a half stone when I came home and I was twelve and a half when I left. I was pretty skinny, pretty ragged-looking. I ripped my uniform off, had a yarn to mother. She got real upset when she saw me, how crook I looked. I went to a party a few weeks later and nobody was interested in anything I said. You could feel it all around you.

A few months later a little kid stepped out of a phone box and he called me a murderer. It turned out to be the son of somebody who I'd known since I was a kid.

ZEV BEN-AVI

I was back six or eight weeks and I took my wife's relatives down to Geelong, in Victoria. There was a whole series of moratoriums in country towns in late 1970 and there was one in Geelong that day. They finished up on the steps of the town hall and these blokes are talking about all these atrocities: killing women and children and using napalm and all the other crap that people used to come out with and, sure, it was true but they were trying to lay it on everybody who went there.

When they were finished anyone who wanted to could go up to the microphone and I thought I can't let this one go by so I got up and I said, 'Everybody is talking about atrocities that our boys are forced to commit in Vietnam. I'd like to set the record straight for a minute. I've just arrived back from Vietnam. I've been in a cavalry unit that saw more of Phuoc Tuy Province than any other unit on the ground because of our role. Now you're trying to tell me that Australian troops are committing atrocities. I'm just going to tell you that I've just spent eleven months, two weeks and three and a half days over there watching those selfsame mothers' sons not committing those atrocities that you say they are doing.' A few people started booing. I said, 'Now before you start booing and carrying on, are you people going to say that I'm talking crap and that you're talking the truth? Because I'm in a position to tell you.

Do you want an eye witness or don't you want an eye witness?' I got a fair hearing, but there was quite an element in the crowd who were yelling out 'baby killer' and 'hey, hey, LBJ, how many boys did you kill today'...the usual expressions.

At that time I couldn't see it, not at all. What atrocities? Despite the fact that I had just participated in a couple. I thought, 'If that's civilians, who wants them?'

RIC

I wandered the streets for about a year, totally confused. I couldn't handle the demonstrations. I was very naive when I came back from Nam, I wasn't politically involved, I had my own little world to live in.

When I got back the first thing I walked into was a demonstration and I got moved along by a policeman. I walked off the train at Spencer Street and I just stopped and I looked. I was very aggravated by what was going on and this cop said to me, 'It's about time you moved along, son.' I looked at him in amazement.

After that it was the confusion. I lost friends, my marriage just disintegrated after Vietnam. I'd get moody, have fits of rage, all that jazz. I'd go through morbid depressions and then I'd get angry and anything would trigger it off.

I went hippy again, absolutely. I mixed with some very neat people. I'd run into a guy in Nam who had a rice farm up in Queensland and he was growing dope so I did about two or three years of touring back and forth from Queensland. He and I shared good company for quite a long time.

I wanted to talk to people about what I went through. I wanted to talk so desperately to someone.

BOB GIBSON

I went straight home to my grandmother's at Kensington and it was the strangest feeling. Everything there was the same, everyone was happy, but I felt different. Everyone was walking on the street like there was no war going on in Vietnam. I mean, it was business as usual, everyone was getting on with life. Even from that day I felt that people thought there was something wrong with me, but for years I wouldn't admit to myself that I had changed. I thought there's something wrong with them motherfuckers, not me.

When I got home the first thing my fiancée's father said to me was, 'How many of the yellow bastards did you kill?' I didn't know what to say. I don't know how many times people have asked me that. I'll never be able to answer that. I still don't know how to answer it. Why does somebody say it?

I got married. We'd got engaged a couple of months before I went to Vietnam. We'd gone together since we were kids. She hadn't changed. She was still the same country girl and she probably thought I was going to be the same country boy.

I wanted to buy a car, but I didn't want to drive in Parramatta Road because there was too much traffic, I couldn't handle that, so I got my cousin to come with me. I bought the car and he drove it back to my grandmother's. Next morning I left with my mother and a friend of hers to go back to Warren, about four hundred mile out west. On the way home this lady friend of my mother's said would we mind if we pulled into the cemetery at Orange, which is halfway. She wanted to see somebody in the cemetery at Orange. And that blew my bubble. I thought, 'No, I don't want to, I don't want to sit around a cemetery.' I didn't say nothing.

They stayed there a half hour. I stayed in the car and I think I cried and then I drove home.

I started drinking heavily and I found myself in the local hotel every night and every day that I wasn't working — getting drunk and getting into fights because there would be something on the television news about Vietnam. Someone would say something like, 'A waste of time you going over there, eh Bomber? They're kicking arse, look at all the bloody Americans they're killing, lost five or six other Australians over there, what a waste of bloody time, you shouldn't have been there in the first place, you just wasted two years of your life.'

And there would be cockies' sons looking at the screen and saying, 'I didn't go, I fooled them; yeah, I got deferred; yeah, I had a bloody good doctor that said I was unfit.'

I felt like I had been used. You'd done something that you thought was expected of you, no more, no less, and the bubble had burst about the grand delusions of the RSL and their little meetings and the hero parades.

I kept hoping that the war was going to be won. I thought it was going to be won in my year and I knew what the fellas who went there in '69 would be thinking, that it might be won in their year.

I hated the people who demonstrated against the war. More than I could ever express I hated those anti-war protesters.

I tried to take up shearing again, but I just never had the patience to put up with kicking sheep. I started getting a rash on my face too and the tension just made it worse. I had to get out of it. I just had to get away from it, from where I was born and bred. What I expected wasn't there, so I left Warren and I tried to hide myself in the city.

I felt that I should have come back with a leg missing or an arm missing. I shouldn't have come back in one piece. I had a terrible time with that. I just felt it wasn't right. I shouldn't have come back in one piece, that something should have been lost. As it turns out something was lost but I couldn't see it.

7

Aftermath

'*This was a war conceived in deceit, nurtured in deceit and it is ending in deceit.*'

Gough Whitlam, 1971

JUDY

She is a widow, who lives in a Victorian country town.

I met John on King Island. He'd been home from Vietnam for two years then. He hadn't been able to live in Melbourne. He had been picked up three times in six weeks for drink-driving when he first came home and he just couldn't cope with Melbourne. King Island seemed an easier place to live. On King Island he was in a lot of fights and he'd lost a lot of jobs, but it wasn't so noticeable down there, among the mining people and the fishermen.

I was pregnant and dad offered him a job up here in the country. He always seemed to want to try and do what he thought was the right thing. He wanted to be a good husband and a good father and do what he thought his family expected of him. He always had ideals that he thought he should live up to, but he just wasn't able to. He was getting really drunk and very violent, very argumentative. I guess I wasn't used to fighting and arguing, the violence. I left John a couple of times but he just seemed to need me so much, he was so dependent on me. But I never felt he gave me anything back.

The Christmas before he died he said he was going to shoot himself and he didn't. He went out with the gun and came back without doing anything. And then he rolled the car and we thought afterwards that probably he'd been trying to run into a tree or something and he just couldn't do it at the last minute.

People up here never accepted him. They're all settled here and quite happy. They don't need a new person as much as a new person needs them. The only people that would have anything to do with him were people that weren't very popular anyway, so he never really fitted in.

He didn't tell me much about Vietnam, just a couple of things that had stuck in his mind. He said they had wrecked a church and he had shot someone who tried to rob him. He had to shoot a little girl because they said she was booby trapped. He was ordered to shoot her and he did. It was something that was hard for him to live with. He said there was an officer who made them keep trying to take a hill that they had no hope of taking and he just kept sending them up and up and they were just getting slaughtered.

John killed himself in February, 1980, just a few days before his birthday.

I thought we'd been getting along pretty well really. I'd gone to work the night before — I worked up at the local hospital — and we were talking quite easily before I went to work. I came home the next morning and went to bed for a few hours while he minded the kids and then he said he was going over to the hotel to get some cigarettes and to ring a man about a job. He didn't come home until three or four hours later, and he didn't say anything but I think maybe he'd rung about the job and hadn't got it. He was pretty desperate to get a job and get out of here. He thought that would solve things.

I forget what we were arguing about now. He came towards me and I sort of jumped back and he didn't like to see me frightened of him, it annoyed him to see that I was frightened, and that made him worse. And then we sort of stopped arguing and I went into the bathroom to try and fix a towel rail that had come down and I could hear him shuffling through the tool box and he'd got this bullet.

I came out and his gun was up on the bench and I said, 'What are you going to do with that?' He said something like, 'You don't need me any more.' He picked up the gun and I said, 'No, you wouldn't do a thing like that,' and he said, 'Pig's arse I wouldn't.'

He just sat down in the chair and put the butt of the gun on the floor and just shot himself. I must have closed my eyes because when I looked at him he was sitting back in the chair.

He didn't die straight away. He lived for about four hours, but I didn't want him to live after that because I thought he'd just see it as another failure and the way he was he couldn't have lived anyway. I'd say his brain was just about a total wreck.

After he died I think I felt what he must have been feeling all along. I couldn't stand anyone to come in here and try to talk to me because I had just so much going around in my head and I think he was that way. I used to sit in the chair like he did and look out the window. I didn't want to go out, didn't want to talk to any people. Lots of things I felt were what I think he probably felt, but I didn't understand at the time.

There's an Eric Bogle song that finishes up with the line, 'I never knew there was worse things than dying,' and that's the way I feel about John, that he didn't have anything else he could do. That was the only way out for him because he had no life the way he was, no future.

BERNARD SZAPIEL

My own experience was one of total unreality. In other words, I never felt that I was there, partly due to the fact that after twelve months you're out ten hours later and back into a totally different environment again. I think the best way to describe it is that it was unreal.

I never killed a person — I'm quite certain of that. If I had the opportunity I would have, I wouldn't have had any qualms, but I was always in the wrong spot at the wrong time.

I feel bitter about the political manipulations which involved Australian troops in Vietnam. I'm also appalled at the political naivety of the whole exercise, even being involved in Vietnam. I'm appalled at the acquiescence of the Roman Catholic Church in condoning those sorts of things, that it's all right to kill.

The thing that I really became involved in after coming back was drinking, and I mean heavy drinking. It wasn't sorrow, it wasn't pity. The only thing I can put it down to is that I wanted to forget something and I don't know what.

I find it very difficult to relate to people now. I don't like going out, meeting people. I don't like talking to people. In fact, if I see someone coming down the street I'll cross the road so I don't have to meet them, and I think to myself, 'What am I doing this for, what's the matter with me?'

Ever since I came back I've been hell-bent on self-destruction. I don't mean outright suicide, although in moments of total desperation if I'd had a gun I think I would have shot myself.

The symptoms that I've got are nausea, dry retching, anxiety, a total inability to concentrate, blurred vision, an inability to take any form of stress or responsibility, loss of appetite — I suppose you could say depression.

I don't feel any self-pity, although occasionally in outbursts when someone says, 'Why are you like this?' I just scream out: 'Well you don't bloody well know what I'm going through.' But then, I don't know what I'm going through myself.

My wife had no idea of what I was going through. I'd come home and just want to be left alone, just totally left alone. I'd break down and cry and then I'd race off to a church at midnight and bang on the parish door for the priest to let me into the chapel just for a bit of peace and quiet.

The priest would look at me as if I was mad. I wanted someone to come up to me and say, 'Can I help you talk to someone, to God?' but this priest would only sit a few aisles back and watch me to make sure that I didn't wreck the church or pinch anything. I found it very difficult to find solace anywhere.

The people I feel for most are the immediate families of the veterans, the wives and the kids. A Vietnam veteran can drown his sorrows but the wife bears the full brunt of the reality that we are going through and so do the kids.

My son is ten. He's got quite severe allergies, very introverted. He's also very aggressive at the same time. I've shown him very little affection. I've found it difficult to relate to him and to my wife. When he's asleep I go into his room and just smother him with affection and kisses, something that I've found very difficult to do. I think to myself, 'You poor kid, why should you be tormented like this?'

If I put a percentage on it I would say it's ruined ninety per cent of my life; that there's about ten per cent left. I'm forty years old now and life has been a misery since I was twenty-four.

PHIL JOHNSTONE

I've lost a daughter. She had only half a heart. That was my first child. David, my eldest boy, he's got perforated ears. He used to lip-read when he was young. He was really a bright kid. He used to lip-read everybody and we didn't realise. We took him to specialists and all they could say was he's a little bit backward or he's a little bit dumb.

We finally got onto it. I think it was about in his second year at school. He was just slipping backwards and backwards. It was hard for him, really hard because all his mates used to call him the dummy. He wasn't. It was just that he couldn't hear properly.

My other son has got incurable skin diseases. They tell me it's hereditary, that's the answer I get from them, but it's nowhere in the family. He comes out in blotches and big scabs. He's also got turned hips, pigeon toes and locked knees.

Kim, my wife, has had three curettes where babies died inside her, and she's miscarried four or five times. She's had a lot of vaginal infections and thrush, that sort of thing. After a while all the antibiotics don't do anything any more.

I don't know whether all these things are associated with the chemicals that were sprayed in Vietnam, but I was definitely sprayed with herbicides and whatever. In fact, I was spraying them myself out of knapsacks. I remember seeing a chopper going over me with a couple of bars hanging out the back and a fog coming off. In 8 Field Ambulance we did fogging every night for mosquitoes and other times we would spray to keep down the weeds. We would mix up the chemicals from one drum to another and away we'd go. I didn't have a clue what was in the drums. They could have told me it was water and I'd have believed them. You did it as a duty. Whether or not that caused problems in my children I really don't know. Everybody just says it's hereditary, all these problems.

I've had health problems too. A valve at the top of my stomach collapsed and they tell me it doesn't usually happen to anyone as young as I am. I used to have a lot of trouble with my eyes when I was driving. I used to work on the road a lot of the time, doing service work, paying off a home, and I'd be driving along and my eyes would be jumping. I couldn't understand what was happening. I went to an eye doctor and he said I had a muscle collapsing in the back of my eyes because of stress.

I work in a coal mine, underground, and I'm happy doing that. I'm playing with 11,000 volts nearly every day, making sure the machines are safe. I think I lost some of my nerve in Vietnam and maybe that's why I work down there, to try and get my nerve back. I don't know. Kim is very good to me. She's stuck by me. A couple of times she's left, times when she had to leave because I couldn't control my emotions, but I think I'd be lost without her.

Vietnam was stupid. Nothing was accomplished as far as I'm concerned, only maiming and killing a lot of people and dumping a whole heap of lead on a nation that didn't really want it.

I've started to worry that if my children have got problems because of me being exposed to chemicals in Vietnam then that could be passed on to their children. I mean, it's like being a leper. Say my kids are meeting their prospective in-laws: 'What did your father do?' 'My father was in Vietnam.' 'Oh, was he? Well, you're not marrying my daughter, mate.'

PETER MOLLOY

I go through stages of depression still. I've contemplated suicide many times. I've had the round up the spout and the barrel against my forehead and my hand on the trigger and just never done it. It's as simple as that. I think about it.

The way the war ended hasn't worried me that much because I know what happened in my mind, I know what went on. It was the politicians that pulled us out. I mean, we won every battle that we ever fought over there. There's not one that we didn't win.

Possibly I still feel bitter about the whole thing, losing my leg, but it's something that happened. I've accepted it. I've got no choice, you've got to accept it. I mean, life's got to go on.

What angers me is the raw deal veterans have had from the Department of Veterans' Affairs, the politicians, the whole Australian government. What they've done for the Vietnam veterans is pathetic. It doesn't matter what you do, you've got to fight for everything.

You go to doctors and all they're interested in is prescribing anti-depressants, sleeping pills, Valium. Whatever you want, virtually.

I've had hell's own trouble with grog. Fits of rage, of temper. I don't know what it is that sparks it off. You go beserk, you throw things, you drive your fist through wardrobe doors, smash things, anything or anybody that gets in your way.

It got to the stage where Gail was being abused with these rages of temper and me full of grog. Then the shame of doing things like that, that gets to you. There's something there, just some sort of inner force driving you to do these type of things. I mean, I was fortunate. I never knuckled my wife, but I slammed her against walls in rages of temper like you wouldn't believe.

It worked out all right. She stuck with me and I now try my best to control my drinking and I don't seem to have those bad fits of rage like I used to.

Was it worth it? No, definitely not. We didn't achieve anything over there, blokes were killed, blokes were maimed physically and mentally, which in turn has affected other people's lives. You only have to talk to some of the wives of Vietnam veterans — the hell that they've been through and their kids.

I am bitter about it, for the simple reason that they used us, just used us. A political pawn, that's all we were.

It doesn't matter what you do through life, if you have a go at something and give it your best shot and you lose you can accept it. But when you give it your best shot and you've been used the whole time, I mean why wouldn't we be bitter.

The only thing I gained out of it was the comradeship of all my mates and I mean they're mates, there's a real bond there.

RON WITTY

Vietnam to me was an experience, it's part of my life, it happened, but it's over. It finished in '75 when Saigon fell. I don't re-live any part of Vietnam, I don't have nightmares about Vietnam, I don't have bitter recollections or flashbacks as some of the blokes do. I'm just facing the problems I've got now and that's enough for me. The problems I've got now make Vietnam look like a teddy bears' picnic.

Up until 1982 I didn't think there was anything in the chemical issue, even though in '77 or '78 I was told by a doctor I had chemical poisoning due to Vietnam. I couldn't believe it, I didn't believe it. I just thought it was a cop out because I've got a brother — or I had a brother, who was also a Vietnam veteran — he started to go troppo about '74 or '75. He ended up in a psychiatric hospital — the same sort of things that I went through six years after him. I used to think to myself that he was just using the problems created through Vietnam as a cop out. There are still times when I say to myself is it a cop out or is it the truth? I don't know. I've been told by doctors that I've got problems and I've got to try and live with them and that they are related to Vietnam service through exposure to chemicals.

I went over in '67–68, and about the time I got back my father went over also and then my brother straight away. They were there in '68–69. My father died a couple of months ago from cancer. He was diagnosed earlier in the year and died in August and my brother committed suicide, self-destructed in '81.

I tried to OD on sleeping tablets, grog and a bit of dope. My marriage had split up, I felt that there was no-one to turn to, no-one to help me, a feeling of isolation I suppose. I think you decide to do something like that and then suddenly you cry out for help, or you want the world to know that you're going out.

I've got rashes under the arms, groin. I get headaches all the time. They get bad. Flashes of temper. It's like a boiler without a pressure–release valve. It builds up and builds up until it explodes. Sometimes with me it takes two weeks, other times it might take six weeks but eventually I explode. I can't mix with people. I've got no sex drive. At one stage I went to the doctor to give me hormone injections, which didn't work. I was married twice. My first wife had quite a few miscarriages. That was back in the early '70s.

I used to pick on the kids, isolate myself from their lives, behave irrationally until it got to a stage where they just couldn't take any more. Unfortunately I realised the problem just a little too late. That's the trouble, when you are having these problems you don't realise it until it is too late.

I was prepared to go back to Vietnam a second time. I didn't because my father and my brother went over there and it got to the stage where it started to destroy my mother. I couldn't have done it to her again. It killed her eventually. In '78 she died from alcohol poisoning. While we were in Vietnam she started to take to the bottle and we were never able to break her of the habit. So really, in my family, it's killed three members and it's only left half of the fourth.

DAVID MILLIGAN

He was a load master with the Airforce in Vietnam in 1970–1.

My main problems were when I got home. I was posted back to 38 Squadron and one of the first times that I had an anxiety attack I was walking down to lunch one day — everything just tilted, as if the whole world had tilted, and I had to grab something. I didn't know what it was, I thought there must be something wrong with my eyes. But after that first one, which was, I suppose, three days after I got back off leave after Vietnam, it just got worse and worse.

I was afraid to walk anywhere, I couldn't stand in a queue, I was afraid to go on parade and I'd be irritable at home, get sick in the stomach for no reason at all. I'd just vomit and vomit until I was that weak I'd just collapse.

I was up on the wing of an aeroplane and I was that scared they had to come and carry me down.

It's hard to explain to someone the feeling in the pit of your stomach. It's a sick, welling feeling — a feeling of helplessness, a feeling that you're going to die.

PETER VANDENBERG

Our first child was born with gross brain abnormalities. If she had lived she would not have been pleasant to look at and she would never have been any good. She would have been permanently and totally retarded and the doctor said that in a sense it was a blessing that she only lived for nine hours.*

ALAN ASHMORE

My skin rash was so bad at times I was losing up to ten layers a week off my face and neck. I was like a lizard. I'd peel in pieces. I had breathing problems with bronchial asthma, conjunctivitis, severe headaches. Tests done by private practitioners showed I had abnormal electroencephalographs, defective chromosomes, abnormal visual-evoke responses. Tests done by Veterans' Affairs at the same time failed to detect any problems at all.

It just got worse and worse until by 1980, '81 I was having a little bit of trouble coping with things. I was getting to the stage where I would break into a sweat for no reason at all, I was hardly sleeping of a night.

*Peter Vandenberg died from a heart-attack, aged forty-three, in September, 1986.

Our eldest boy has been diagnosed as having acute lymphatic leukaemia, and I have been told by a doctor that the cancer could be directly attributable to my exposure to chemicals in Vietnam. I guess I find that pretty abhorrent.

The other thing that peeves me off is that from March '79, when questions were first being asked in Parliament about Australians using herbicides in Vietnam, the government continually denied all knowledge of it. I guess it was on that basis that a lot of us decided that we should pursue the class action in the United States. It wasn't until December '82, when Sinclair as Defence Minister tabled his report in the Parliament, that the government for the first time admitted that we had used herbicides. So from March '79 to December '82 complete denial. Why did they tell lies for so long?

A lot of insurance companies won't touch Vietnam veterans, a lot of employers won't touch Vietnam veterans either. In fact, you ask any Vietnam veteran, when they go for a job, do they say they're returned servicemen, which is supposed to help you? Vietnam veterans don't mention that they've ever been to Vietnam because employers don't want Vietnam veterans.

I guess as a Christian I've always believed any experience in life is worth living provided you don't bear permanent scars, up until the late '70s I didn't believe there were any permanent scars, but I guess we're going to reap the repercussions for years to come.

BOB MILLARD

For so long I just never told anyone I was a veteran. I didn't want to talk about it, I felt no-one else wanted to talk about it. When I joined the Vietnam Veterans Association I took a step towards saying that 'I am a Vietnam veteran and I respect the fact that I am.' A lot of blokes have tried to forget about Vietnam, but you really can't take a year or two out of your life and pretend it didn't happen.

The blokes from the Second World War probably went through the same thing, but when it was over they came back to a fanfare. They had done something, they had won a war and freed the world. All we had done was stuff up a country and kill a lot of people. You had to live with that. It was a dirty war. I suppose all wars are dirty, but Vietnam was the first one that was shown on television.

MARK ROSE

I copped a lot of flak when I came back. Family friends or people I knew wouldn't talk to me. I had an uncle who didn't think we should have been in Vietnam, who openly wished me dead, all because I'd been a soldier in Vietnam and I had volunteered to go there. Here's me still trying to wave the flag saying, 'We were right, we were right, we were right,' and at that stage the whole country was saying, 'You were wrong, you were wrong, you were wrong.' That really affected me.

When I joined the Army I was looking for a great cause and a great purpose and a great adventure, but it had to be right. Like, good guys versus bad guys and I would be one of the good guys. And then you came back saying, 'Jesus, were we?'

I went back to school to see if I could do something. I lasted about a term. I went to Queensland for a short time, couldn't get work there, then I went up to New Guinea where I was loading planes. From there I flew to Manila, got a visa and went back to Vietnam.

I'd been away from the place for a couple of years, but the war wasn't yet at the winding-down stage. I didn't know what I'd find specifically. I wanted to have a look at it again. I'd only seen it as a soldier, just the heat and the stink of the bush. And part of me wanted to get back into it, to go there and somehow grab the flag again and go charge up the hill and do something.

I had known a girl there too and I wanted to see if she was all right. I was just so uptight about the whole thing.

I went from Saigon to Vung Tau by taxi, looked up members of the Training Team and went back to Nui Dat, which at that stage was virtually disbanded except for SAS Hill. I found all the buildings pulled down, cattle wandering through the place, all the wire trampled down. There was a unit of ARVN up on SAS Hill and that was all.

It was such a transition. When I was there as a soldier it was such a bustling place. It was a small compound if you compared it with places the Americans had at Long Binh or something like that, but for the Australian Army it was a big place where there were troops and vehicles and aircraft coming and going. It was a military camp.

I went back to where our company area had been and there were still signs hanging around with the number of enemy kills on them, but it was non-existent, everything else was gone. It left me with a very empty feeling. It was like saying here we were and it was for nothing.

I went north to Dalat, Qui Nhon, Danang and I went to Hue, the imperial city. I was there for a couple of days and I felt like something sort of beautiful had been smashed up.

I went back to Saigon after that, then to Phnom Penh in Cambodia and then I flew to Vientiane in Laos. I had it in my mind to go back into Vietnam for POWs. I don't know how I was going to do it. That's the way my mind was. I was all screwed up.

I had a fixation with Vietnam for a long time, until it went under. When that happened I threw all my campaign medals in the Yarra and burnt my mention in despatches. I've been out of work since November '83. I've got an alcohol problem and according to the psychs a personality disorder. I've been at Heidelberg Repatriation Hospital and Bundoora psychiatric hospital. When I got sent to Bundoora I thought, 'Fuck, you've hit rock bottom now.' I'll be forty this year. I receive a pension that says I'm temporarily incapacitated.

MICHAEL

I was involved in South Africa for a few years after I came back from Vietnam. It was the only other place paying. There were two places paying well in those days, that was South Africa or Vietnam again.

I could have gone back to Vietnam. I had an airfare paid to go back and a job lined up as soon as I'd gained my discharge here, employed by the Americans. If you had your wits about you over there it was easy to get a job lined up, if you were quite serious and you had the right skills.

I decided not to go back. I could see that things were folding up, from what things were like in-country before we pulled out. I had a feeling it wouldn't have been a nice place to have gone back to for very long. I couldn't see surviving there for too long. I had a great distrust of the people and the politics of the country, and I knew there was no way the South Vietnamese government could control the country after the Americans and the Australians and the other allies had pulled out. I didn't see a great future there.

I was contracted to go to South Africa. I was attached to the Rhodesian Light Infantry for a while and then the Grey Scouts. The majority of the RLIs in those days were mercenaries, if you like to call them that, and the Grey Scouts were virtually the same, but a more elite unit.

I guess I was looking for the fulfilment I felt in Vietnam, and the enjoyment as well, and there was communism involved so that was a good excuse. I still hate communism.

I didn't like what was going on there, sure, but there wasn't nobody paying me better over here.

I'll always look back on it as one hell of an experience and one that I would not have missed. I enjoyed what I was doing; I was good at my job and I did it well. If you could say you love another man I guess there are blokes that I really loved spending that time with and had a deep feeling for and wouldn't forget. You had to be there to make friends like that.

JOHN QUINCEY

I don't work. I get the service pension. I've got a deterioration of the heart muscle, called a cardiomyopathy. There are many causes for it, but in my case they couldn't pinpoint a cause. It could have been caused by chemicals or infective agents or a virus that I contracted in Vietnam and lay dormant all these years. My hearing has slowly deteriorated. Up until about 1972 big blisters used to break out on my feet and around my ankles and just fill up with pus.

That went away and now I get a rash like dermatitis on my hands and in my groin and under my arms. I have sleeping problems. I take sleeping pills now to sleep. The little girl was born with a murmur of the heart but things seem to be okay now.

The first ten years after Vietnam there wouldn't have been a week go past without me having a dream about Vietnam. The dream always ended with me firing a gun and the bullets not reaching the enemy. They'd be coming towards me and the bullets would always pour out the end of the gun and never reach them.

Once, the kids gave me a shirt on Father's Day. It was the day after Father's Day and for some bloody reason something upset me and I got the shirt and I ripped it into pieces. My wife just stood there with her mouth open and after I had done it I couldn't believe that I had done it. I just couldn't believe it.

RAY STOCK

I woke up the other day and realised I am thirty-nine years of age. Where did my twenties and thirties go? As far as enjoying my life I feel that it stopped at twenty-two, when I came back from Vietnam.

BARRY ROE

I was asleep and I just looked at the doorway and he was there, a young Vietnamese bloke, the typical nog you'd see hanging around Vungers or any of the villages, Baria or anywhere like that.

He had a little bit of a fringe, the jet-black hair parted down the centre, a full-grown moustache and trying to grow a beard down the side, a typical nog face. He was only a short arse, only a little fella. It just scared the hell out of me when I saw him there.

There's other times when I've had an imaginary gun in the bed with me and he's been standing there, and as I've grabbed the gun to shoot him he just disappears. Then I start screaming and my wife will wake me up and I'm saying, 'He was at the doorway', and she's saying, 'No-one's there.' When I see him I think I'm fully awake, but I know it's in my dreams. I can see everything as plain as day and he's just standing there. He's not smiling or nothing, he's just there and he's saying sometimes, 'I've come to get you.'

RAY CALDWELL

I find that today, all these years later, I don't go anywhere near Richmond in Melbourne because it reminds me now of the streets of Saigon. I still hate them, you see.

FRANK HUNT

I'm one of the fortunate ones. People can see me wearing callipers and they can see the way I walk with a limp and they say, 'Poor bastard, look what happened to him in Vietnam.' But the veteran who is suffering from anxiety or depression or who is in and out of mental homes, they call him a malingerer.

There was a fellow on Anzac Day in Narooma last year. He arrived at the cenotaph in jeans and a black T-shirt with his medals hanging off this black T-shirt. The last post was playing and he broke ranks, jumped down an embankment and stopped the traffic on the Princes Highway. He took his medals off and threw them on the highway and then he started to kick and punch cars. No-one wanted to know him.

BOB WALKER

I go to Anzac Day, but I don't wear medals. I keep them in my pocket to get into a room or something.

I did wear them once and I came face to face with an old guy in Victoria, at Mordialloc RSL, and this guy had I think about five rows of six medals on each row and he said, 'Put those things in your pocket, son.' This guy had everything, he was unreal. 'We earned it,' he said. '*You* didn't. Wait until you've earned some.' He was an old Rat of Tobruk so I guess he was entitled to say that.

MORGAN QUINN

I have trouble sleeping, I've got headaches all the time, hot and cold chills, rashes. I'm forty-three and I feel like an old man.

I was from a pretty quiet Catholic family. I had government jobs in Mackay up until I joined the Airforce. I did four years of college.

I played a lot of sport when I was young — Rugby League and athletics and boxing. I was always sports-minded. I've got cups for athletics and for football. I was captain of the Point Cook Rugby League team in '64. I never was a slob before Vietnam. I wasn't born to be a slob.

Going to Vietnam was the worst thing I could have ever done in my life. I feel so guilty about everything. Guilty for leaving Diane and the kids here on their own for a war that was unnecessary and unjust and I don't know whether if we'd have won it would have made any difference either.

I got out of the Airforce in October '72 and we went to Queensland and I fucked up. I was still on the piss then and I screwed up quite a bit there. I was in a partnership that busted up because me and the other bloke were on the grog, then I worked for myself for a while and couldn't make a go of it, then I was picking pineapples. I did quite a few things, job to job, but couldn't hold them.

I ended up working for a bloke that had a pig farm. I used to sleep in his little shed out the back and he'd give me a few dollars, enough to keep me in piss and my keep, which wasn't that much.

I came back to Melbourne and got a job with the Government Aircraft Factory. I had that for three years, the longest job I ever had.

My missus was always telling me that there was something wrong with me, that I wasn't just a slob but I needed help. I tried AA when I was up in Queensland, but I only ever went twice. I didn't cop the way they ran their meetings.

I started a boxing gym in the backyard, because there's not much for kids in this area. I did pretty well at that. I had a few Victorian champions and I took Lester Ellis to three Australian championships. I had to give it away though. I couldn't handle the nervous side of it and the noise and the kids' parents. Lester was a responsibility, too.

I was in the nut house three times, out at the Repatriation

Hospital. The first time was for three months.

Whenever I go out I always carry a knuckle-duster and a flick-knife. I don't know why. The area's not the best, but that's not the reason. I don't like people. I don't like being around people.

I've stressed all along to the doctors and psychiatrists at the Veterans' Affairs and at the Repat that I never ever fired a shot in anger, I was never out in the jungles fighting like the infantry were. I get a pension for post-traumatic stress, but I believe I was poisoned by chemicals, not frightened.

JIM CHALLENGER

I get a fifty per cent pension for nerves and a lower spinal injury. I've got Meniere's disease, epilepsy, high blood pressure, neuro-dermatitis across the stomach and back of the neck that comes out every twelve months. I have bad dreams, I sweat at night, I get very depressed at times and want to get away from everyone.

They say, 'Forget about Vietnam, forget about Vietnam,' but the point is it keeps coming back into my mind all the time.

I had a nervous breakdown about two years after I came back. They shoved me in hospital for a bit over a week. My nerves were just shattered. I was sitting there one night and I just broke down, couldn't do anything about it, burst out crying. I was thinking about back there, Vietnam.

BARRY and SUE KELLY

SUE: We went to school together, grew up together. He was always placid-natured, always a practical joker, good for a laugh, never a dull moment. When he came back he was more serious, which you'd expect. You can't see your mates blown up and not have fits of depression now and again. That's what I put it down to. He didn't drink heavily to start off with. As the years wore on there were family pressures, more kids, work pressures, then he started to drink, then the violence started.

BARRY: I'm still very confused about the whole issue. I was so sure that we did the right thing, that we were the good guys. When we left Garden Island we had a ticker-tape reception, we had streamers hanging down from the aircraft-carrier, an escort ship and there was a big water cannon going and bands playing; it was razzmatazz like you wouldn't believe: speeches, crowds and hallelujah baby you're the greatest thing since sliced bread. There was none of that when we came home. When we came back we were lower than the little earthworm.

SUE: I used to always go and clean up the broken glass and explain that it had got broken accidentally or dropped off the shelf or something. I covered for him, because nobody would have believed it.

The kids never knew anything about it until he came home one night and turned the place upside down. He had me up against the door and the youngest boy, Darren, flew at him with a penknife. That was enough to stop him. I left everything the way it was. He woke up before I did, I was asleep on the couch, and he saw all the mess. He said, 'I want you to tell me what I did.' I got to the point of saying, 'Your son was going to kill you.' He just cracked, broke down and said, 'Ring the shrink.' He was at the Repat for six weeks.

BARRY: The rash comes and goes. That's been with me during Nam and since Nam and it just doesn't go away. It was a prickly rash and you didn't worry about it too much, you just got used to it after a while. But the headaches were the big thing. It was headaches followed by everything else. Headaches went into tantrums went into rage and when you got aggressive and smashed up the joint you'd then go into a depression. It just went round and round and round and the only way out was to hit the bottle. Hit it hard and hit it fast and every day.

SUE: I was three days in labour with the first child. She weighed only eighteen pounds at twelve months, had a tightened stomach muscle and congenital heart disease. The second child has had two operations for deafness and has a heart murmur. The third one has a curvature of the spine and pelvis, a heart murmur and she suffers from rashes. And the fourth one has undefined skin rashes, asthma, hyperactivity, learning difficulties and deafness.

Fred, the eldest boy, he never seemed to do as he was told. The two girls would do as they were told but he never seemed to, so he would get a smack. He was asked, then he was warned, then he was smacked. And I could see the look of disillusionment on his face, wondering why. But then he would look at the girls and realise what they had done and he would copy his older and younger sisters. That's the part that hurts. I'd pick up the two girls and cuddle them and I was always calling him a naughty boy: 'You don't listen, you won't do as you're asked.'

To find out that he was deaf, I still feel the guilt. We had a specialist who was a great guy. He was about six feet tall and six feet wide and he just hugged him and said, 'You poor little bastard, you've gone through hell.'

BARRY: One minute you were the hero and the next minute you're the villain. You go back to '64. You do your basic training, you win awards. Three awards they had there, you take two of them. Your dad comes up to watch you march out after fifteen weeks and he sees a kid turn into a man. He sees this kid march out with the rest of the platoon and lead the platoon. That's not too bad. Whatever you did you put your best into it and did as best you could for the service, for the corps and for yourself. You'd wear your uniform home with all the decor- ations on it and people respected the uniform and they'd always say g'day to you. You'd get onto a train or a tram and it was always 'G'day digger.' It was something that was good.

And then after Nam, after we came back from that, things were so different. You couldn't wear your uniform because of the moratoriums. They handed out leaflets at state schools about the war in Vietnam so everybody from the kids in nappies upwards were against us. All of a sudden all of Australia, it seemed, turned against us. When we came home the word Vietnam was a dirty word and the words Vietnam veteran were words of derision. You didn't say the words Vietnam veteran, you spat them out.

WAYNE

I'm only thirty-six years of age. I'm separated from my wife because she's got sick and tired of me. When she brought me to the hospital last time she told them that unless they can get me a hundred and fifty per cent fit she doesn't want me back. She said she didn't care whether they put me in a hole, or scrapped me, but she didn't want me back. I've got a little girl. She hates me now because I tried to commit suicide.

We were in the gardens in the city and there were Australian and Vietnamese kids there and I freaked out. I thought I saw the little Vietnamese girl I wanted to bring to Australia. I was crying my eyes out and I went up and kissed one of these Vietnamese kids and the teacher went crook on me.

I can't hold a job, I've got no future. Thirty-six years of age and I'm rooted.

MALCOLM McLEAN

I burnt all my Army gear when I got discharged. The only thing I kept was the overcoat, mainly for wet days. The slouch hat, the battalion lanyards and all that, I just had a sacrificial fire one afternoon.

It was just something that got in my head. I didn't want anything else to remind me of it and I just burnt the lot in the backyard, threw it all in the drum and doused it. I felt like part of the crazy system that got me involved in the first place was being burnt along with it. I felt that's part of your life that's behind you and you've got to try now and get on with the rest of it.

Everything that I grew up and believed in and was taught from an early age was a lie. Everything from school, right through the whole system.

Vietnam was a country that had known no unification. All those people had known was foreign intervention, foreign invasion. All they wanted was their own self-determination, their own democracy, their own freedom. We would do exactly the same thing in this country. Americans did it two hundred years ago.

JIM RICHMOND

He served as an infantry soldier in Vietnam in 1966. He lives at Mt Isa, Queensland, and works as a fitter in the mine.

I still get bad dreams, my chest plays up quite a bit. If I see things on TV I might start bawling. I've got to walk out of the room quite often. I just start crying and I like to be alone when I'm crying. Well, I suppose it's a bit embarrassing, although I'm not ashamed of it. Sometimes in my dreams I can see the blokes' faces again, my mates who were killed there. I try to tell them it's only a dream, that I'm only dreaming and when I wake up they'll wake up too. Others are a bit worse, but that's the one I dream most. I just see their faces all the time.

MICK and MAREE CRAWFORD

MICK: There have been times when I've treated Ree and the kids really bad, flown off the handle for no reason at all. Since I got home I've tried lots of things. I went into business with the old man and I couldn't make that work. It just seems that every time I'm going to get up something knocks me down again.

MAREE: I left him. We separated for eight months. There wasn't a lot of physical damage, it was more emotional because I couldn't talk to him. I didn't understand it either, I didn't know what was happening to him. Mick rarely, even now, speaks about Vietnam and I didn't know what he went through.

He is a totally different guy than the one who went to Vietnam. I've known Mick since I was eleven years old and before he went over he was playing in a band and real sort of happy-go-lucky. Nothing really bothered him that much and he really got on well with people. That's one problem I've noticed since he came home: Mick can't make friends, he doesn't like to get involved with other people.

MICK: I was on the dole for twelve months and I couldn't be bothered finding a job because that meant I had to get out amongst people again. I just didn't want to leave here. I was quite happy just to sit here with Ree and the kids and not see anybody.

I didn't want to make any friends because something might happen to them, like things happened to them in Vietnam. So I'd just sit out here on my little farm and fool around with my animals and I was quite happy.

MAREE: When he first came home from Vietnam it was great, but I miscarried between the birth of the two boys and I think our problems started then. It's hard to describe the problems. They're just little things. I'd leave him tomorrow if it wasn't for the kids.

I blame myself. I should be able to cope better with his moods, his anger. But I can't. I'm only human.

MICK: I often think, 'Should we have been there, why were we there?' We should have been able to do more. Sometimes I think other people are right when they say that we just wasted our time. It's still communist now isn't it. I mean, we didn't change a damn thing.

I guess I feel that the government owes us something somewhere along the line. They've knocked us back on everything we've gone for and these Second World War guys go up there and get the lot. I mean they deserve it too, don't get me wrong, but the unfairness of it, just because theirs was a great war.

AL ROBINSON

He served in Vietnam in 1965.

I used to work with a young chap down at the Royal Brisbane Hospital when I was with security. I think he was in Vietnam with 6RAR in 1966.

We used to talk about it quite a lot, Vietnam. He always used to think about it. Every discussion we used to have would always be about Vietnam. Nothing about the security of the hospital or anything like that. He'd start talking about Vietnam.

Finally he took his own life. He bought himself an automatic .22 pistol and taped back the sear and pulled the trigger on himself one night. They don't know whether it was the first round or the other six that killed him.

BRUCE and DIANE POULTON

BRUCE: All my nightmares are about Vietnam. I'll wake up screaming, yelling out. If I wake up in a dark room, out of a nightmare, it's very hard for me to orientate myself and get back to reality. A lot of times I'll sleep in the lounge-room with the TV going so I can relate.

DIANE: I met Bruce in Newcastle when I was twenty-one. He'd not long come back from Vietnam and I suppose he struck me as sort of different from anybody else I'd ever met, very aggressive. I'd been married before to a really docile sort of person and I think his aggressiveness seemed mannish; it intrigued me a little.

I was having problems with my divorce and I decided to go away for a while and when I came back Bruce was in hospital with an overdose. That was my first experience with him OD-ing, before we ever got together as a couple.

He'd taken all these pills, fallen over and cut his ear half off. I went down there and he looked terrible. They sent him off to Concord and he was there for three or four months. I used to go down every weekend. He was pretty bad that time.

BRUCE: I got shot out of a lot of towns for fighting, breaking into joints, shit like that. I didn't give a fuck about nothing. I had no morals. All my morals were knocked out of me when I was nineteen.

I was in Darwin in jail and I tried to hang myself. I had nothing to jump off so I just sat down. I tied a blanket around my neck and on the bar and sat down, tried to slowly strangle myself. Then I started OD-ing and crap like that. That started about 1973.

I've been in jail forty times I suppose, mainly for drunkenness, assault. I've been separated from Diane three or four times. I've tried to kill myself maybe ten times, as recently as three weeks ago. I swallowed fifty Sinequan tablets that should have killed me. I parked the car in the scrub and dropped them, but I'd been drinking and I vomited them up.

DIANE: When he started really going off I thought, 'God, what have I struck here?' I could never understand and I'd think, 'Why is he doing this to me, why?' I'd sit there and I'd cry and I'd carry on and he'd be swinging telephones around the room and smashing walls.

There was one particular night he went right out of his tree.

He had me in a corner and he was totally somewhere else, and I thought I'm gone, I'm really gone. He was screaming at the top of his voice, 'You don't understand, you don't understand.' I don't know exactly the words he was saying, but he wasn't looking at me, he wasn't talking to me. He seemed to be talking to someone else. He wasn't yelling out like he was in gunfire in the bush or anything like that, but he was somewhere else in his own mind.

BRUCE: I woke up after taking an overdose of Valium and someone with glasses was talking to me and he says, 'We're sending you to hospital.' It didn't dawn on me that he was talking about sending me to a lock-up ward at Morisset psychiatric hospital.

When I woke up again there were four coppers plus a doctor and he said to me again that I was going to Morisset and I said, 'I'm not going.' A copper, who was the oldest of the four, put his hand on my shoulder and said, 'You have to go.' They walked me out by the arms because someone had hit me with a needle. I could feel myself starting to move backwards.

When we got to the hospital they took me in and they said things like, 'Here's another one for you.' They took me and locked me in a cell.

They give you pyjamas, and the tops are a different colour from the pants and they're too big for you. They shower you and shave you. They watch you all the time. They take you out to the meal room and you sit at a table where they've got your name written. And when you've finished, and all the knives and forks and spoons and plates are accounted for, they tell you to stand up, put the chairs up on the table, then they march you out into this room where they lock you up all day. Everything is locked up. You just sit there, or you might go out to the courtyard and there would be blokes punching one another out. It's a real weird joint.

The next day I wasn't too bad. I was starting to think a bit clearer and that was bad because all these other people stayed the same. They're mad and they're going to stay that way for the rest of their lives, punching shit out of one another.

I talked to two shrinks and they said that they couldn't see any reason why I should be in that place, that the only problem I had was that I went to Vietnam.

It blew me out being put in Morisset and it's on my record

now that I was committed on a Schedule 2A, which means 'committal under police escort'. No-one would ever put me back in there.

DIANE: I think I've become hard. There was nothing that Bruce could do to me one time that would make me turn against him — and he's tried a lot of things — but now I find it harder to be compassionate and feel sympathy. I switch off. It's just that if you don't close your mind off you'll go insane yourself. I've got to the point where I'm angry about the whole thing. No-one will do anything about it, no-one can give me any answers. Now if he says something about Concord Hospital or he wants to talk about overseas I say, 'I don't want to hear it, don't tell me about it, I don't want to know.' I have heard it and heard it for twelve years until I am fed up with hearing it.

BRUCE: You feel sort of hopeless. There doesn't seem to be a purpose to your life. I'll be thirty-six in August. I should be a confident, well-adjusted, secure family man with a future. I shouldn't have to rely on talking to shrinks to get through a day, I should be able to work things out for myself. I shouldn't have to rely on the government for money. My kids work money out as 'cheque days'. 'We can't have anything this week because it's not cheque day.' At thirty-six you shouldn't have to live like that.

When I see other veterans suffering I suffer with them, because I know what they go through. I think about different people that I've known and how they are today. I saw them going over there and they were young, confident people and today you see them and they're cracking up and crying and there's no answer to it. What you feel is that there's really no answer.

DIANE: It seems like they can't get rid of their anger, their hate. Have you ever looked in their eyes? It frightens me.

BOB GIBSON

Doug was one of the few blokes that ever really talked about how he wanted to march on Anzac Day when he got home. The one thing he wanted to do was march in front of his father and mother on Anzac Day and show everybody how proud he was. We used to talk about that a lot, and we made a pact if anything happened to him I was to visit his parents and if anything happened to me he was going to do the same.

He was killed, and when I got home, with the anti-war protests and stuff going on, I just couldn't go down to Victoria and see his parents. I thought, 'What do they think about him dying, do they think he was worthwhile, are they marching with the people in Melbourne, are they with the activists that are against the war?' The last thing I wanted was to knock on a door and to have somebody related to a mate of mine that had been killed there throw something at me or abuse me or something like that.

I used to march on every Anzac Day and it was the most emotional and the most harrowing day I'd ever put in. But I wouldn't miss it because I wasn't marching really so much for myself, I was marching more for Doug because he didn't get back.

It was like carrying a bag of wheat on each shoulder because I had never gone down to see his parents, I didn't know where he was buried, I didn't know whether he'd had a full military funeral, I didn't know if he'd got everything he deserved. I don't know really, honestly, how one of those Anzac Days I didn't commit suicide. I almost did it. I don't know why I didn't because right through the march and afterwards, having a drink with the fellas, I used to think about him, wonder where he was buried, wonder what his parents thought.

In my mind I fantasised that they were fantastic Australian people, that they were the real good dinky-di Aussie people that he was — and they must have been because he was a great bloke.

I started going to this psychiatrist about seven years ago, in Macquarie Street, and he said that even though it was going to be a lot of pain to me that I should make an effort to track down his family even after all those years and make peace with myself and make peace with them if that was the case.

I finally went down to his mum and dad's place and it was the typical Australian house: weatherboard, little wire fence out the front. I opened up the front gate and it was unbelievable. I walked in that thing and it was something that I knew I should have done regardless of anti-war protesters, regardless of opinions. I knew it was something I should have done for myself and for Doug years and years before.

I knocked on the door and his father said, 'You must be Bob Gibson.' I said, 'Yeah, I am.' He said. 'Welcome. Come on in, mum's in here waiting to meet you.'

I walked in and the lounge-room was like a shrine to Doug. They had a big photograph of him on the wall the same way as I remembered him, as a twenty-year-old. He hadn't aged. And even in the dreams I have now he's still twenty and I'm the age I am now. There were all those photographs of him up across the mantelpiece and I thought, 'Jesus, he's going to walk out into the room here in a minute.'

His mother came over and gave me a hug and a kiss and said, 'It's been a long time,' and I said, 'Yeah, I know. I should have done it a long time ago.'

The sister came across and the brother was there and they brought out some letters that Doug had written home about me and what we were going to do when we got together. His sister said, 'You remember Doug telling you that I was going to have a baby?' I said, 'Yeah, oh Jesus we got drunk that night. He was so happy you were going to call him Douglas Jnr.' And she said, 'Dougie, come in here,' and this thirteen-year-old boy walked in: 'This is Douglas Jnr.' Oh Jesus, it was unreal.

His father took me aside later on when my wife and his mother and sister were talking and he said, 'You know what happened to Doug's younger brother, don't you?' I said, 'No, I don't. What happened?' He said, 'Well, he turned eighteen and joined the Army, and every time he was off duty he would go to the Springvale crematorium and he'd sit by his brother's grave. He was the youngest one and he always looked up to his brother, being a soldier. He wanted to be a soldier like his brother. He never got over his brother's death — none of the family did. In 1975 he shot himself with a .303, right through the heart.'

At the end of the day I went to the cemetery and I walked over to the grave-site and I stood there and the feeling...I still can't explain the feeling of not just seeing Doug there but his younger brother buried alongside him and I thought, 'My God, what has this war done?'

GARRY

I had this dream the other night. It was just a lot of bodies and then more bodies and then more bodies. I wasn't involved. I don't know where it was. It was just a war where they sent them in and they got mowed down, and they would send another lot in and they would get mowed down and it was just a never-ending procession of people coming up to die. I was just on the sidelines looking on, had no involvement with either side and the blood just kept on getting higher and higher where I was standing. I can't honestly remember where it ended. When the blood got up pretty high it just stopped. It was vivid. It was like I was there.

TOMMY BROWN

It was really good to get home, but people would always point the finger at you about things you were supposed to have done over there. They'd call you a rapist and a murderer and you'd think, 'Christ, what are they having a go at me for? I didn't kill anyone over there.' You think, 'Am I going to be condemned all my life because I went to Vietnam?'

TREVOR MORRIS

You could never be the same again, never. And no-one cared. No-one was interested, you couldn't talk to anyone and a lot of blokes wouldn't talk. But no-one was interested to hear that you were one of the unfortunate ones that went away, because there were thousands of blokes that didn't go. It's hard to put into words, but you were never the same.

In hindsight now you see what's going on with the Yanks, how Vietnam started, what they did over the years and how it progressed to the stage it did. And they're still doing it. They're doing it in Latin America, doing it all over the bloody world.

I just feel I got conned.

Chronology

1950   Ho Chi Minh declared on 14 January that the Democratic Republic of Vietnam was the only legal government. It was recognised by the Soviet Union and China.

On 8 February, Australia extended diplomatic recognition to the French-sponsored government of Vietnam headed by former puppet emperor Bao Dai.

On 9 March, External Affairs Minister, Percy Spender, told Parliament if Vietnam 'came under the heel of communist China' then Malaya, Thailand, Burma and Indonesia would 'become the next direct object of further communist activities.' The United States announced, 8 May, it would provide military and economic aid to the French in Indochina, starting with a grant of $10 million.

1954   French defeated by Viet Minh forces at Dien Bien Phu, 7 May, after a siege lasting fifty-five days. The defeat signalled an end to French presence in Indochina.

South-East Asia Treaty Organisation (SEATO) formed by US, Britain, France, Australia, New Zealand, Pakistan, Thailand and Philippines, 8 September.

French forces left Hanoi, 9 October.

1955   US began to funnel aid directly to Saigon government, agreed to train South Vietnamese army.

1957   In September, South Vietnam's President Ngo Dinh Diem visited Australia. Menzies reaffirmed support for his regime. Diem had also visited US, in May.

1960   Hanoi leaders formed National Liberation Front for South Vietnam, 20 December, which Saigon regime dubbed 'Viet Cong', meaning communist Vietnamese.

1961   On 17 November, US government sought an indication through diplomatic channels of Australia's willingness to assist in Vietnam.

1962   Defoliation program Operation Ranch Hand began in South Vietnam, 13 January.

On 24 May, Australia's Minister for Defence, Athol Townley, said that thirty military advisers would be sent to Vietnam. Advisers arrived there July-August.

1963   An adviser, William Francis Hacking, accidentally killed in Vietnam, 1 June, forty miles west of Hue — the first Australian killed in Vietnam.

By year's end, 15,000 American military advisers were in South Vietnam, which had received $500 million in aid during the year.

1964   In June, Prime Minister Menzies visited Washington, where talks centred on Vietnam.

An adviser, Kevin George Conway, became first Australian killed in action in Vietnam, 6 July, at Nam Dong, thirty miles west of Danang.

North Vietnamese patrol boats attacked US destroyer *Maddox* in Tonkin Gulf, 2 August. A doubtful second incident involving the *Turner Joy* reported two days later.

On 7 August, US Congress passed Tonkin Gulf Resolution, giving President Johnson extraordinary powers to act in South-East Asia.

Australian government introduced conscription, 10 November.

1965   In January, the defoliant Agent Orange introduced in South Vietnam.

Menzies government announced commitment of Australian combat troops to Vietnam, 29 April.

First battalion, comprising eight hundred men, arrived at Bien Hoa in May-June as US troop level passed 50,000.

In September, Morgan Gallup Poll found fifty-six per cent of those polled were in favour of continuing the war in Vietnam, twenty-eight per cent wanted forces brought back to Australia, sixteen per cent were undecided.

Police arrested sixty-five people during a demonstration against the war in Sydney, 22 October.

1966   Harold Holt succeeded Menzies as Liberal leader and Prime Minister, 26 January.

On 8 March, Holt announced that a self-contained task force of two battalions, an SAS regiment and combat support units would be established in Phuoc Tuy Province and that conscripts would go to Vietnam.

In Washington, Holt pledges to go 'all the way with LBJ', 30 June.

Errol Wayne Noack first conscript killed in Vietnam, 24 May.
Battle of Long Tan, 18 August. Australians suffered eighteen killed for 245 Viet Cong and North Vietnamese in single biggest contact of Australia's war.
Morgan Gallup Poll, 19 November, found sixty-three per cent of those polled were in favour of conscription, but only thirty-seven per cent favoured sending national servicemen to Vietnam.

1967   In May, Morgan Gallup Poll found sixty-two per cent of those polled were in favour of continuing the war in Vietnam, twenty-four per cent wanted forces brought back to Australia, fourteen per cent were undecided.
Holt presumed drowned, 17 November. His deputy, Country Party leader John McEwan, sworn in as Prime Minister, 19 December.
Australia's military commitment to Vietnam peaked at 8,300 troops, November-December.

1968   John Grey Gorton sworn in as Prime Minister following election as Liberal Party leader, 10 January.
On 31 January, Tet Offensive began as Viet Cong and North Vietnamese troops attacked South Vietnamese cities and towns.
On 12 February, Gorton indicated that Australia would not increase its commitment to Vietnam.
Massacre of civilians by American soldiers at My Lai, 16 March. At least 450 unarmed South Vietnamese were killed. The massacre was not revealed until 16 November, 1969.
In May, National Service Act amended to impose two-year civil jail term for draft evaders.
By year's end, US forces in Vietnam totalled 536,000. Numbers killed in combat totalled 14,592 for the year.

1969   In August, Morgan Gallup Poll found fifty-five per cent of those polled wanted forces brought back to Australia, forty per cent were in favour of continuing the war, six per cent were undecided.
Ho Chi Minh died in Hanoi, aged seventy-nine, 3 September.
Gallup Poll on 4 October found fifty-eight per cent of Americans polled believed the war was a mistake.
Massive anti-war demonstrations in Washington, 15 October.

1970 On 22 April, Australian government announced that a battalion would be withdrawn from Vietnam.

Large anti-war protests spread across United States. National guardsmen killed four students at Kent State University in Ohio, 4 May.

On 8 May, about 120,000 people throughout Australia demonstrated for an end to the war in Vietnam. The biggest of the moratorium marches was in Melbourne, where 70,000 people occupied the streets.

On 18 September, about 100,000 people throughout Australia took part in a second moratorium. The biggest march again was in Melbourne where 50,000 marched. More than three hundred demonstrators were arrested in Sydney and Adelaide.

1971 William McMahon replaced Gorton as Liberal leader and Prime Minister, 10 March.

Australian government announced, 30 March, that a further one thousand men would be withdrawn from Vietnam.

Third and last of the big anti-war rallies, 30 June. About 110,000 demonstrated in state capitals.

On 18 August, McMahon announced that most Australian troops would be home by Christmas.

Last major withdrawal of Australian troops from Vietnam, 17 December.

1972 Australian Labor Party elected to government after twenty-three years in opposition, 2 December.

Conscription ended, 5 December; draft resisters released from jail and pending prosecutions for draft resistance dropped.

Last Australian troops left Vietnam, 8 December.

Last Australian advisers left Vietnam, 18 December, as US President Nixon ordered renewed bombing of Hanoi-Haiphong area.

1973 On 23 January, Nixon announced agreement had been reached for 'peace with honour'. Ceasefire began, 27 January.

On 26 February, Prime Minister Whitlam announced establishment of diplomatic relations with Hanoi, but retained recognition of the government of South Vietnam.

Last US troops left Vietnam, 29 March.

Last American prisoner of war released in Hanoi, 1 April.

1974   South Vietnam's President Nguyen Van Thieu declared, 4 January, that war had begun again.

1975   In Cambodia, Phnom Penh fell to Khmer Rouge, 17 April.
Australia closed its embassy in Saigon, completing withdrawal from Vietnam, 25 April.
Communist forces captured Saigon as last Americans evacuated, 30 April.

1983   In June, four thousand Australian veterans joined a class action in New York State against the manufacturers of herbicides sprayed in Vietnam.

1984   In January, royal commission headed by Mr Justice Evatt began looking into the health of veterans and the effect of exposure to chemicals in Vietnam.

1985   In July, Evatt royal commission found Agent Orange 'not guilty' of causing illnesses among veterans. The Vietnam Veterans Association rejected the finding.

Glossary

AK-47	Soviet-made assault rifle used by the North Vietnamese Army and Viet Cong
APC	armoured personnel carrier
Armalite	American-made lightweight rifle
ARVN	Army of the Republic of Vietnam; the South Vietnamese Army
AWOL	Absent Without Official Leave
bodybag	olive-green plastic bag in which bodies were placed for convenient transportation
canister	*see* splintex
Cannungra	Australian Army base in Queensland where Australian soldiers did their final three weeks battle efficiency training before leaving for Vietnam
Charlie	Viet Cong; short for radio code 'Victor Charlie'
Chicom mine	Chinese communist-built mine
chieu hoi	open arms surrender; an enemy soldier who has surrendered
claymore	command detonated anti-personnel mine which fired about 700 steel balls in an outward arc
CMF	Citizen Military Force (forerunner to Army Reserve)
C-rations	American field rations

crunchy	*see* grunt
CSM	company sergeant-major
Dat, the	Nui Dat, headquarters for Australian forces in Vietnam
didi mau	Vietnamese for 'go away', or 'move quickly'
DMZ	demilitarised zone dividing North and South Vietnam at the 17th Parallel
dust off	evacuation of wounded and dead by helicopter
Enoggera	Australian Army base in Brisbane
fire-support base	a temporary, fortified base in the bush, used as a support base for battalion operations
GP boots	general purpose boots
grunt	infantryman
greens	Army working clothes
gunship	a helicopter fitted with rockets and machine-guns capable of firing six thousand rounds a minute
harbour up	to set up camp at night in the bush
hoi chanh	a surrender program aimed at communist soldiers; an enemy soldier who has surrendered
hoochie	tents or shacks used to house military personnel
in-country	in Vietnam

Ingleburn	Australian Army base in New South Wales
jumping jack	American-made anti-personnel mine which would burst out of the ground like a jack-in-box, forward of the trigger point and explode at waist height
Kapooka	training base for conscripts in New South Wales
KIA	killed in action
klick	kilometre
lewie	lieutenant
LCT	amphibious landing craft
LZ	land zone; usually a small clearing secured temporarily for helicopters to land
M-16	American-made assault rifle
M-60	American-made machine-gun
M-79	American-made grenade launcher
mama-san	pidgin for any older Vietnamese woman
medevac	medical evacuation by helicopter
nasho	a conscripted soldier; national service
NCO	non-commissioned officer, e.g. a corporal
Nigel	slang for nog

nog	enemy soldier, but derogatory for any Vietnamese
NVA	North Vietnamese Army
OC	officer commanding
picket	sentry duty
Puff the Magic Dragon	a DC3 plane fitted with Gatling guns; so named after the saccharine song of the same name
Puckapunyal	Australian Army base in Victoria
RAP	regimental aid post; a medical centre
RAR	Royal Australian Regiment. So, 1RAR is First Battalion, Royal Australian Regiment etc.
R&C	recreation and convalescent leave in Vietnam, normally 36 hours in Vung Tau; also referred to as rec leave
reg	a regular soldier; an enlisted man
reo	reinforcement; a newly arrived soldier
RPG	rocket propelled grenade used by the Viet Cong and NVA
R&R	rest and recreation leave, up to seven days which could be taken out of Vietnam
RSM	regimental sergeant-major
RTA	return to Australia

Saigon tea	cold tea in a glass for a bar girl; payment for her company
SAS	Special Air Service; an elite Australian force
Scheyville	officer training base in New South Wales
short time	the final weeks of a tour of duty in Vietnam
sig(s)	radio operator; signal corps
Singleton	Australian Army base in New South Wales
SLR	self loading rifle
splintex	razor-sharp slivers of steel contained in canister round fired by tanks and artillery
Spooky	*see* Puff the Magic Dragon
TAOR	tactical area of responsibility
tail-end Charlie	last man in a patrol
tracer	phosphorous tipped bullets which glow as they travel to let the firer know the direction of his aim
track	slang for armoured personnel carrier
Uc Dai Loi	Vietnamese for Australian
VC	*see* Viet Cong

Viet Cong	Vietnamese communist; name adopted by South Vietnamese communist guerrilla forces; the successors of the Viet Minh
Viet Minh	nationalist resistance movement established by Ho Chi Minh during Second World War
wallaby	regular Australian Airforce flights from Saigon to Nui Dat and Vung Tau
WIA	wounded in action